GUIDE TO FINANCIAL MANAGEMENT

OTHER ECONOMIST BOOKS

Guide to Analysing Companies
Guide to Business Modelling
Guide to Business Planning
Guide to Cash Management
Guide to Commodities
Guide to Decision Making
Guide to Economic Indicators
Guide to the European Union
Guide to Financial Markets
Guide to Hedge Funds
Guide to Investment Strategy
Guide to Management Ideas and Gurus
Guide to Managing Growth
Guide to Organisation Design
Guide to Project Management
Guide to Supply Chain Management
Numbers Guide
Style Guide

Book of Business Quotations
Book of Isms
Book of Obituaries
Brands and Branding
Business Consulting
Business Strategy
Buying Professional Services
Doing Business in China
Economics
Emerging Markets
Managing Uncertainty
Marketing
Managing Uncertainty
Megachange – the world in 2050
Modern Warfare, Intelligence and Deterrence
Organisation Culture
Successful Strategy Execution
The World of Business

Directors: an A–Z Guide
Economics: an A–Z Guide
Investment: an A–Z Guide
Negotiation: an A–Z Guide

Pocket World in Figures

GUIDE TO FINANCIAL MANAGEMENT

Principles and Practice

John Tennent

PublicAffairs
New York

Typeset in EcoType by MacGuru Ltd.
info@macguru.org.uk

Library of Congress Control Number: 2013948990

ISBN 978-1-61039-393-5 (PB)
ISBN 978-1-16039-394-2 (EB)

First Edition

10 9 8 7 6 5 4 3 2 1

Contents

Preface

EFFECTIVE FINANCIAL MANAGEMENT is essential for a business to succeed; many have failed for want of it. All too often a career aspiration falters, not for lack of effort or ability in a chosen field, but for not being able to understand the financial impacts of decisions and ultimately a failure to "deliver the numbers". Managers who find themselves in a senior role unable to ask questions of others – which might imply their own ignorance – have wished that they had got to grips with really understanding financial matters earlier in their career.

This guide to financial management is designed to take you through financial principles and illustrate their application, providing a toolkit for managing financial responsibilities. Each chapter is written from an operational perspective in establishing and running a business. Before the index is a glossary of the financial terms used in the book. There is also a list of companies used in examples. The names are those in existence at the time of writing; merger and acquisition activity will inevitably change this.

All books are not just the work of the author but the results of contributions of many others. I am grateful to clients and colleagues who provided the opportunity to explore aspects of business, complete research and develop my thinking. In particular I would like to thank my colleagues at Corporate Edge for their insights and contributions, and Mandy Aston for her work on the original script and many of the diagrams; Mike Samuel for his support and the time he dedicated to reviewing and commenting upon the first edition; Nick Insall for his review of this edition; and Profile Books for the help they gave me, particularly Stephen Brough, Penny Williams and Jonathan Harley.

Special thanks to my wife, Angela, and my two sons, William and George, who have supported my enthusiasm for writing, even on holidays. Also to my parents, particularly my father, a chartered accountant, who always encouraged my career, and gave me the passion and interest in business.

I would welcome feedback and can be contacted on the following e-mail address: John-Tennent@CorporateEdge.co.uk

John Tennent
May 2013

1   Defining a successful business

EVERY ENTREPRENEUR ASPIRES to create a successful business and investors certainly want management to run successful businesses. So what determines whether a business is being successful? Before answering this question it is helpful to define what a business is and the various forms it can take.

A business is a commercial operation that provides products or services with the aim of making a profit for the benefit of its owners. The significant point is "for the benefit of its owners", which differentiates it from a government or not-for-profit organisation, such as a charity, where the activity is conducted for the benefit of the people it serves.

A profit is an essential element of running a successful business. It is a trading surplus whereby the revenues earned exceed the costs. This surplus belongs to the owners of the business to use as they choose: to take for themselves, to reinvest back in the business, or a mixture of the two. For a government organisation or charity any surplus is reinvested in the activities to further benefit the people it serves.

Business structure

A business can take many forms ranging from a sole trader to a large multinational company. The principal aim of making a profit for its owners is still the same.

A person starting out and setting up a business will take all the risk and reward as the venture gets under way. As the business grows it can be advantageous to share the risk with others and separate the business activities from those of the owner by establishing a company.

A company is a legal entity in its own right that is separate from its owners. An investor is risking only the money paid for buying some shares in the company. If the company ceases trading, the shareholders (owners) are not liable to make up any shortfall between the value of the company's assets and its liabilities.

There are five broad categories of business:

■ **Sole trader.** Someone who sets up a business alone and takes all the risk and reward of running it, and who may employ staff.

■ **Partnership.** Two or more people who set up a business together. The partners have joint ownership and share the risk and reward of running the business. Like a sole trader they may employ staff.

■ **Limited liability partnership (LLP).** A hybrid of a partnership and a company which provides the owners with the limited risk of a company and the shared ownership and tax status of a partnership.

■ **Private company.** Usually a small organisation raising its money from a few private investors. The shares may be difficult to trade as they are not listed on any stockmarket. Investors' liability in private and public companies is limited to the amount of their investment.

■ **Public company.** Typically a large organisation that is usually listed on a stock exchange. Because of its size it may require significant investment, and hence it may need to draw investment from many investors.

In this book the focus is mainly on companies, though the principles can be equally well applied to a sole trader, a partnership and indeed not-for-profit organisations.

The role of the board

The directors of a company are people hired (and at times fired) by the shareholders to be stewards of their investment. However, they need to balance this with their primary fiduciary duty as a director which is to act in the best interests of the company. Collectively, a board of directors has overall responsibility for running a company successfully. This is achieved by setting and implementing its strategy.

In fulfilling the strategic aims of the company, the board will be responsible for making sure not only that the company has the necessary resources in terms of investment, assets and people, but also that there are appropriate operating controls and procedures for managing business risk and making sure that all monies that flow through the business are properly accounted for.

What is a successful business?

The media love to report on successful entrepreneurs and tell of how they beat the odds as they built their business and became household names. The media also enjoy revelling in the collapse of mighty organisations and unpicking the journey to their downfall. So what is it that defines business success or failure?

Many descriptions are used to describe success, including "the business is profitable", "revenue is growing" and "the share price is rising". All these attributes are elements of success though individually they do not embrace the totality. To be successful in business is to "create a sustainable superior return on investment".

The core element of this definition is "return on investment" (ROI). The business, having been built from money provided by investors, has a responsibility to reward those investors for risking their money in the venture. The ROI is a measure of the reward being generated. The concept is similar to a savings account where an amount of money is placed on deposit with a bank and the investor earns interest on it. Despite the banking crisis of 2008 and its aftermath, the investment in a savings account is still seen as low risk and consequently the return that the investor will make is similarly low.

$$\text{ROI for a savings account} = \frac{\text{Interest}}{\text{Investment}} \%$$

Therefore, if a deposit of $1,000 is placed in a bank and the gross interest earned over a year is $30, the ROI can be expressed as being 3%.

For a business to be successful it needs to reward investors by making them wealthier than they would be by putting their money in a savings account. Why should they accept the greater risk of investing in a business, with all the uncertainty it faces, if they are not going to be any better off? The return that investors would require might be double or more than a savings account depending on the perceived risk, which will be related to factors such as the nature and maturity of the business.

The return in a business is derived from the profit it generates compared with the money invested to achieve that profit.

$$\text{ROI for a business} = \frac{\text{Profit}}{\text{Investment}} \%$$

Therefore, if investors place \$1,000 in a business and the operating profit over a year is \$200, the ROI can be expressed as being 20%. Some examples of the returns achieved by companies in 2012 and stated in their annual reports are Walmart (a retailer) 18.2%, ExxonMobil (an oil company) 25.4% and Anglo American (an international mining company) 13.3%.

Generating a "superior" return is to achieve a ROI that is greater than the rate achieved by businesses running similar activities in similar markets, and so to be successful is to generate a return that is at least as good as that achieved by your competitors, but ideally better than them.

A "sustainable" superior return is perhaps the most difficult objective to achieve. It means generating a superior rate of return year in, year out. A business may be flying high when its products or services are in fashion. But the fall can be swift when its products or services are no longer in vogue and the business has gone from producing superior returns to producing inferior ones. To be sustainable is to continuously develop the business proposition in a way that keeps customers buying the company's products or services in preference to those of its competitors. Innovation, technology and cost reduction are all activities that can help maintain a sustainable return.

For example, the returns generated by Nokia in 2006 were almost 46%. They resulted from a pre-eminence in a growing market coupled

FIG 1.1 **Return on investment, %**

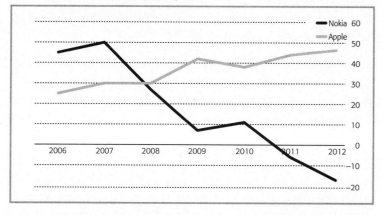

with an ability to continue to introduce new technology and ignite passion for the company's latest products. Subsequently, Nokia failed to offer leading technology and was late in offering smartphones. As a result it lost customers and the superior returns declined; in 2012 Nokia reported losses of €2.3 billion.

At the same time as Nokia was declining Apple, its American rival, was rising. The two companies' ROI between 2006 and 2012 is shown in Figure 1.1.

On creating a superior ROI the directors of a company have two choices. They can either distribute the wealth to the investors or retain it in the business. The second option depends on whether the directors can identify further investment opportunities that will create even more wealth in the future. Profits can be retained in a company while investment opportunities are identified. However, this is only in the short term as investors (particularly in public companies) will demand the cash be "earning or returning".

Wealth is created for investors in a business in two ways:

- annual income – a distribution of profit to the investor (by way of a dividend);
- capital growth – a reinvestment back in the business to increase its value (share price).

Shareholder value

The term "shareholder value" is also used to describe success. Two definitions of shareholder value are:

■ a concept that focuses strategic and operational decision-making on steadily increasing a company's value for shareholders;

■ maximising shareholder benefit by focusing on raising company earnings and the share price.

These definitions focus more on increasing the value of a business in the long term rather than delivering a profit in the short term. An example would be Amazon, one of the best-known online retailers, where the initial strategy was to invest in building the distribution network and customer base as the foundation of the business. Once customer numbers grew the profits would emerge. Throughout its early years the company was creating long-term value while making large losses. During this period Amazon's share price was volatile as it reflected changing views on the future benefits that would arise for investors.

For a mature business, an example would be its investment in research and development to provide the products and revenue streams of the future. This investment can create shareholder value because of the potential it is judged to provide. However, the danger is that success is built on a future promise, and in a fast-changing world the future is always uncertain. For example, a pharmaceutical company that has taken years to develop a new drug only to find it fails to meet Food and Drug Administration (FDA) regulatory requirements.

For a company that is quoted on a stockmarket, there is the expectation to achieve a sufficient ROI every year while also investing to create future value. Once the business has started to make profits, any performance that is worse than the previous year is likely to meet with an adverse reaction from analysts and investors, which in many instances leads to a forced change of management. After many years of substantial losses Amazon made its first profit in 2002, and profit expectations have been greater in every year thereafter. It joined the ranks of other global companies in a battle to produce the ever more superior results that stockmarket investors look for.

The details of the measures used to monitor ROI and shareholder value creation are explained in Chapter 12.

Describing success

Although the definition of success given above may be at the heart of a business, many companies prefer a softer approach to defining what they are in business to achieve. For example, Microsoft, a software giant, states that its mission is: "To enable people and businesses throughout the world to realize their full potential."

There is no mention of the investors here. Among the exceptions are:

■ FedEx, a logistics company, states: "We will produce superior financial returns for shareowners by providing high value-added supply chain, transportation, business and related information services through focused operating companies."

■ Avon, a cosmetics company, states: "We will deliver superior returns to our shareholders by tirelessly pursuing new growth opportunities while continually improving our profitability."

A business as a corporate citizen

An increasing preoccupation in business is corporate social responsibility (CSR), whereby a business's pursuit of success should benefit its shareholders in a way that respects (and benefits) the other stakeholders that make it possible: employees, suppliers, customers and the wider community. Being a good corporate citizen is also about a business taking responsibility for the impact it has on the world in areas such as the environment, including the consumption of global resources, pollution, carbon footprint and the generation of waste. For example, Citigroup, a financial services corporation, said in its mission statement: "Like any other public company, we're obligated to deliver profits and growth to our shareholders. Of equal importance is to deliver those profits and generate growth responsibly."

The CSR argument is that only by working in harmony with all these external influences can a business achieve true success and contribute to an ethical goal of prosperity for all. A company to overtly embrace success within this context is Ben and Jerry's, an American ice-cream company that is now part of Unilever. It has three interrelated parts to its mission:

- Economic – To operate the company on a sustainable financial basis of profitable growth, increasing value for our stakeholders and expanding opportunities for development and career growth for our employees.

- Product – To make, distribute and sell the finest quality all natural ice cream and euphoric concoctions with a continued commitment to incorporating wholesome, natural ingredients and promoting business practices that respect the earth and the environment.

- Social mission – To operate the company in a way that actively recognises the central role that business plays in society by initiating innovative ways to improve the quality of life locally, nationally and internationally.

The third part is perhaps the most altruistic in recognising that the role of a business is to "improve the quality of life". Cynics might say that this is just good marketing: by giving the business strong ethical credentials it attracts certain types of loyal customers and boosts sales. Whichever view you take, there is growing momentum behind the desire for businesses to balance their duty to shareholders with their responsibility to other stakeholders. Paying insufficient attention to the latter, especially if that results in adverse media coverage, will undermine the long-term sustainability of the business and ultimately shareholder value.

Setting up a new business

When starting a business, the founders need to raise money to cover the costs of setting up and running the business until it is generating sufficient revenues to cover its costs. To get this initial capital the directors must convince potential investors and other providers of finance of the robustness of the business proposition and the returns that can realistically be expected. There are two options to raise the money to set up in business:

■ **Loan.** The founders could put together a business plan showing how they anticipate being successful, making enough money to pay interest on a loan and ultimately repay the principal. However, if the business has just started there will be nothing to provide security for the loan should the venture fail. The risk to the provider of the loan is high and repayment depends on the founders being able to carry out their business plan. The loan provider would therefore want the founders to put some of their own money into the business, not only sharing the risk but also demonstrating their belief and commitment to the venture. Alternatively, it would require some security from them – a charge on their homes, for example, which could mean the founders losing their homes if the business does not work out.

■ **Equity (or share) capital.** A company is owned by its shareholders, so if the founders want to part own the business, they need to invest some of their own money to buy shares in addition to attracting outside investors. Any profits that the business generates belong to the shareholders (the owners) and any losses are borne by the shareholders (up to the amount invested). The shareholders are therefore the ones that take the highest risk in a business, but they also have the potential for the highest reward. Should the business fail, any assets it owns will be sold to pay the creditors (in the first instance secured lenders and then unsecured creditors such as suppliers and other payables). Only after all debts are satisfied will the shareholders get any of their investment back.

With a significant amount of share capital invested to take the primary risk of the business, a bank will be more willing to provide loans and on more favourable terms.

Weighted average cost of capital

In Figure 1.2 the business has a pool of money, the "capital invested". To invest this wisely, the first stage is to determine what the average dollar in the pool costs as derived from the returns that the various investors are seeking. Knowing this average rate enables the directors to make choices about the activities and projects they select to invest in.

FIG 1.2 **Sources of money to establish a business**

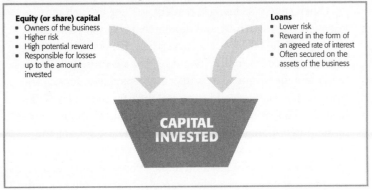

Equity (or share) capital
- Owners of the business
- Higher risk
- High potential reward
- Responsible for losses
  up to the amount
  invested

Loans
- Lower risk
- Reward in the form of
  an agreed rate of interest
- Often secured on the
  assets of the business

CAPITAL INVESTED

For example, a business has raised $70,000 of equity capital and a $30,000 loan. If the shareholders require 20% return on their money and the bank wants 8%, the average dollar would cost the business 16.4%, which is calculated as follows:

		Annual cost ($)
Shareholders	$70,000 @ 20%	14,000
Debt	$30,000 @ 8%	2,400
Total	$100,000	16,400

Therefore the average cost of a dollar $= 16,400/100,000 = 16.4\%$

This is known as the weighted average cost of capital (WACC). For a business to be successful and satisfy its investors it must earn at least this rate on its operating activities.

A combination of the two sources of finance provides an optimal way to raise funds and build a business. A business with debt usually has a lower WACC than one without. A low WACC can therefore create more value for the shareholders out of the projects it chooses to invest in.

This is a simplified formula for the purposes of illustrating the concept. To calculate the actual returns required for shareholders and banks, the optimal proportions of each source and the effect of tax are explained in more detail in Chapter 6.

FIG 1.3 **The selection of investment projects**

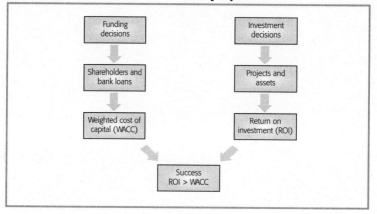

Selecting successful activities

Any project that can earn a business a ROI that is greater than the WACC will help the business be successful.

It is rare that a business will publicly quote its WACC, as it is the determinant of investment selection and therefore valuable competitive information when bidding against others for opportunities. However, some years ago Coca-Cola, an American drinks company, said in its annual report: "Our criteria for investment are simple: New investments should directly enhance our existing operations and generally be expected to provide cash returns that exceed our long-term, after-tax, weighted average cost of capital, currently estimated at between 8% and 10%."

An executive of British Airways, the UK's largest airline, once described the business as "a group of investment projects flying in close formation". This is an apt description of a business, illustrating that any organisation is a collection of business decisions, all intended to generate returns that exceed the cost of funding them.

As anyone who has worked in business will know, the returns anticipated by business plans are not always achieved and it is the shortfalls that cause businesses to fail. The WACC is a fairly constant and predictable percentage compared with the volatility of a project's performance in which the investment is placed. For example, an

FIG 1.4 **Growth in shareholder value**

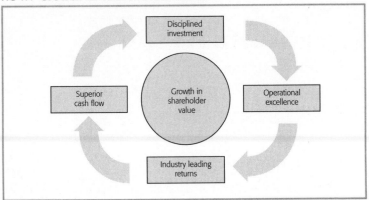

Source: *ExxonMobil*, analyst meeting, 2010

ice-cream business excels in a hot summer, but in a cold and wet summer sales volumes are much lower. The WACC for both scenarios will be the same.

Once a project has been selected (see Figure 1.3) the implementation needs to be managed well to achieve the expected returns. Shareholder value is created by following the cycle in Figure 1.4. Starting at the top, select projects that are rigorously evaluated and promise high returns. Manage these projects excellently to fulfil their promise. Combining the first two items should enable superior returns on investment to be achieved. The superior returns should generate substantial cash flow which will provide the resource for future investment opportunities.

Overall success

Success can therefore be achieved by understanding and satisfying investors' requirements, which can be interpreted as "creating a sustainable superior return on investment". To do this directors need the vision, business sense and confidence to invest in ideas and opportunities that they believe will produce a ROI that is greater than the WACC.

2 Business structures

FOR A BUSINESS to be successful it needs to develop a revenue stream by providing a product or service that customers will buy. The criteria for this customer proposition are to:

■ have a product or service that meets a specific need for a customer such that they will want to buy it;

■ provide the product or service better than a competitor so the business will be chosen in preference to others;

■ charge a price that offers value to the customer yet enables the business to earn a profit.

These criteria are difficult to combine in practice. A product or service that is better than a competitor's is, because of its differentiating factors, likely to cost more to provide. However, the additional cost may not be able to be passed on to the customer in the price, and this will reduce the profit. Many firms in the same line of business seek to prosper by exploiting the criteria in different ways; for example, a scheduled airline providing a high-quality service at a relatively high price and a low-cost carrier relying on low fares and no frills.

The business model

Building businesses that can generate a revenue stream requires investment to pay for infrastructure, equipment and staff. Figure 2.1 illustrates how a business is structured to provide a customer proposition.

The model is built on five activities:

FIG 2.1 **The fundamental business model**

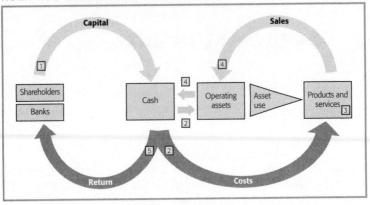

1 Starting on the left, the investors provide the capital for the business. The cash received will be held in a bank account.

2 The cash in the business can be:
- converted into another type of asset that will be used in the business such as equipment or goods for sale (inventory); or
- spent on running costs such as staff and utilities.

3 The combination of the business resources (assets and staff) provides the basis for producing the products or services that are available for customers to buy.

4 The sale of a product or service to a customer generates what is called a receivable which, once collected, will produce more cash for the business.

5 This new cash is used to pay interest on loans from any debt providers. The rest can be sent round the cycle again by being converted into further assets or spent on running costs (back to stage 2). Providing the whole process earns more money than it consumes, a profit will be generated on which tax will have to be paid. Any surplus after tax can continue to be reinvested in the cycle or paid out to the shareholders as a "return" on their investment.

The model illustrates the way money flows around a business and provides the basis of accounting, which is the collecting, recording, analysing and communicating of all the financial activity in the business.

To manage a business effectively, it is important to know how the cash has been spent and how profitable the products or services have been to the business. The availability of this historic information helps management to make judgments on how to improve the performance of business.

Crucial elements

To make a business successful requires three crucial elements:

- **Cash.** The money that it is used in the cycle described above. Without sufficient cash it is difficult for any business to start or maintain the cycle (see *The Economist Guide to Cash Management*, John Tennent, 2012).
- **People.** The means of creating the products, providing the service and running the business. The quality of the skills of the people in the business is crucial in achieving success.
- **Customers.** A business cannot survive without customers. Attracting customers is where the process begins, but retaining customers by continuing to satisfy their needs is just as important. Existing and satisfied customers not only provide revenue but may also become advocates for the business.

Types of business

Although the fundamental business model does not vary, there are infinite ways of applying it to provide the range of products and services that make up the business world. However, the range of products and services can be summarised in seven broad categories (see Figure 2.2 and Table 2.1).

FIG 2.2 **The seven types of business**

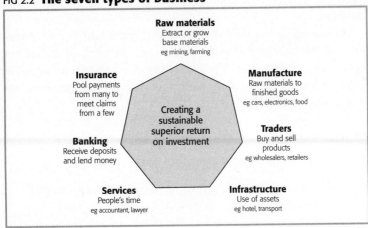

TABLE 2.1 **The seven types of business**

Type	Activity	Structure	Examples
Raw materials	Growing or extracting raw materials	Buying blocks of land and using them to provide raw materials	Farming Mining Oil
Manufacture	Designing products, aggregating components and assembling finished products	Taking raw materials and using equipment and staff to convert them into finished goods	Vehicle assembly Construction Engineering Electricity Food and drink Chemicals Media Pharmaceuticals Water
Trader	Buying and selling products	Buying a range of raw materials and manufactured goods and consolidating them, making them available for sale in locations near to their customers or online for delivery	Wholesaler Retailer

Type	Activity	Structure	Examples
Infrastructure	Selling the utilisation of infrastructure	Buying and operating assets (typically large assets); selling occupancy often in combination with services	Transport (airport operator, airlines, trains, ferries, buses) Hotels Telecoms Sports facilities Property management
Services	Selling people's time	Hiring skilled staff and selling their time	Software development Accounting Legal
Financial	Depositing, lending and investing money	Accepting cash from depositors and paying them interest; using the money to provide loans to borrowers, charging them fees and a higher rate of interest than the depositors receive	Bank Investment house
Insurance	Pooling premiums of many to meet claims of a few	Collecting cash from many customers; investing the money to pay the losses experienced by a few customers. By understanding the risk accepted and the likelihood of a claim, more premium income can be earned than claims paid	Insurance

All these activities are a combination of a product and a service proposition to a customer. The raw material producer is primarily a product-based business, but the service element emerges in the way the materials are sold, the speed of response to orders and the manner with which customer relationships are built. At the other end of the spectrum is a service provider which is primarily a people business, but the way this type of business can develop efficiencies is by using products such as, in the case of an accountant, a software package to process tax returns.

The mix of product and service elements in the customer proposition will define the need for acquiring assets and hiring staff.

Structuring a business for flexibility

The investment of cash in assets and staff will define the flexibility that a business will have in responding to a changing business environment. A rapid increase in the need for assets and staff can be difficult to meet, particularly if they are specialist in nature. The assets may need to be built by a manufacturer and the staff may need to be trained.

A business with substantial non-cash assets will find it difficult to adjust to a decrease in sales volume; for example, in the aftermath of terrorist events airlines have found themselves owning assets they could neither fill with passengers nor sell. A business with high staff costs may be able to respond more quickly to a downturn by laying off people, particularly if it has employed staff on short-term contracts (for example, the software industry where programmers are often hired on short-term contracts), but labour laws can make this costly.

In seeking greater flexibility to cope with changing circumstances, businesses may choose to outsource parts of their operations, particularly non-core activities. This is the process of letting another business acquire and operate the assets, and provide services or products on a contractual basis. For example, businesses may find that outsourcing their cleaning and catering provides much greater flexibility than recruiting and managing their own staff. As there are many businesses supplying such services, the prices are likely to be competitive and service quality forced upwards.

Management of any business needs to identify the optimum structure that will enable long-term success to be achieved. This may be done by combining owned resources with outsourced resources to provide the products and services.

Because of constraints on how quickly a business can respond to significant changes, careful planning is essential. This involves making projections about demand and making sure an appropriate business infrastructure is in place. As events unfold, the judgments made need to be refined in the light of new information and opportunities.

Causes of failure

The high proportion of businesses that fail never seems to deter entrepreneurs. Failure is often a result of one of the following three events:

- **Insufficient revenue.** Producing products or services that customers do not buy in sufficient quantities. This is often caused by entrepreneurs not really understanding the needs of customers. An example is what marketers call "a musical ash tray", a product that meets no specific need and relies wholly on customers making whimsical purchases.

- **Excess fixed cost.** A high cost base in a business that does not enable a profit to be made; or a cost base that is not flexible enough to adapt to changing volumes if sales decline. Many airlines struggle to survive because of the way that demand for air travel can suddenly slump.

- **Poor quality and service.** The inability of managers and staff to plan, control and operate the business effectively. This affects the quality and reliability of the business, ultimately leading to a decline in its revenue. Many have experienced examples of this in poorly run restaurants and have left saying "never again". The word spreads and that business continues its downward spiral.

3 The role of the finance department

THE DIRECTORS OF A COMPANY have a legal responsibility for ensuring that the company keeps appropriate accounting records which enable them to report the financial position of the business to investors, regulators and tax authorities.

This responsibility is normally delegated to the finance director. Until the end of the 20th century, the finance director would be in charge of the "accounts department", often a large team of people whose primary role was book-keeping. They manually recorded every transaction in ledgers for purchases, sales, cash and a host of other details.

Today the transaction recording is as much about computer systems as it is about accounting. Large organisations choose highly integrated systems that have direct data feeds with customers and suppliers, continually reducing the need for paperwork and human intervention. The accounts department has become the "finance department", where the role is about adding value to the numbers by providing decision support such as cost analysis, trends, investment appraisal and business plans.

The finance department is still responsible for record keeping and financial reporting, but it has evolved into a service department that supports the rest of the business, taking a lead in strategic planning and putting together the business plan.

Some organisations find they can split these responsibilities into transactional work (routine record keeping) and transformational work (the added-value services). With so much of the transactional work being electronically generated and transmitted, the location of these services is no longer required at the centre of decision-making (head office). Many organisations now outsource this work to locations or countries where wages are lower. A robust data connection back to head office enables the transformational work to continue without any time lag.

Financial and management reporting

In adding value to the transactional information that is recorded there are two types of reporting:

■ Financial reporting. Summarising historic information to report externally on how the business performed (for example, the annual report that is distributed to all investors).

■ Management reporting. Using analysis of historic information and judgment to provide the basis of future decisions (for example, an investment appraisal to justify buying a new piece of equipment).

Table 3.1 lists the differences between these two areas.

TABLE 3.1 **Financial reporting and management reporting**

Area	Financial reporting	Management reporting
Users of information	Investors and other stakeholders	Business managers
Reports	Summarised and general	Detailed and specific
Purpose	Investor protection and regulation	Decision support
Regulation	Highly prescriptive regulation on the format and underlying accounting practices used	No regulation, the report is fit for purpose
Validity	Independently audited	Potentially subject to internal review
Frequency	Annual, half-yearly and quarterly	As required
Information used	Specific historic monetary amounts	Historic results as well as estimates, judgment and non-financial indicators
Perspective	Records results	Contributes to the future results

This book is primarily concerned with management reporting and the operation of the business, but Chapter 15 covers some of the important principles and details of financial reporting.

What managers need to know

In an organisation financial acumen is a skill that will support any manager in their career. The skill is not about knowing the intricacies of transaction recording or the details of financial reporting; it is about having the ability to do six things:

■ Engage with the business strategy – know the organisation's mission, objectives, strategy and tactics at a macro level to make sure that all actions that are taken align with these overarching principles.

■ Understand performance indicators – know the portfolio of measures that are used to monitor business performance at a company, department and project level. This includes knowing how the indicators are calculated to make sure that actions taken can be translated into how the indicators will be affected.

■ Read and interpret financial reports – be able to read the financial reports that are generated within the business. This includes company, department, budget area and projects. The skill is being able to assess strengths and weaknesses and identify appropriate actions that will improve performance.

■ Contribute to the budgetary process – participate in the budgetary process, the setting of budgets and the monitoring of performance through the financial year. At a detailed level this includes using variance analysis to interpret the causes of deviation from budget predictions and producing year-end forecasts that predict the likely outturn for the year.

■ Know the financial consequences of the decisions – identify the financial implication of decisions through the creation and evaluation of a business case that takes into account the likely financial effects of the changes to the business that will take place as a result of any decision. This involves venturing beyond finance into judgment, but the judgment is made on the basis of experience and sound evidence.

■ Seek ways to add value not cost – continually improve the performance of the products and services by adding customer value while eliminating cost and waste in their provision.

Although strength in these six abilities is by no means a fast-track ticket up through an organisation, the opposite is almost certainly true. Weakness in them will hold back even the most ambitious individual.

Other abilities are important, depending on the role of the manager in the organisation; for example, sales people may find it helpful to be able to read published financial statements to complete credit checks, and those in manufacturing should know cost allocation techniques to be able to build up a product cost. These other abilities build on the foundation of the six abilities outlined above.

Designing management information

In many organisations the finance department is the fount of all financial knowledge. Reports are regularly produced, often referred to anonymously as, for example, the "Blue Book". They are published on a set day, such as six working days after the month end, and crafted by analysts who toil with their spreadsheet "front ends" to drill down into the database. These reports are often based on standard templates that have been used for several years, only ever added to and rarely thinned out.

This is fine if managers have the skills to assess strengths and weaknesses and identify appropriate actions that will improve performance. Unfortunately, it often results in "so what?" being asked and does not help drive future action or produce change. This is frequently characterised by management reports presented with content and style that generate more heat than light.

The deficiency is often in the quality of the narrative that supports the report. This can be because a finance department finds it easy to mechanise the tables of data but may not have the business insight to interpret them in a valuable way. Too often the narrative will suffer from "elevator syndrome", simply stating the numbers that are going up, going down or not moving at all. This information can be obvious from the data, but what is needed is to understand why the movements are taking place and what is being done about the numbers that indicate there are problems.

As well as standard monthly reporting, self-generated reporting is becoming increasingly common as system access in organisations becomes more sophisticated. Managers from all functions have access to the accounting system and can view transactions, monitor budgets and raise purchase orders. This can reduce, if not eliminate, the need for printed reports and instead move the business to providing more tailored information, which is less cumbersome, more action oriented and allows a more efficient use of management time.

To create these tailored reports requires intelligent design and communication. The reports may be the responsibility of the financial analyst, but it is also up to the managers who are going to read and use them to specify requirements and provide feedback on how they can be improved.

The first stage in designing any report is to identify its purpose and/or the questions that it seeks to answer. Typical questions might be: "What proportion of the budget has been spent?"; "Which transactions are over a specific amount?"; "Which customer invoices are unpaid after 60 days?" Once the purpose has been defined it is a simple matter to create an appropriate report for distribution as frequently as required.

Where there are many questions to answer, a type of "dashboard" can be created which summarises on one page the most important items of data and performance measures. The typical measures are summarised in Chapter 12 and may be in the form of a balanced business scorecard.

A helpful way to summarise significant amounts of data is through exception reporting. This involves stripping out data that meet specific acceptance criteria, leaving only the items that fail and require action. An example might be a series of cost-centre account codes that in month three have overspent their budget. An analysis criterion might be all areas that have spent more than a quarter of their budget. Even using this criterion may generate too much information, particularly for areas that have an uneven spend profile. Minor overspends can be eliminated by only reporting areas that have spent more than four-twelfths of the annual total or are more than, say, $1,000 overspent at the end of month three.

Working with finance

As managers build their financial acumen and experience, they should see their finance colleagues as "business partners" who are there to help complete the financial analysis and reports required to support decisions. For this collaborative approach to work, the operational managers need to have a good relationship with and to communicate effectively with their finance colleagues. This involves four things:

- Briefing – describing the decision to be made and the analysis support that is required.

- Co-inventing – working together on the required analysis so that its findings can be interpreted and challenged.

- Implementing – identifying the impact on such business resources as cash and people, including how they will be sourced.

- Communicating – presenting the proposed action plans (with supporting analysis) to more senior management for approval.

This process assumes that the finance team has the capability and staff numbers to provide the business partner with support. Finance managers often have limited exposure to or experience in operational areas. Therefore the co-invention stage really is a joint activity, with the finance manager providing the finance skills and the operational manager providing the operational experience.

Presentation of management information

Financial results can be presented in a bland way that many may find difficult to interpret usefully. Alternatively, they can be presented with an engaging analysis that is supported by pictorial or graphical charts to convey important information. In his book *A Primer in Data Reduction* (Wiley, 1982), A.S.C. Ehrenberg describes several methods for communicating data through tables and charts that make it easier to read, assimilate and act upon. Some of his techniques are as follows:

Rounding

Most people cannot manipulate long numbers in their heads, so to enable readers to analyse the data presented it can be helpful to round each number to two digits. This may seem a reduction in detail, but it will probably be sufficient to support the decision-making it is intended to instigate.

For example, if the margins for two products are 18.86% and 38.12%, it can be difficult to compare them easily. However, with just two digits these become 19% and 38%, making it quicker to see that one number is half the other.

Tables of data

Tables of data are much easier to read if they are sorted into ascending or descending order of the most critical item, such that the top few items of data convey the critical information. It can also be helpful to put a gap every few rows to enable the reader's eyes to travel across the table without jumping a row.

TABLE 3.2 **Sales by country ($ '000)**

	2009	2010	2011	2012
Canada	578.1	553.2	654.2	765.4
France	177.9	241.4	472.9	632.8
Germany	384.1	429.4	556.1	642.9
India	185.4	278.3	335.6	432.8
Japan	165.4	145.2	185.4	176.4
Spain	0.0	0.0	25.2	64.1
UK	153.2	171.6	183.6	234.6
US	1,473.2	1,321.5	1,659.0	1,854.3

Table 3.2 would be better presented (as it is in Table 3.3) rounded to two significant figures without a decimal point, sorted by size of sales in 2012 (not alphabetically by country) with a gap inserted between the two blocks of four rows.

TABLE 3.3 **Sales by country ($ '000)**

	2009	2010	2011	2012
USA	1,500	1,300	1,700	1,900
Canada	580	550	650	770
Germany	380	430	560	640
France	180	240	470	630
India	190	280	340	430
UK	150	170	180	230
Japan	170	150	190	180
Spain	0	0	25	60

Rows versus columns

It is usually easier to read down a column of numbers than across a row. This is because the leading digits in each number are then close to each other for direct comparison (see Table 3.4).

TABLE 3.4 **Age profile of customers**

	Under 15	15–30	30–50	Over 50
Buyers	8%	23%	48%	21%

If Table 3.4 is swapped around it is much easier to see where the most valuable segment of the market resides. Also the superfluous percentage sign has been removed and added to the heading, making the numbers clearer.

TABLE 3.5 **Age profile of customers**

	Buyers (%)
Under 15	8
15–30	23
30–50	48
Over 50	21

FIG 3.1 **Sales, $m**

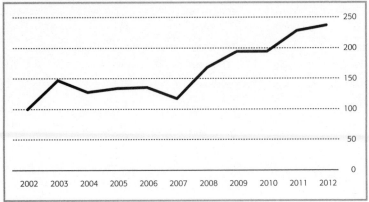

Graphs

Graphs are useful to tell a story, not necessarily to convey detail (for which a table would be better). For clarity, keep a graph to a maximum of three lines (or stacks on a bar chart) and then summarise the trend that emerges to help the reader interpret what is being shown. Avoid a detailed description of each up and down on the line.

In the graph shown in Figure 3.1 an appropriate narrative might be: "The sales rise by an average of 9% per year over the ten years though much of the growth is achieved in the last five years."

Sarbanes-Oxley Act

Throughout the world there is an increasing focus on risk management initiated by the collapse of high-profile businesses such as Barings Bank, brought down by a rogue trader, and Enron, which entered into complex financial arrangements to inflate profits.

Risk comes down to the potential to lose money and in particular to destroy investors' capital. To prevent unreasonable risks being taken by directors and managers within organisations, tighter internal controls have been introduced, especially for publicly traded companies in the United States and all publicly traded non-US companies that require a listing in the United States. The Sarbanes-Oxley Act of 2002 requires these companies to submit an annual assessment of the effectiveness of their internal financial controls to the Securities and Exchange Commission (SEC). Additionally, each company's external auditors are required to audit and report on the management's internal control reports.

Sarbanes-Oxley has introduced a much tighter regime for the management of financial data and financial reporting. All companies that have to comply with the act must now have a financial accounting framework that can generate financial reports that are readily verifiable with traceable source data, which must remain intact without undocumented revisions. Even for those businesses around the world that do not have to comply with the act, its financial accounting rules provide a framework for governance of organisations.

4 Financial statements and accounting systems

ALL BUSINESSES NEED A SYSTEM of recording transactions and presenting them in a coherent way which is widely understandable. The fundamental business model, introduced in Chapter 2 and reproduced here as Figure 4.1, shows the flow of transactions round the business.

The underlying transactions can be grouped into four categories as set out in Table 4.1. The two columns split transactions according to whether they involve money coming into the business or money going out of the business. The two rows are split according to whether the effect of the transaction has either a future or a current impact.

These categories provide the basis for the three core statements that make up a set of accounts:

FIG 4.1 **The fundamental business model**

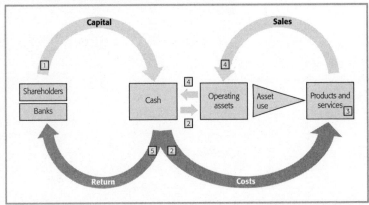

- **Statement of financial position (or balance sheet).** A snapshot of the business showing the assets owned, the liabilities owed and the money put in by investors. It represents the items that will provide a future benefit or have a future claim on the business.

- **Income (or profit and loss) statement.** A trading statement that summarises the revenue earned and the costs incurred for a period. The costs comprise all the items that have been consumed or have been spent in earning the revenue. For example, the cost of telephone calls would be shown as a cost in the income statement, as the benefit is derived at the time they are made and there is no future benefit to be derived. However, the purchase of telephone equipment such as a handset is an asset that will appear on the statement of financial position, as the business will be able to continue deriving benefit from this equipment in the future.

- **Cash flow.** A summary of the cash received and paid for a period. This is effectively a summarised bank statement showing money in and money out.

TABLE 4.1 **Categories of transactions**

	Money coming in	Money going out
Future benefit or claim	Equity/loans Customer receivables	Buildings Equipment Inventory Supplier payables
Current benefit or cost (with no future consequence or impact)	Sales revenue	Employees (payroll) Utilities Services

As shown in Figure 4.2, the statement of financial position is drawn up at a point in time whereas the income statement and cash flow summarise the activity over a period of time (typically a month or year). The priorities of three crucial items on these statements can be summarised by the adage that:

FIG 4.2 **The relationship of three statements**

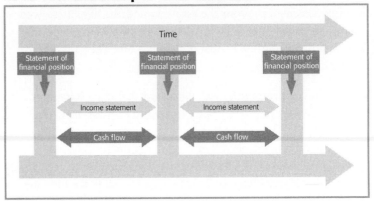

- Revenue is vanity
- Profit is sanity
- Cash is reality

Thus revenue that does not generate a profit or provide a basis for earning future profit (a loss leader) may flatter a business in terms of growth, but generates no shareholder value. Profit that has been earned but is tied up in receivables cannot be reinvested until it is turned into cash. Without cash a business cannot survive in the longer term.

The statements in practice

To illustrate the construction of the three statements, take an example of a door-to-door salesman, Peter Jones, who sets up a cleaning products business with $500. He goes to a wholesaler and buys 200 dusters for $2 each and a holdall for $50. After a hard day on the road, spending $20 on bus fares and finding only a few customers, he has sold 50 of the dusters for $5 each. At the end of the first day he has a lot of dusters left, some cash and some used bus tickets. Has it been a successful day?

The statement of financial position – day 1

Adding up the items in his possession at the end of the day that have a future benefit for the next day and beyond, he would produce the following.

	$	
Holdall	50	
Inventory	300	150 dusters at cost of $2 each
Cash	280	Analysed in the cash flow
Total assets	630	

He would not include the bus tickets as they have been used and there is no future benefit to be derived from them.

To evaluate whether the day has been successful, he needs to compare the assets of the business with the amount originally invested.

	$	
Original capital	500	
Profit	130	Analysed in the income statement
Total equity	630	

The increase in value is the profit that has been earned. This can be analysed in more detail in the income statement.

The income statement – day 1

The profit has been earned by selling the dusters at more than they cost to purchase. Money was also spent on an item that has no future benefit (the bus fares) and therefore this must be deducted in arriving at the profit earned.

	$	
Sales	250	50 dusters at $5 each
Less: cost of dusters sold	(100)	50 dusters at $2 each
Less: bus fares	(20)	
Total profit	130	

Only the cost of the dusters that were sold is deducted in arriving at the profit. The cost of the other 150 dusters originally purchased is shown as inventory on the statement of financial position as it will provide the basis for future trading.

In financial statements, the convention for showing negative numbers is to put them in brackets. Hence in calculating the profit, the cost of the dusters and the bus fares is deducted from the revenue received.

The cash flow – day 1

The cash flow is like a bank statement, though in this example it is a summary of the physical cash payments and receipts. It starts with the original capital invested and shows all the cash received and paid out.

	$	
Capital invested	500	
Add: sales	250	50 dusters at $5 each
Less: dusters bought	(400)	200 dusters at $2 each
Less: holdall	(50)	
Less: bus fares	(20)	
Closing balance	280	

Day 2

On day two the business becomes more successful, but also more complicated. Travelling further on buses for $30, Peter sold 60 dusters for $5 each. He also sold 30 dusters to a part-time office cleaner for $4 each, but the office cleaner promised to pay for them at the end of the week when he received his next pay cheque. Running low on dusters for day three, he went back to the wholesaler, opened an account and purchased 100 more dusters on credit. At the end of the month he will have to pay the wholesaler.

The statement of financial position – day 2

Again adding up the items in his possession at the end of the day that have future benefit for the next day and beyond, he would produce the following:

	$	
Holdall	50	
Inventory	320	160 dusters at $2 each
Money due from customer	120	30 dusters at $4
Cash	550	Analysed in the cash flow
Total assets	1,040	

It is valid to include the money due in the statement of financial position as the customer has taken some of the stock on the basis that he will pay for it in the future. Therefore there is a future benefit of the cash receipt.

Although this accumulation of assets looks successful, the obligation to the wholesaler also needs to be included as it is a future claim on the business.

	$	
Money due to supplier	200	
Original capital	500	
Profit	340	Analysed in the income statement
Total liabilities	1,040	

The income statement – day 2

The income statement summarises a period of trade and in this example covers day 2. The profit for day 1 is added on at the end of the statement to arrive at the total profit earned by the business.

	$	
Sales: cash	300	60 dusters at $5 each
Sales: credit	120	30 dusters at $4 each
Total sales	420	
Less: cost of dusters sold	(180)	90 dusters at $2 each
Less: bus fares	(30)	
Profit: day 2	210	
Profit: day 1	130	
Total profit	340	

The sale on credit can be included in revenue at this stage as the goods have been delivered and the business has performed all it needs to do to fulfil its part of the transaction. The only matter outstanding is to collect the cash which, until it is received, puts the business at risk.

The cash flow – day 2

The cash flow continues where it finished the day before with the opening balance for day two being the closing balance for day one. The new cash received and that paid out during day two are the only items shown.

	$	
Opening balance	280	
Add: sales	300	60 dusters at $5 each
Less: bus fares	(30)	
Closing balance	550	

Having introduced the core elements involved in the three statements, the next stage is to look at the details of the complete statements.

The statement of financial position

The statement of financial position provides a snapshot of the business showing the assets owned, liabilities owed and the money put in by investors at a particular moment in time, typically the end of a month or year as follows:

- **An asset** is something that is owned by the business and has a future value either through its conversion to cash (such as inventory or receivables) or by its use in the business (such as a piece of property, plant or equipment).

- **A liability** is an obligation to pay a business or individual at a future date. This can be either short term (such as payables due to suppliers) or long term (such as debt).

Ironically, a business does not create wealth for itself. Any profit that is generated belongs to the investors who risked their capital in establishing the business. Therefore any profit earned becomes a liability of the business as it belongs to the investors. Through this principle the assets in a business will always equal the liabilities and a statement of financial position, previously known as a balance sheet, will indeed balance.

The statement of financial position does not value a company as many assets are recorded at their original cost (known as historic cost) when they were first acquired. Hence after many years, even allowing for depreciation (see Chapter 5), items such as property, plant and equipment may on the statement of financial position have a much lower value than what they are worth to the business or indeed their market value. The value of a company is its future potential as an earning machine rather than the historic collection of assets it has amassed. See Chapter 13 for techniques to value a company.

The typical structure of a statement of financial position is shown in Table 4.2.

TABLE 4.2 **Structure of a statement of financial position**

US terms	UK terms	Amount	Explanation
Property, plant and equipment	Tangible fixed assets	150	Items that are owned and used in the business such as premises, vehicles and machines. These assets are depreciated to reflect their wearing out over time. The value shown on the statement is known as the net book value after depreciation
Intangible assets	Intangible assets	100	Similar to tangible fixed assets except they are valuable rights and are usually paper-based, such as patents, trade marks and brands. Their treatment is covered in Chapter 5
Goodwill	Goodwill	50	A type of intangible asset that arises on the acquisition of a business. It represents the value of the acquisition over and above its specific net assets and covers items such as brand, reputation, customer base, employees. The concept is covered in Chapter 16
Current assets	Current assets		A collective term for the short-term assets which are likely to be converted into cash within one year
Inventory	Stock	50	Items ready or being constructed for sale, consisting of raw materials, work in progress and finished goods
Receivables	Debtors	40	Amounts owed to the business from customers for sales it made on credit
Cash	Cash	10	The bank balance (and any physical cash held)
Total assets		400	

US terms	UK terms	Amount	Explanation
Current liabilities	Current liabilities		A collective term for the short-term liabilities that must be settled within one year
Payables	Creditors	30	Amounts owed to suppliers for products purchased on credit
Loans	Loans	120	Money borrowed from banks
Provisions	Provisions	60	A future obligation that is uncertain in amount and timing, such as the funding of a shortfall in a company pension fund
Common stock	Ordinary shares	100	The money raised by the business when it issued its shares
Retained earnings	Reserves (retained profit)	90	Profits made by the business that have not been distributed to shareholder by way of dividends
Total liabilities		400	

Equity is the total of the shareholders' investment which comprises the common stock or ordinary shares and the retained earnings.

Working capital is the total of the short-term items covering inventory plus receivables less payables. This is the money tied up in the business that will be released by selling the inventory, collecting the receivables and settling the payables.

The income statement

The income or profit and loss statement provides a summary of the revenue earned and the costs incurred over a period of time, which is usually a month or a year. The statement starts with the trading activities, covering the revenue and direct costs incurred in earning that revenue. These are followed by the indirect or overhead costs to derive the operating income:

	$	
Revenue	100	
Direct costs	(60)	Costs incurred in providing products or services such as raw materials and packaging
Gross profit	40	Also known as trading profit
Indirect costs	(25)	Costs incurred in running the business such as rent, IT and payroll
Operating income	15	Also known as EBIT (earnings before interest and tax)

For example, most retailers earn revenue from selling bought-in products. The direct costs are easily identified as the costs charged by the manufacturer of those products. Subtracting the direct costs from the revenue gives the gross profit or trading profit. Deducting the indirect or non-trading costs such as rent and payroll costs gives the operating income.

The split between what is classified as direct and indirect is up to the business to decide and is not always obvious. For a retailer, are the delivery costs direct (as they relate to moving the products) or indirect (as they are a consequence of the main activity)? The answer is a commercial judgment and there is inconsistent treatment in the retail sector. Therefore comparison of gross profit levels between businesses is not as easy as you might expect it to be because of the ways different businesses categorise their costs. Hence most comparisons are done at the operating income level when all costs have been accounted for and the judgment element removed.

The structure of an income statement is shown in Table 4.3. In the past dividends used to be shown at the foot of an income statement as a distribution of profit. These are now shown separately in financial statements as a movement in shareholders' equity. Furthermore, in published accounts the income statement is extended to include a statement of comprehensive income. The purpose of this is to show the non-operating items such as gains in property values or foreign-exchange movements. This is explained more fully in Chapter 15.

TABLE 4.3 **Structure of an income statement**

US terms	UK terms	Amount	Explanation
Revenue	Sales	300	The value of all products and services sold to customers
Cost of sales	Cost of sales	(260)	The costs involved in making and producing the products that have been sold, sometimes known as the cost of goods sold
Gross profit	Gross profit	40	Revenue less cost of sales gives gross profit
Selling, general and administration	Expenses	(15)	The overheads of the business that do not specifically relate to producing products or providing services, including rent, telephone and other head office costs
Operating income	Operating profit	25	Gross profit less expenses gives operating income
Interest	Interest	(5)	Interest charged on the business's borrowings
Income tax	Tax	(5)	Tax charged on the business's profits
Net income/ earnings	Earnings	15	The profit available for shareholders once all costs have been met

Cash flow

The cash flow statement summarises the cash received and paid out during a period of time which, as in the case of an income statement, is usually a month or a year. As many of the items in an income statement are paid for in cash, the cash flow statement could just repeat the same information. To simplify the detail, the cash flow statement usually starts with the operating income that has been earned and then adjusts for non-cash items and movements in working capital. As a business grows, it uses more cash (inventory levels rise and more customer balances are tied up in receivables). Consequently, as a business shrinks, it generates considerable cash as the money tied up in the working capital is released. Success is achieved when a business starts to generate more cash than is needed to fund the growth. The structure of a cash flow statement is shown in Table 4.4.

TABLE 4.4 **Structure of a cash flow statement**

US terms	UK terms	Amount	Explanation
Operating income	Operating profit	25	The operating income from the income statement
Add back depreciation and other non-cash deductions	Add back depreciation and other non-cash deductions	10	In arriving at operating income, several items have been deducted that do not involve cash leaving the business, including depreciation, amortisation and provisions. Hence these need to be added back
Movement in inventory	Movement in stock	3	The money tied up in funding an increase in inventory (or released on a reduction in inventory)
Movement in receivables	Movement in debtors	(5)	The money tied up in funding an increase in receivables (or released on a reduction in receivables)
Movement in payables	Movement in creditors	(3)	The money made available by increasing payables (or spent by reducing payables)
Cash from operations	Cash from operations	30	The cash generated from trading
Tax paid	Tax paid	(5)	Tax paid to a government, which typically lags behind the cost shown in the income statement. This is because the full cost cannot be worked out until the profits have been calculated
Investing activities	Investing activities	(40)	Cash spent on buying (or received on selling) fixed assets or business acquisitions
Financing activities	Financing activities	25	Cash raised on drawing down of further loans or issuing of additional share capital (or from repaying either of these sources of finance). Also includes any interest and dividends paid to investors
Change in cash in the business	Change in cash in the business	10	Surplus cash available for the following year

For a business to be successful it needs to be able to generate a positive cash flow before investing activities; in other words, it needs to generate surplus cash from trading. Failure at this point means the business is reliant upon investors to contribute additional funding to keep operations going, which is unsustainable in the long term. A surplus can be used to fund the purchase of new assets that not only maintain the business infrastructure but also support growth.

EBITDA

An approximation to the cash from operations is EBITDA, which stands for earnings before interest, tax, depreciation and amortisation. This is valid only if the movements in working capital are small or even self-cancelling (for example, an increase in receivables is matched with an increase in payables). It is a measure that is widely used by investment banks and analysts to understand a business's ability to generate cash and service debt.

Some organisations will also use a measure of EBITDARL, where the R and L stand for rentals and leases. This type of measure is useful for businesses such as airlines, where a substantial number of their assets are rented or leased, lease payments being equivalent to the depreciation and interest payments on owned assets.

Alternative language and layout

Around the world the essence of financial statements is the same. However, the language and layout vary. In the analysis above the American and British structure and terms have been used but other countries do things differently; for example, in France and Germany the statement of financial position for assets is typically presented the other way up, in liquidity order, with cash being the most liquid at the top and assets being the most illiquid at the bottom.

Although International Accounting Standards (IAS) try to harmonise the presentation, language and layout, there will always be variations. When working with statements from different countries, it is more important to know what the words mean rather than where they appear on the page.

Accounting systems

Every business needs to establish a system for co-ordinating the capture and recording of its transactions to produce these statements. This requires efficient collation of all purchase invoices, sales invoices, cash transactions and an array of other entries including payroll and petty cash. The system needs to be robust to ensure completeness and accuracy of the information that is gathered. It is from this database of information that the financial management reports are compiled on which performance is reviewed and many decisions are made.

Although financial management systems are now largely computerised, their structure, design and terminology have changed little since the days of manual book-keeping. At their heart is a system of double entry, where every transaction has a cause and effect. This means that two items in a statement of financial position are affected every time a transaction takes place.

The following series of transactions shows the build-up of this principle through a series of transactions.

A business issues 1,000 shares of $1 each raising $1,000. The cash in the business would rise and the liability to the investor would increase.

Assets ($)		Liabilities ($)	
Cash	1,000	Shares	1,000

A machine is purchased by the business for $600. The cash in the business will go down and be replaced by a fixed asset. The machine is a fixed asset as it will be used in the business rather than being sold (if it was purchased for resale then it would be inventory).

Assets ($)		Liabilities ($)	
Fixed asset	600	Shares	1,000
Cash	400		
	1,000		1,000

Inventory worth $500 is purchased on credit for resale. The asset of the inventory becomes part of the business as well as the liability to pay the supplier. Without the use of credit the transaction would not be able to take place as there is insufficient cash in the business.

Assets ($)		Liabilities ($)	
Fixed asset	600	Shares	1,000
Inventory	500	Payables	500
Cash	400		
	1,500		1,500

Half of the inventory is sold on credit for $400. Recording this requires the combination of two separate transactions: the disposal of inventory of $250; and the recognition of the profit on the sale of $150. Both transactions are added together in receivables as the customer owes the business $400. The profit belongs to the shareholders and hence it is shown as a liability for the business to pay this surplus to them at a future date. Profit is recognised when a product or service is delivered rather than when cash is received. This is explained in more detail in Chapter 5.

Assets ($)		Liabilities ($)	
Fixed asset	600	Shares	1,000
Inventory	250	Profit	150
Receivables	400	Payables	500
Cash	400		
	1,650		1,650

The business pays $80 for staff and utilities. This is an expense and will reduce the profit that has been earned. In paying for these items the cash will also be reduced.

Assets ($)		Liabilities ($)	
Fixed asset	600	Shares	1,000
Inventory	250	Profit	70
Receivables	400	Payables	500
Cash	320		
	1,570		1,570

These five transactions illustrate how the statement of financial position has been built by the process of double-entry book-keeping. Every transaction has affected two numbers and the totals of the two sides have remained balanced throughout.

As the example has progressed the details of the transactions have become lost. In a business this would make it impossible to find errors and check the validity of the items presented. Therefore to support each item there is a detailed account that records all the individual transactions (much like a bank statement). It is only the final balance on that account that is being shown on the statement of financial position.

The detailed accounts are known as "T" accounts as they are presented in a T shape. Taking cash as an example, the cash received is recorded on the left and the cash paid is recorded on the right. When all the transactions are entered a balance is struck to even up both sides. The net balance of all the transactions is the amount of cash held at the end of the example. In T accounts the items on the left are known as debits and those on the right are known as credits. In book-keeping there is always a credit for every debit.

TABLE 4.5 **T account**

CASH ACCOUNT

Initial investment	1,000	Purchase of asset	600
		Expenses	80
		Balance to carry down	320
	1,000		1,000
Balance brought down	320		

So far the example has shown only the statement of financial position, as the income statement is just an expansion of the profit line to explain how it was derived.

The income statement would be as follows:

Revenue	400
Cost of sales	(250)
Gross profit	150
Expenses	(80)
Net income (profit)	70

In reality, like the statement of financial position, the income statement would be drawn up from a set of T accounts that are used to record the accumulation of all the individual transactions in the business under various income and expense headings.

The cash flow statement records the transactions from the start of the year to the end and as described above is presented as follows rather than as a bank statement:

Net income	70
Increase in inventory	(250)
Increase in receivables	(400)
Increase in payables	500
Cash from operations	(80)
Purchase of new fixed assets	(600)
Investment by shareholders	1,000
Movement in cash	320

FIG 4.3 **A typical accounting system**

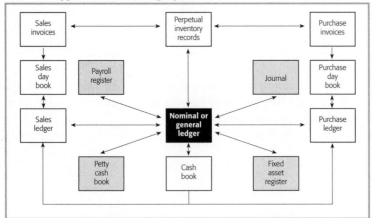

To manage this process of recording transactions for large organisations the business activity is separated into transaction types. Sub-systems are used to manage the volume of paperwork and detail. For example, a sales ledger, consisting of a T account for each customer, is used to record all the balances owed by customers. The addition of all the individual customer balances gives the total amount of receivables. Similarly, a fixed asset register is used to list all the assets owned by the business (for tracking purposes the ledger would also keep details of the current location of the asset and so on).

An example of a complete system is shown in Figure 4.3. Each of the registers is used as in Table 4.6.

TABLE 4.6 **Registers and their purpose**

Register	Purpose
Nominal or general ledger	The heart of the system where all the separate accounts for each item in the income statement and statement of financial position are kept and the transactions affecting each item are recorded. Control totals for all the other ledgers are also held here. The three principal financial statements are drawn up from the information kept in this ledger
Sales invoices	The individual customer invoices. A copy of each invoice (often stored electronically) is kept as evidence of customer transactions
Sales day book	A record of invoices issued each day to customers. This register has been dispensed with in many businesses where it can be easily compiled from the invoice data held in the system
Sales ledger	Individual customer accounts showing how much each customer owes the business. This enables a business to monitor when payment is due, and thus make sure that payments due are chased in good time so that cash continues to flow through the business as it should according to the terms of business agreed with customers
Purchase invoices	Invoices from suppliers which should be matched against the purchase orders raised to sanction the expenditure .
Purchase day book	Summarises all the purchases made each day. Like the sales day book, this has been dispensed with in many companies where the information can be extracted from the database
Purchase ledger	Also known as the bought ledger. This has individual supplier accounts showing how much is owed to each supplier. Payment runs are often done on set dates to pay the accounts as they fall due

Register	Purpose
Perpetual inventory records	Sitting between the sales and purchasing systems, the perpetual inventory records are updated as items are sold and can be set to automatically trigger purchases when inventory levels are low. This system is never completely reliable as most organisations experience "shrinkage" (waste, damage or theft) that requires regular inventory counts to ensure the accounting system accurately records the level of inventory
Payroll register	Accounts for the pay, overtime, taxation and benefits of all employees, providing a monthly feed of data
Journal	Provides information about any non-standard transaction that the business has experienced such as a bad debt or damaged stock that is written off
Petty cash book	Records the transactions in physical cash that take place for generally small-scale sundry business expenditure
Fixed asset register	A record of all the tangible fixed assets which is used to track age, depreciation and perhaps maintenance
Cash book	Unlike petty cash, the cash book is concerned with bank transactions and is used to update other registers; for example, cash received is reflected in the sales ledger and payments are matched against the purchase ledger.

Many software providers have created modular packages to support businesses. For smaller businesses, there are suites of packages ranging from those suitable for sole traders to more dynamic, integrated packages suitable for national businesses. For many multinational companies, software provided by SAP, a German company, has become the cornerstone of their accounting and information system. The software provides highly integrated business support. For example, the sales ledger does not just track invoices and cash receipts, but can be used to track all contact and correspondence with a customer, providing fast access to an entire relationship history. The perpetual inventory record can be linked directly to suppliers' computer systems to ensure that replenishment orders efficiently reflect lead times and suppliers' delivery schedules. All these enhancements enable a business to provide higher quality and more efficient service.

These highly integrated systems with total operational dependency also increase business risk because when they go wrong the business can struggle to maintain continuity.

This book aims to help with the understanding and management of finance within a business and not the detailed mechanics of transaction recording. The descriptions in this chapter should provide readers with an appreciation of the system used in many businesses, but the remaining chapters focus more on using the output from the system rather than its internal mechanics.

Actions for success

The three statements each have their use in understanding how the business is performing, but the route to success is to work through each line and constantly challenge the value being derived from the assets being used and costs incurred. A structured review can be completed as shown in Table 4.7.

TABLE 4.7 **A structured review**

Statement of financial position

Tangible fixed assets	■ Sweat the assets to make them work hard for the business (such as running production for more than eight hours a day and five days a week)
	■ If the machine is not working hard, it may be more effective to dispose of it and hire equipment for the occasions that it is used
	■ To avoid having a significant amount of cash tied up in assets, it may be more cost effective to rent or lease them
	■ Select equipment that has the lowest life-cycle cost, not necessarily the lowest purchase price. Maintain the equipment to extend the usable life
Inventory	■ Strive towards just-in-time delivery of inventory to keep the business's inventory levels low, although this needs to reflect lead times in supply and order quantities that are economic (see Chapter 14)
	■ Increase customer service levels by improving response times and being able to deliver on time in full
Receivables	■ Accelerate payment from customers; make sure that invoices are accurate and include the correct information (such as their purchase order numbers)

Cash	■ Investors in the business seek to earn a superior ROI. Some cash needs to be available to meet obligations, but having lots of cash will not necessarily make a business successful
Payables	■ Agree payment terms that defer payment and minimise the amount of funding required in the business

Income statement

Revenue	■ Look for opportunities to achieve revenue growth: more customers, more sales per customer and price increases based on the value added ■ Expand product range, market segments, channels to market and places/countries of operation ■ Invest in research to stay ahead of the market ■ Use marketing effectively to increase customer awareness and activity
Costs	■ Ensure value for money and seek economies to bring down costs ■ Seek to reduce unit manufacturing costs, but not by degrading the consumer proposition ■ Investigate cheaper administrative processes that do not reduce quality; these might include centralisation of overheads, and relocation, outsourcing or offshoring of some activities to lower-cost areas ■ Encourage staff to focus more on shareholder value by implementing share incentive or share option schemes

Cash flow

Cash from operations	■ Focus on cash flow, not cash; cash needs to arrive in the business ahead of its going out, and thus managing receivables and payables is critical to maintaining sufficient cash flow ■ Longer term, a surplus is needed to enable funding of reinvestment and growth. Cash over and above this requirement should be returned to investors

These are the actions that are critical for success in a business, and so it is helpful to have measures of performance for each of them – for example, a measure that records the average time inventory is held in the business. If this time is extending, the implication is that more cash is being tied up, but more importantly it may mean that customers are buying less of one or more product lines. Chapter 12 explores the calculation and use of this and a range of other measures that are used to monitor and manage a business.

5 Accounting concepts and principles

CHAPTER 4 LOOKED at creating financial statements for a business by recording the effect of the transactions that had taken place. This chapter looks at principles that are used to present business performance in a true and fair way.

For example, when should a business recognise the sale of a product or service? The options lie between the points when an order is placed by a customer through to when that customer settles the invoice. As this span of events could take place over a period of a year or more, a principle is needed to ensure that a sale, and business performance more widely, is consistently reported.

Four accounting concepts

Below are four accounting concepts which provide the basis for much of the world's accounting policies and practice.

Going concern

An assumption is made in accounting that a business will continue in existence for the foreseeable future. Therefore the value of the assets in the business does not have to be adjusted to a liquidation value (as if they had to be sold today). For example, the cost of equipment can be spread over its useful life using the concept of depreciation (explained in more detail on pages 62–9). This principle is particularly relevant for computers, where the useful life may be five years yet within a few months of purchase the market value can be minimal compared with the cost.

Similarly, if a business has an amount of receivables owed, it does not need to discount them to a value that it would get for immediate settlement. The business can show the amount that will be collectable with continuance of trade.

Prudence

The principle behind this concept is one of caution when prescribing suitable accounting policies. Revenues and profits should not be anticipated. They should be included only once they are realisable with reasonable certainty. For example, revenue is not recognised until it has been earned. To declare revenue when a customer places an order would be premature, particularly if the customer subsequently cancels the order. However, once a service or product has been delivered to a customer the business has fulfilled its obligation and is entitled to payment. At this point it would be prudent to declare that revenue has been genuinely earned.

Applying this concept is also important for costs, as it would be wrong to avoid disclosing liabilities or potential liabilities that were known to the business. For example, if a pension benefit has been granted to staff as part of their employment package, the amount of the commitment and the potential performance of the investment fund set up to fulfil the commitment may be unknown, but it is still prudent to declare any liability the business may have to make sure that the pension obligations are met. Even if the calculation of an obligation is difficult, a best estimate is still required to ensure that financial statements present a true and fair view of a business.

Accruals or matching

When the results for a business are declared, they should reflect the activity of the business not just the transactions. For example, if a hotel customer stays for two weeks spanning the business's year end (the first week in one year, the second week in the following year), even though the invoice is paid when the customer leaves, it does not fairly reflect the business activity if all the revenue is taken in the later year, so half the income should be accrued in the earlier year.

Similarly with matching: the costs for providing goods and services should be recognised in the same year as the revenue relating to those goods and services is recognised. Therefore in a retail environment the cost of the inventory sold should be recognised in the same time period as the revenue. It would be misleading to declare profits that did not include all the operating costs that were incurred in generating the declared revenue.

Consistency

This principle aims to ensure that when comparing the business results achieved in one period with those of another, the basis on which the information is prepared is the same. Therefore any comparisons of financial performance that are made between two periods are valid. For example, if a piece of equipment is depreciated over ten years in one period, this policy should be consistently applied and not extended or shortened for the next set of accounts.

Changes in accounting policies are allowed but should be infrequent. Any significant change requires the previous year's figures to be restated using the new policy, so that performance can be compared on a like-for-like basis.

Applying the accounting concepts

These four accounting concepts are straightforward in their purpose, but they can be applied in many – and sometimes conflicting – ways. For example, prudence suggests deferring revenue until it is reasonably certain, yet the accruals or matching concept suggests that accounts should reflect the activity of the business, not just the transactions.

The rest of this chapter will look at the practical application of the concepts.

Revenue recognition

When should a business recognise income? For example, an oil company has many definable points in its processes that could be used when it has "earned" its money. These include when:

- an oil field is discovered;
- crude oil is extracted;
- the crude oil is refined into finished products such as gasoline;

■ a customer places an order;
■ a product is delivered;
■ an invoice is raised;
■ the customer pays for the product.

Each of these events happens at different times (some being years apart). Therefore the point at which revenue is recognised will advance or retard the point when a venture becomes profitable.

Although effort and resources are invested at all these stages, there is no revenue until there is a sale to a customer. This may narrow the options, but there can still be some ambiguity. Should the revenue be taken on an intended sale to a customer or a fulfilled sale? The answer is that revenue is realised when the "obligations to a customer are substantially complete" – for example, when products are delivered to a customer or services completed.

In the case of an oil company, the application of this principle would mean revenue being recognised when products are delivered, even though the invoice may not have been raised or the cash received as these final two events require minimal resources to complete them. It is of course the case that until the customer pays the oil company will be at risk of bad debt and should be vigilant in chasing payments as they fall due.

Shell's policy for revenue recognition is: "Sales of oil, natural gas, chemicals and all other products are recorded when title passes to the customer." In other words, "when the goods are delivered".

The timing of when revenue should be recognised described here is typical of most businesses, but sometimes matters are more complicated.

Revenue received in advance

Airline seats are usually booked and paid for ahead of the departure date and often many months ahead. However, when the airline receives payment it has not transported the passenger and cannot say that its "obligations to the customer are substantially complete". Therefore the revenue should be recognised in the accounts only when the passenger travels and not on the receipt of cash. For a return flight the fare should be split, with perhaps half being recognised when the outbound flight is taken and the other half being recognised when the inbound flight is taken.

To account for the booking, the airline would show the cash received in its cash flow but also a liability on the statement of financial position of prepaid revenue that is potentially repayable to the customer until departure. On take-off the fare can be transferred out of liabilities and into earned revenue.

British Airways' policy for revenue recognition is: "Passenger and cargo sales revenue is recognised when the transportation service is provided. Passenger tickets, net of discounts, are recorded as current liabilities in the 'sales in advance of carriage account' until recognised as revenue." The amount of prepaid revenue in the company's accounts at December 31st 2012 was £853m for a business that has flown revenues of nearly £11 billion. Without this accounting policy the results would be significantly different.

Recognising revenue for continual service provision

Subscribers to a telecommunication business receive continual service so there is no one point of service delivery. Customers may be invoiced quarterly for usage during the previous three months, but the service is provided as each call is made and should be recognised as revenue in the same way. Therefore in the statement of financial position of a telecommunications company there would be two types of receivables:

- unbilled receivables – for calls made by customers but not yet invoiced to them;
- billed receivables – for invoices sent out and waiting for payment to be received.

When an invoice is sent to a customer the value of the invoice is moved from unbilled receivables to billed receivables.

The policy of France Telecom (known as Orange) for recognising call revenue is: "Revenues from charges for incoming and outgoing telephone calls are recognised in revenue when the service is rendered." This is regardless of whether it is paid for in advance (a prepaid mobile) or in arrears (a domestic fixed line).

Revenue from subscriptions

Subscribers to a magazine might make an annual payment in advance and then receive a copy every month or week for the next 12 months. In this example the service is being provided in a piecemeal format, so revenue should be similarly recognised. If the annual subscription for a monthly journal is $120, the publisher should recognise $10 a month over the life of subscription. In the accounts the advanced revenue would be held as a payable on the statement of financial position in a similar manner to the airline example above.

For Pearson (part owner of *The Economist*) the policy for recognising subscription revenue is: "Subscription revenue is recognised on a straight-line basis over the life of the subscription." Straight line means evenly over the period of the subscription.

Cancellable revenue

Although revenue is declared when the "obligations to a customer are substantially complete", this statement needs to be balanced with any policy that exists for customers to return goods. This is separate from guarantees or faulty products (which are covered under warranties below) – it is a simple change of mind by the customer after paying for the goods. In this situation the product is returned, a full refund is given and the product is put back on display for sale again. If significant quantities of products are involved, it would be wrong for a business to declare all the sales it made only to see some of them being cancelled. In this case, some sales should be held back to match the rate of return typically experienced. For example, if 5% of a retailer's sales were returned within four weeks, a provision should be made for these returns, lowering revenue and making appropriate adjustments as the actual returns rate materialised. The percentage used to calculate the provision would be constantly revised in the light of experience.

Marks & Spencer, a UK retailer, says that revenue in its accounts is: "Sales of goods to customers less an appropriate deduction for actual and expected returns."

Consignment inventory

A manufacturer that wishes to encourage a retailer to sell its products may distribute them using a consignment process. The retailer takes delivery of products and displays them, but does not purchase them; the manufacturer retains ownership of the products. The retailer will purchase the goods only when it sells them to a customer. Any goods left unsold can be returned to the manufacturer. In the meantime, the manufacturer must account in its statement of financial position for inventory it owns being held by the retailer and only recognise revenue on its income statement when the retailer has made a sale.

Cost of sales

The accounting concept of matching described above requires that when revenue is recognised, the costs associated with earning that revenue are also declared. By this process the revenue is matched with its costs and a genuine profit can be identified. The inclusion of cost in a different time period to the revenue will clearly distort the amount of profit. The difficulty is to define cost.

In retailing the principle is easy to apply. When a product that cost a business $80 is sold for $100, the income can be matched against the cost to produce a profit of $20.

However, if the cost of the product rose such that there were two items on the shelf, one costing $75 and the other, which had been bought after the price increase, costing $80, it would be tempting to assume the customer bought the cheaper one and the business made more profit. Therefore a rule is required to decide which one was bought first. The principle typically applied is known as FIFO (first in, first out), which means the product bought first is sold first regardless of which item was actually bought and even whether the cost is rising or falling.

Pirelli, an Italian tyre manufacturer, has the following accounting policy for inventory: "Inventories are measured at the lower of cost, determined according to the FIFO method, and their estimated realisable value." This means that if items of inventory have a lower market value than the price paid for them, they should be valued at that lower market value.

In the United States, LIFO (last in, first out) is also permitted as a basis of managing inventory. Hence the inventory comprises the oldest items.

ExxonMobil, an American oil company, has the following accounting policy for inventory: "Inventories of crude oil, products, and merchandise are carried at the lower of current market value or cost (generally determined under the last-in, first-out method or LIFO)."

Although this is an accounting policy for inventory, the principle directly relates to cost of sales as this is the basis upon which the items remaining on the shelf are valued. Depending on the chosen method, LIFO or FIFO, the one sold will be the one that has been owned either the shortest or the longest.

Warranties

The definition of cost should not only cover what happens at the point of sale but also the full obligation attached to the sale. For example, if a manufacturing business sold a product that was faulty and had provided a guarantee, the business would have the obligation to rectify the fault at its own cost. Depending on the length of the guarantee, the cost of these repairs could fall in a later time period to the one when the profit was recognised, as would be the case for sales made with, say, three-year warranties. Therefore manufacturing businesses set aside a proportion of every sale to meet the cost of future warranty obligations.

For example, if a business sold 10,000 products and on average 2% of these required warranty repairs, a warranty provision would be required to mend 200 products. If each repair averaged $200, a provision of $40,000, or $4 per product sold, would be required. The provision would be a cost on the income statement at the point of sale to ensure that profits were not overstated. On the statement of financial position the provision is a type of liability set up to pay the future repair costs.

As the actual costs of repairs materialise they will be charged against the provision rather than the income statement. However, the provision is unlikely to be exactly the right amount – the fault rate may be higher or lower as may the cost of each repair. This results in an additional cost being incurred or a release of an excessive provision. Experience should enable the provision to be calculated more accurately in future years.

Renault, a French vehicle-maker, has the following accounting policy with regard to warranties: "The estimated or incurred costs relating to product or part warranties not covered by insurance are charged to expenses when the sales are recorded. In the event of product recalls relating to incidents that come to light after the vehicle has been on the market, provisions are established to cover the costs involved as soon as the decision to undertake the recall campaign has been made."

Therefore the costs of any warranty work are anticipated and charged against profits in the year the car is sold rather than being left until they are incurred.

Overall, the focus in a business should be not just how to make the provision more accurate but also to find the source of any faults, improve quality and reduce the incidence of repair.

Abandonment

The principle of recognising future obligations attached to a sale can be extended still further to what happens when a business ceases trading. For example, a nuclear power station may operate for 50 years, but once it is decommissioned the cost of clearing the site is immense, with no future income from that power station to cover the cost. Such future costs should therefore be charged to the income statement during the profitable years to create a provision that can cover this future expenditure.

EDF Energy's accounting policy for decommissioning nuclear power stations is: "Provisions for decommissioning of nuclear power plants result from management's best estimates. They cover the full cost of decommissioning and are measured on the basis of existing techniques and methods that are most likely to be used for application of current regulations."

The provision can be created on:

■ an annual basis, with a fixed amount for each year of operation; or

■ a unit basis, taking the expected abandonment cost and dividing it by the expected output over the life of the business. This will produce a provision amount that is required per unit of output. Therefore the provision can build in direct proportion to the income earned.

Other industries that need this type of provisioning are those involved in extraction (mining and oil) and waste management, making good after a waste site has been filled. A smaller-scale example would be dilapidations that are paid on the exit of a property lease. It would be prudent to accrue an amount for these over the term of the lease, rather than incur the full cost on exit.

Accruals and prepayments

In preparing a set of accounts it is important that under the "matching" concept there is completeness of both revenues and costs. Otherwise the profit that is reported will be inaccurate and misleading. Accruals and prepayments are used to move costs into the accounting period where the benefit of the expenditure is derived by the business.

Accruals

An accrual is where a business has had the benefit of goods or services, yet at the end of the accounting period there is no invoice or paperwork to record the cost. An example would be electricity that is invoiced quarterly or advertising that is invoiced in arrears. In both examples the cost shown in the accounts could be understated, leading to an overstatement of profit.

To correct for this understatement of costs an estimate is made for the amount of benefit derived. For example, if the most recent quarterly electricity invoice was for $3,000 and it was received a month before the year end, it would be reasonable to assume that the business consumed $1,000 of electricity a month and this was the amount due for the last month of the year. The accounting effect would be to increase electricity costs by $1,000 and increase accruals (a liability) by $1,000.

FIG 5.1 **Accruals and prepayments**

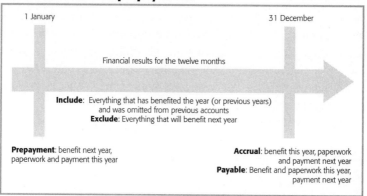

1 January   31 December

Financial results for the twelve months

Include: Everything that has benefited the year (or previous years)
and was omitted from previous accounts
Exclude: Everything that will benefit next year

Prepayment: benefit next year,
paperwork and payment this year

Accrual: benefit this year, paperwork
and payment next year
Payable: Benefit and paperwork this year,
payment next year

An accrued expense is in effect an estimated payable. Once the paperwork arrives the accrual can be reversed and the actual invoice recorded as a true payable.

Bank interest is an area where an accrual is required to ensure that a full 365 days of interest is shown in the accounts rather than just the quarterly or monthly payments as they fall due.

Prepayments

A prepayment is where a business has incurred the cost of a service but has not received the benefit. Examples are insurance and rent, which are both usually paid in advance of receiving the benefit. If the benefit were to arise in the next accounting period, it would lead to the current accounting period incurring costs unjustly, resulting in an understatement of profit.

To correct for this, the expenditure is shown as a prepayment, a type of receivable (although it is unlikely ever to be received as cash), rather than taken as a cost in the income statement. For example, if $12,000 is spent on next year's insurance, the expenditure will be recorded as a prepayment of $12,000. The accounting effect will be to increase prepayments (an asset) and reduce cash by $12,000.

As the benefit is being derived the prepayment is reversed and cost is incurred (the accounting effect being to reduce prepayments and increase the insurance cost). However, this may be done monthly at a rate of $1,000 so it shows as a constant monthly cost.

Depreciation

When a company purchases a fixed asset, such as a piece of plant or equipment, it will initially record it on its statement of financial position at cost. As the asset is used in the business it will start to wear out. Eventually the asset will be either sold or scrapped. With the exception of property, the business is unlikely to recover its original investment on disposal.

For example, a car that costs $20,000 new is sold four years later for $8,000. The business will have lost $12,000 during the period of ownership. How should this cost be treated in the accounts? Potentially there are three options:

■ Take the cost at the end, once the full loss is known. This, however, is contrary to the principle of prudence outlined above. Losses should be recorded as soon as they are known.

■ Take the cost as an expense on the purchase and not show an asset at all. However, it would seem rather harsh that the profits in the year of purchase should be hit so hard when there may be many years of benefit derived from the asset.

■ Recognise the cost of the asset over its useful life in the business. This is the most logical option and is in line with the accounting concept of matching. The asset is being used to generate income for the business so a proportion of its cost is recognised at the same time. This is the concept of depreciation.

Depreciation is the process of spreading the cost of owning an asset over the years that benefit from its use. This is a straightforward application of the matching concept.

In making the decision four factors should be taken into account:

■ the original cost;
■ the useful life of the asset;
■ the potential disposal value or residual value;
■ the method of spreading cost over the useful life.

The original cost

The cost of the asset will in most circumstances be the purchase price. But where considerable installation or acquisition costs are incurred it would be reasonable to capitalise the total cost and depreciate this higher amount over the years that benefit.

The inclusion of all costs that are directly attributable to bringing the asset into working condition for its intended use should be considered. This can be difficult if an organisation constructs its own assets. For example, a telecommunications business might build its network using its own staff, so it would be reasonable to include the cost of all the materials and the staff and management time used in construction, with the total sum being depreciated over the period that the network will be used.

British Telecom's accounting policy for the cost of an asset is: "Costs for network infrastructure and equipment are direct and indirect labour costs, materials and directly attributable overheads."

Some organisations also include the cost of interest on the finance for the construction of the asset up to the point of its being brought into service. For example, Boeing says: "Property, plant and equipment are recorded at cost, including applicable construction-period interest."

The capitalisation of these construction costs is appropriate as a business has two ways of acquiring an asset: purchase or build. If it purchases, it is effectively paying for another organisation to complete the construction and the purchase price will reflect not only these component costs but also the construction company's profit. If it decides to construct its own assets, it can accumulate the costs of doing so and have an asset of the amount invested.

During its life an asset may be enhanced by improvements, such as constructing new offices in a building, which are an addition to the cost.

The *de minimis* (a Latin expression meaning "little things") principle applies here. It means that low-value assets should not be subject to the depreciation process as the administration involved does not justify the benefit. Therefore businesses will have a rule that excludes any item from being capitalised if its cost is below, say, $1,000.

Useful life

When deciding how to spread the cost of an asset over its expected useful life, management needs to determine how long they will derive value from the asset. Some assets, such as computers, will have short lives because of technical obsolescence, whereas others, such as buildings, will last for many years. Therefore organisations pool similar types of assets and set a standard period for their expected useful life.

For example, Tui, a travel business, sets the following periods for its asset lives:

Hotel buildings	30–40 years
Other buildings	up to 50 years
Cruise ships	20–30 years
Yachts	5–15 years
Motorboats	15–24 years
Aircraft:	
fuselages and engines	up to 18 years
engine overhaul	depending on intervals, up to 5 years
major overhaul	depending on intervals, up to 5 years
spare parts	12 years
Other machinery and fixtures	up to 40 years
Operating and business equipment	up to 10 years

The reason for using time spans rather than a fixed period is that within each category there are sub-classifications. For example, "business equipment" includes office furniture that may have a ten-year life compared with computers that may have a five-year life. It is unusual for businesses to fully disclose all the detailed categories in their accounts.

Other organisations use similar periods for their asset lives.

Residual values

At disposal an asset may well have a resale value and hence its cost should not be depreciated below this amount – vehicles and some equipment fall into this category. In many businesses the assets will be used for their full life and have to be scrapped at the end.

In some businesses there may be a cost for disposing of the asset at the end of its useful life. This implies that the residual value is in fact a payment rather than a receipt. An example would be a machine involved with hazardous materials where there is a clean-up cost at the end of its useful life. The process of building a provision for a future known liability is explained under abandonment (see page 59).

Depreciation method

Four methods are commonly used to spread the cost of an asset over its estimated useful life:

- Straight line – this will allocate the cost of ownership equally for each year of the useful life.

- Reducing balance – reflecting that many assets, other than property, typically lose more of their value in their early years than in their later years. This is particularly the case for computer equipment.

- Sum of digits – similar to reducing balance with less complicated mathematics.

- Unit of production – depreciating the asset in proportion to the amount of revenue that the asset has helped to generate.

In the short term each of these methods will result in different annual charges and hence an acceleration or deceleration of profit. However, in the long term the effects will be the same as all three methods spread the same amount of cost over the same period of time (see Figure 5.2).

Figure 5.3 illustrates the typical profile of an asset (other than property) over its life in terms of market value. It shows how straight-line depreciation reaches the same destination, although it takes a different route.

FIG 5.2 **The three depreciation methods compared**

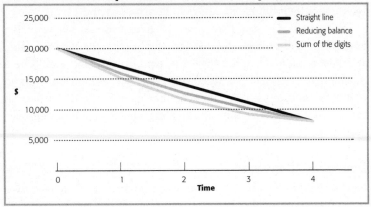

Straight-line depreciation

Returning to the example introduced earlier, a car costs $20,000 new and is sold four years later for $8,000. If straight-line depreciation is used, the loss of $12,000 will be spread evenly over the four years at the rate of $3,000 per year.

The calculation for this is:

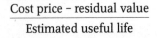

$$\frac{\text{Cost price} - \text{residual value}}{\text{Estimated useful life}}$$

FIG 5.3 **The typical profile of a depreciating asset**

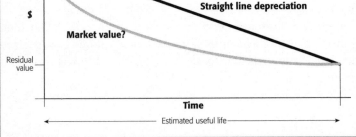

The business's accounts would look like this:

	Year 1	Year 2	Year 3	Year 4
Statement of financial position extract				
Fixed asset cost	20,000	20,000	20,000	20,000
Accumulated depreciation	(3,000)	(6,000)	(9,000)	(12,000)
Net book value	17,000	14,000	11,000	8,000
Income statement extract				
Depreciation	3,000	3,000	3,000	3,000

At the end of the four years the asset may be sold for slightly more or less than the anticipated value. This will result in a small profit or loss on disposal.

Reducing-balance depreciation

This method takes a fixed percentage of the previous year's net book value. The effect is to produce a profile of value that more closely reflects the market value of the asset.

The calculation for this percentage is:

$$\left(1 - \left(\sqrt[\text{Asset life}]{\frac{\text{Residual value}}{\text{Cost}}} \right) \right) \times 100$$

Applying the formula to the example, the reducing-balance percentage would be:

$$\left(1 - \left(\sqrt[4]{\frac{8,000}{20,000}} \right) \right) \times 100$$

This results in a value of 20.473%. Each year the net book value will be depreciated by this amount as follows:

	Year 1	Year 2	Year 3	Year 4
Statement of financial position extract				
Fixed asset cost	20,000	20,000	20,000	20,000
Accumulated depreciation	(4,095)	(7,351)	(9,941)	(12,000)
Net book value	15,905	12,649	10,059	8,000
Income statement extract				
Depreciation	4,095	3,256	2,590	2,059

Sum of digits depreciation

This uses the principle of accelerating depreciation by taking the years in reverse order and expressing them as a fraction of the sum of the digits of the years (4 + 3 + 2 + 1 = 10) in the example. Thus in year one 4/10 of the loss in value will be recognised, in year two 3/10 will be recognised and so on.

The results for the example will be as follows:

	Year 1	Year 2	Year 3	Year 4
Statement of financial position extract				
Fixed asset cost	20,000	20,000	20,000	20,000
Accumulated depreciation	(4,800)	(8,400)	(10,800)	(12,000)
Net book value	15,200	11,600	9,200	8,000
Income statement extract				
Depreciation	4,800	3,600	2,400	1,200

With the complexity of calculation and the acceleration effect of cost in two of these methods it is little surprise that the majority of businesses opt for the straight-line method of depreciation.

Boeing's policy is a rare mixture of all three methods: "The principal methods of depreciation are: buildings and land improvements, declining balance; and machinery and equipment, sum-of-the-years' digits. Capitalised internal use software is included using the straight-line method over five years."

Unit of production method

This method is used primarily in natural resources businesses where the cost of establishing an oil well or mine is depreciated over the expected reserves to be extracted. For example, if a mine costs $100m to construct and there are an estimated 50m tonnes of ore to extract, it would be reasonable to suggest that as each tonne is lifted $2 of depreciation should be recognised.

This method most closely follows the principle of matching described earlier, although the data capture required to apply it makes it suitable only for large-scale assets such as mines. Businesses using this method need to watch carefully the level of remaining recoverable reserves as a large write-off would have to be made should the extraction cease to be viable with half the cost still left to depreciate.

BP's policy on depreciation is: "Oil and and natural gas properties, including related pipelines, are depreciated using a unit-of-production method." But the company uses the straight-line method for all other property, plant and equipment.

Reserves or provisions

Much of this chapter focuses on the principle of matching and this extends to understanding how future events will affect the current results of the business – for example, the way the cost of abandonment for a nuclear power business needs to be accounted for during the life of the asset (see page 59).

A provision is a probable liability that a business will have to pay. It is of uncertain amount and timing. The indefinable nature requires judgment that is both prudent and realistic. Some common examples are as follows.

Vouchers

Where a business issues coupons or rewards to encourage sales it would be prudent to make a provision for the cost of their redemption. Therefore the income that triggered the "gift" is matched with the cost of its fulfilment. An example is frequent flyer points or miles. Delta Air Lines's policy is: "We defer revenue from the mileage credit component of passenger ticket sales and recognise it as passenger revenue when miles are redeemed and services are provided." On December 31st 2012 the liability in the company's accounts was $1,806m with an undisclosed number of miles.

For these "gifts" the business needs to identify the conversion value and ensure it has made a sufficient provision. Experience will make it possible to improve the assumptions and refine the provision.

Bad debts

A bad debt occurs when a customer, who purchases on credit, does not pay their invoice. Using the going concern concept the results of a business are prepared with the expectation that the receivables will be received. However, it is likely that not all will be, and experience and judgment should be used to estimate a prudent bad debt provision that can be included in the accounts.

The collection of loan receivables is critical to a bank's performance. Citigroup, one of the world's largest banking groups, states: "Allowance for loan losses represents management's best estimate of probable losses inherent in the portfolio, as well as probable losses related to large individually evaluated impaired loans and troubled debt restructurings." In 2012 Citigroup earned net interest revenue of $48 billion and increased its provision for loan losses by just under $11 billion. Cautious or optimistic views on debt delinquency can substantially change the profit declared to investors, as many banks found in 2007 when the credit squeeze and American subprime mortgages substantially increased bad debt levels. The loan losses in 2007, 2008, 2009 and 2010 were $18 billion, $35 billion, $40 billion and $26 billion respectively.

Inventory

Inventory is normally valued at cost – using the first in, first out (FIFO) method described above – unless its net realisable value would be lower. In a high-technology business, products quickly lose their saleable value as competitive new products come onto the market or simply because old models have little value. The prudence concept requires these to be written down to a low or zero amount to ensure their value is not overstated. The cost of this reduction in inventory value is a direct cost that reduces profit.

Intel, a large silicon chip manufacturer, states: "The valuation of inventory requires us to estimate obsolete or excess inventory as well as inventory that is not of saleable quality. The determination of obsolete or excess inventory requires us to estimate the future demand for our products." Therefore the costs of products that are more than six months old are likely to be written off as there is little or no expectation of them being sold.

In managing the valuation of inventory it is also important to validate its existence. Regular inventory counting to check that the records are accurate will identify inventory that has been lost through operational errors or theft. Inventory losses need to be written off and where these are significant, procedures should be implemented to improve control and security.

The cost of improving security needs to be proportional to the losses. High-value and easily resold items should be held securely, with the remainder being held in a less secure environment. A system of control known as ABC can be used to manage this (see Table 5.1).

TABLE 5.1 **ABC inventory control system**

A	High-value and easily resold items	Tight control and high security	80% of sales and 20% of the range
B	Bulky items with low resale values	Lower control and security	15% of sales and 30% of range
C	Consumables with low stock turn and resale value	Little or no control	5% of sales and 50% of range

This approach should make sure that a cost-effective amount of recording, validation, security and checking will be in place. The percentages are merely indicative and need to be adapted to the nature of the inventory being held.

Traditionally, businesses would have a full inventory count at regular intervals when trade would cease and everything would be counted. These days it is more common for organisations to operate a perpetual product inventory (PPI) system which requires a random selection of products to be counted each day and validated. The random selection is biased to have the high-value items counted more frequently than the lower-value items and for every item to be counted over a six month period. PPI can be automated with handheld terminals reading bar codes, enabling a business to operate more continuously than would be the case if it had to close to complete a full inventory count.

The use of RFID (radio frequency identification) tags can be an efficient way to monitor and keep track of inventory, as RFID readers can be positioned at critical points along the supply chain, allowing individual items to be constantly located during storage and distribution. The cost of the technology makes this process viable only for high-value items; it is typically used by such businesses as mobile phone companies to control their inventory. This technology is overtaking bar codes as the most efficient way to track products.

Impairment

As seen in the previous section, inventory is specifically tested against its net realisable value so that it is not overstated. Similarly, all other assets on the statement of financial position are tested against any permanent diminution of value or impairment.

Hewlett-Packard, an IT company, states that its "in-process research and development' is initially capitalised at fair value as an intangible asset with an indefinite life and assessed for impairment thereafter". It also applies the same principle to its acquisitions: "Goodwill and purchased intangible assets with indefinite useful lives are not amortised but are tested for impairment at least annually." In 2012 the company took a total impairment charge of $18 billion, mainly relating to its acquisition of Automony. Goodwill is covered in more detail in Chapter 16.

This process forces management to review the assets each year and prudently consider the changes in circumstances that would leave assets overstated on the statement of financial position.

Legal claims

This is perhaps the most contentious area, where a provision can disrupt the legal process. If a business is sued or prosecuted and found at fault or guilty, it is likely to have to pay compensation. Therefore if a business has any outstanding cases to defend, prudence would suggest that a provision should be made for the potential financial costs. However, lawyers would argue that a provision would imply an acceptance of fault or guilt by preparing for the verdict to go against the business.

BAT, a global tobacco company, has a policy which states that group companies "are defendants in tobacco-related and other litigation. Provision for this litigation would be made at such time as an unfavourable outcome became probable and the amount could be reasonably estimated." Therefore no provision is held until late in the legal process.

Where a business has insurance for a legal claim, such as a personal injury to a member of staff or a visitor to its site, any liability will not necessarily have an impact on the financial results. Therefore no provision would be necessary regardless of the outcome of the claim.

Pensions/post-retirement plans

As part of staff remuneration packages many businesses offer a pension scheme. With "defined benefit schemes" that prescribe the amount of pension employees receive on retirement (normally a percentage of their final salary), building up sufficient funds to meet this liability requires a business to contribute annually to a separately administered pension fund. Actuaries are used to calculate the amount of contribution required each year based on assumptions for fund performance, pension payments and life expectancy of staff. Should the assumptions differ from reality, such as poor fund performance or longer life expectancy, the fund required to pay the pensions can be insufficient to meet expected obligations. At this point a deficit is declared, but the question is how to close the deficit.

AkzoNobel, a chemicals company, declared in its 2012 accounts that its future pension liabilities were €16.9 billion and the value of the assets to meet those liabilities was €15.4 billion, which meant there was a pension-funding deficit of €1.5 billion. Under accounting rules a company must show this deficit in its accounts.

The deficit can be tackled in a number of ways. To reduce the liability, either future pension benefits need to be scaled back or employees are required to retire later. To increase the assets, either more contributions are required or better fund performance is sought. None of these are easy options and most businesses opt for a combination of all four.

Ultimately, the liability will become payable far into the future and much can change in the intervening period to make radical short-term actions unnecessary. Therefore these deficits are set to run for many years with a planned gradual narrowing. However, the size of the deficit on some statements of financial position is such that it can deter investors. Investing to narrow a pension deficit is unlikely to be as rewarding as investing in growth activities. Thus it is imperative that those businesses with large deficits bring the gap under control to enable the focus on operating activities to return.

Ironically, in the late 1990s it was not uncommon for many of the schemes to be overfunded, with more assets than liabilities. In those years of plenty many businesses took "pension holidays", which meant they suspended their contributions. With hindsight, a constant level of contributions would have put many schemes in a stronger position today.

As a result of the problems that have arisen with regard to pension funding, many businesses have changed from having "defined benefit" pension schemes to having "defined contribution" schemes, under which a fixed amount is paid into a fund and whatever value it reaches on retirement will determine the level of pension received. This change has transferred the investment performance and the longevity risk from the business to the employee.

Insurance loss reserves

The insurance industry provides a good example of accounting for provisions. Customers pay premiums (often in advance of the time period covered) and at some future date a proportion of the policyholders will make a claim. The insurance company's business model depends on it calculating the likely frequency and size of claims and setting premiums at a level that will leave the desired profit after paying out claims. Errors in the risk assessment calculations can result in insurance companies paying out more than they earn.

To manage this type of business there needs to be a constant assessment of the amount of premium income that needs to be held in a provision for future claims. AXA, a French insurance company, has the following accounting policy note: "Claims reserves are based on historical claim data, current trends and actual payment patterns for all insurance business lines as well as expected changes in inflation, regulatory environment or anything else that could impact amounts to be paid." Essentially, the profit declared by an insurance company is entirely based on its provisioning judgment.

This judgment is made more difficult by potential liabilities that are far into the future. Insurance companies categorise their obligations into "short tail" and "long tail" business:

- Short tail relates to policies where claims will arise within the policy period. Examples are motor and household. Cover is for a year and if no claims are received within that period, there is no future obligation.

- Long tail relates to policies where claims may arise a long time after the policy period for events that happened during the policy period. For example, under employers' liability, insurers have to pay out large amounts on claims relating to asbestosis where employees become ill many years after their employment.

Research and development

Applying the principle of matching to the cost of research and development, it would seem sensible for the accumulated costs in advance of a product launch to be treated as an intangible asset and then spread over the years in which revenue is earned. This would be similar to the way in which depreciation spreads the cost of a physical asset over the years that benefit from its use.

However, as a research project progresses and the costs are accumulated, there is no guarantee that the project will succeed or even generate any revenue. Therefore prudence should prevail and no accumulation of cost should be made until the outcome of the research is known with some certainty. Until this point the research costs should be charged to the income statement as they are incurred.

The second stage is known as development and the costs for this can be accumulated as an intangible asset and spread over a product's life.

GSK (GlaxoSmithKline), a large pharmaceutical company, invests heavily in drug research and its policy for treating research and development costs is: "Research and development expenditure is charged to the income statement in the period in which it is incurred. Development expenditure is capitalised when the criteria for recognising it as an asset are met, usually when regulatory filing has been made in a major market and approval is considered highly probable."

Summary

The four accounting principles covered in this chapter may seem straightforward, but considerable judgment is required in their application and at times the principles can conflict. When presenting financial information that reports the performance of a business it should be prepared with prudence and in a consistent manner, and wherever possible the revenue and costs for the provision of products and services should be matched so that a fair profit for each sale is declared.

6 Investors

IN CHAPTER 1 two broad categories of investor were identified (shareholders and banks) as was the concept of the weighted average cost of capital (WACC), which is the average cost to the business of the pool of funds invested. From these funds management needs to create their sustainable superior return on investment (ROI), hence their quest to create a ROI that is greater than the WACC (see Figure 1.3 on page 11).

For example, a business with a WACC of 12% needs to make sure that all its projects and investments generate at least this rate for it to stand a chance of meeting its investors' expectations. If the business's actual ROI is 18%, it is delivering real shareholder value of six percentage points (or 50%) more than the rate required by its investors. To improve the shareholder value still further, management need to focus as much effort on enhancing ROI as they should on reducing WACC. Much of this book looks at the former, but this chapter explores the variety of funding sources and their impact on WACC. It looks at the types of equity and debt available, and the purposes to which each can be applied. The mix of equity and debt will determine both the funding cost to the business and the risk exposure for the investors.

Selecting finance

In selecting the most appropriate type of finance for a business there are two main determinants: duration and cost.

Duration

For how long is the funding required? The repayment of funding should match the profile of the investment it is used to finance. For example, the purchase of property, which may have long-term use in the business, should be funded by long-term finance with repayments matching the revenue expectations. Potentially, these can be spread far into the future. This type of long-term funding would be inappropriate for a business that needed to cover a short-term funding requirement while waiting for a receivable to be paid.

Cost

What is the cost of the funding? The greater the risks taken by the providers of funding, the higher is the rate of return they require. For example, if a provider of funds is promised that it would be the first to be repaid if the business were in difficulty and that it can take a charge over the physical assets (such as property that it could sell to clear the debt), it has a low risk of losing its money and thus the business would expect the cost of this funding to be relatively low.

However, lowering the risk to one provider of funds increases the risk to another. With the assets all used as security for one party, another will have no security that its money will be repaid in event of difficulty. For this higher risk a higher return will be required. The cost of funding is therefore determined by the level of risk to each type of funding.

Types of funding

There are three main types of funding:

- **Equity.** This is capital put in by investors – the owners of business. They are the last to be repaid if the business is in trouble and have to accept the risk that they may lose all the money they put into the business (but no more than that). In return they are entitled to the profits generated by the business, and to a potentially limitless return.

- **Debt instruments.** These long-term borrowings are typically used to fund investments such as the purchase of property. The

FIG 6.1 **Types of funding**

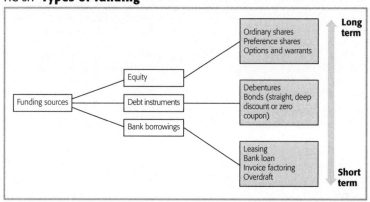

lenders will have priority if the business runs into trouble and may even have some protection by taking security on the asset funded. Their reward will be a predetermined rate of interest that is either fixed or linked to a central bank index.

- **Bank borrowing.** This typically short-term funding is used to cover temporary shortfalls and timing differences. The borrowing may be unsecured and consequently carry an interest rate above that of a debt instrument. A business may organise a borrowing facility with a bank to enable it to draw on this type of funding at short notice without the need for further discussion with the bank.

These three types of funding can be split further into a variety of instruments to meet specific needs in the business (see Figure 6.1). The characteristics of each are shown in Table 6.1.

TABLE 6.1 **Characteristics of different types of funding**

Type	Duration	Cost	Risk	Purpose
Ordinary shares/ common stock	Permanent finance, although there are legal processes available to allow redemption through a share buy-back	Usually through dividends paid out of earnings	Ordinary shareholders are the last to be paid in event of a winding up and have highest risk of losing their money	Ordinary shareholders own the company and provide its core long-term funding. The equity also provides security for the debt providers
Preference shares/ preferred stock	Sometimes given a repayment date, otherwise like ordinary shares	Usually a fixed percentage dividend. May be cumulative should the company be unable to pay in any one year	Holders are paid out before ordinary shareholders	Usually issued to raise share capital without diluting control. Preference shareholders do not normally have voting rights
Options and warrants	Provide the right but not the obligation to buy ordinary shares at a future date at a set price	No cost until exercised, at which point they become ordinary shares on which dividends may be paid	No cost at issue and if the exercise price at the due date is not attractive they lapse. If purchased on the market, they have no value other than for resale	Either issued with ordinary shares as an incentive to buy ordinary shares or used as an incentive for executives
Debentures	Fixed with a predetermined repayment date	Fixed rate of interest	Secured on the property of the company, usually freehold buildings	Effectively a commercial mortgage to provide long-term loan finance for assets

Type	Duration	Cost	Risk	Purpose
Bonds	Fixed with a predetermined repayment date	Fixed interest rate. Varieties are straight, deep discount and zero-coupon. Interest may be paid during the life of the bond, at the end, or a mixture of the two	The bond is issued in certificate form that can be traded like shares. Bondholders are paid out before all shareholders	Long-term loan finance with a cash flow profile to match the cash profile of a project in which the funding is invested
Convertibles	Permanent capital first as debt then as equity. There can be a repayment option if the share price at conversion is not attractive	Low interest rate for a set period, followed by conversion into ordinary shares provided the share price has achieved a specified level	Although a form of debt, convertibles usually rank after other debt. Once converted to ordinary shares the risk is the same as for other shares	Long-term finance that has a low initial cost
Leasing	For the life of the asset being leased	Normally a fixed interest rate cost implicit in the monthly payment	Secured on the asset being leased	To fund specific asset purchases without an up-front purchase. There can be tax and replacement benefits
Loans	Often fixed with a predetermined repayment date and sometimes interim repayments	An arrangement fee as well as a percentage return that can be fixed or variable. The variable rate is usually linked to a central bank rate plus an increment	Ranks before all shareholders and will sometimes be secured on assets with a fixed or floating charge	Funding for projects which will generate sufficient funds to allow repayment

Type	Duration	Cost	Risk	Purpose
Factoring	The outsourcing of debt collection and hence its duration is for the life of the contract	The debts being factored are discounted to take account of the interest cost of the money advanced for the time taken to collect the debt. There is also a management fee	Secured on the debts. Factoring can be done with recourse (any bad debts passed back to the business) or without recourse (the lender accepts liability for any bad debts, but will charge a higher fee for doing so)	To accelerate the collection of receivables and prevent cash being tied up in working capital. It can also be used to reduce overhead costs as it outsources part of the accounting function
Overdrafts	Rolling facilities that normally have a fixed time period	A facility fee as well as a variable rate at a significant increment over a central bank rate	Depends on security arrangements but can rank behind other forms of debt	To bridge day-to-day working capital gaps between receivables and payables

Funding duration

The duration of the funding has a significant influence on which will be most suitable. In principle, long-term assets should be funded by long-term finance and short-term requirements by short-term finance. For example, the fixed assets of property or equipment might be funded by equity or debt instruments as they are both for long-term duration, whereas an increase in working capital, such as receivables or inventory as a consequence of seasonal business activity, might be funded by a bank overdraft as the cash investment should be repayable within a few months. Table 6.2 gives some guidelines.

The equity and debt amounts referred to in Table 6.2 would be minimums for public offerings. Private raising of smaller sums is managed with a single or syndicated group of investors.

Potentially in conflict with this approach is the funding of working capital (the net balance of inventory, receivables and payables). Although these are short-term assets and liabilities, there can be a

TABLE 6.2 **Guide to funding duration**

Over 15 years	Use a form of equity funding (providing the amount is over $20m as the cost of raising this funding can be expensive)
5–15 years	Consider a debt instrument (providing the amount is over $10m)
Under 5 years	Bank loans usually provide the cheapest and most flexible source (potentially fixed rate to remove an uncontrollable uncertainty – the central bank rate)
Under 1 year	Bank overdraft

rolling long-term balance which could be funded more cheaply with long-term funding. An example is an engineering company that may average 90 days of inventory. If suppliers are paid after 60 days, there will still be 30 days of inventory plus receivables being funded on an almost permanent basis that could be covered by long-term finance.

Share events

Share issue

A share issue takes place in order to raise money from investors to create a business or allow it to grow. There are normally three types:

- a private issue – where founder shareholders invest in a private business;

- an initial public offering (IPO) – which is the first time a company comes to the market;

- a rights issue – the issue of additional shares for a company that already has existing shares (see below).

An IPO is the sale of shares to the public in advance of them trading on an exchange for the first time. This is not the only way in which a company can start trading in its securities, but it is the most common. The shares offered in an IPO are usually a new issue, but they may also be shares being sold by the founder shareholders, or a combination of both.

The process involves issuing a prospectus and an application form for shares. The prospectus is similar to a brochure: it describes the background to the business, the expectations for the future and the details of the offer. To compensate for the lack of a track record as a listed company, a business's disclosure during an IPO is often extremely detailed and can be better than that of similar companies that are already listed.

The price at which the shares are sold will be either predetermined by a company valuation or determined by an auction to interested investors. An IPO also needs a mechanism for deciding how to distribute shares should there be too many applications (the offer is oversubscribed). This may be done by pro-rata allocation or by using an auction process. An IPO is usually priced low enough to ensure that the entire offer is taken up by new investors and is also underwritten by investment banks to ensure all the shares are sold.

The fees paid to advisers and underwriters for an IPO are substantial and, along with mergers and acquisitions, are a major source of revenue for investment banks, especially when bullish markets and high valuations tempt private companies to list. Because of the cost of the issue, this method is appropriate only if substantial sums of money need to be raised.

Rights issue

A rights issue is used by a company already quoted on an exchange to sell additional shares to raise further capital. Shares are offered to existing shareholders in proportion to their current shareholding. This pre-emption "right" means that any investor can retain their ownership proportion of a business should they choose to. Alternatively, they can sell their right as a tradable security if they do not want to subscribe to the additional shares.

The price at which the new shares are offered is usually at a discount to the current share price, giving investors an incentive to buy the new shares. However, the market price of the company's shares after the new ones have been issued will fall to a weighted average of the original as follows:

$$\frac{(CP \times ES) + (NP \times NS)}{ES + NS} = \text{Average price of all shares after the rights issue}$$

The attributes are as follows:

- NS is the number of new shares issued for every ES (existing share). For example, if 2 new shares were offered for every 7 existing shares, NS would be 2 and ES would be 7
- CP is the closing price on the last day the shares traded with entitlement to the rights issue (known as the cum-rights price)
- NP is the price of each new share

For example, if a share was trading at $2 and a rights issue offered one new share for every two shares held at a price of $1.55, the share price after the offer would become:

$$\frac{(2.00 \times 2) + (1.55 \times 1)}{2 + 1} = 1.85$$

The same adjustment needs to be made to per share measures such as earnings per share (EPS) if they are to remain comparable.

Bonus, scrip or capitalisation issue

These are three descriptions given to the issue of new shares to existing shareholders, in proportion to their existing shareholding, at no charge.

The term capitalisation is less common but more accurate than the terms scrip or bonus issue. It reflects what happens in the books of the company. The share capital (on the statement of financial position) has to increase by the nominal value of the newly issued shares. This is balanced by an equal decrease in another part of the shareholders' funds, such as retained earnings.

A bonus issue is therefore a book-keeping exercise and the value of any shareholding is unchanged despite the increase in the number of shares held. For example, if an investor held ten shares of $20 each, the investment would be worth $200. If a bonus issue was three shares for every share held, the investor would receive an additional 30 shares. The value of each share would reduce proportionally to $5 making the investment worth the same amount (40 shares of $5 = $200 in total).

The purpose of this exercise is as follows:

■ A gesture of confidence. The amount available to pay dividends is reduced, so it can be inferred that the management of the company is sure that the amount capitalised will be used to grow the assets and will not be needed to pay dividends.

■ To improve the liquidity of highly priced shares when trading small blocks becomes difficult. A share price of $500 means investors wanting to put $750 into a company can only invest less or more than they want to. However, a share price of $5 provides investors with more permutations.

Debt to equity proportions

In building the pool of funds for the business it is important to balance and optimise the proportions of debt and equity. The relationship between total debt and total equity is referred to as leverage or gearing.

If there is too much debt, a business becomes highly leveraged with the following implications:

■ Repayment risk. The risk to debt providers increases as there is less of an equity buffer to absorb losses that the business may make.

■ Interest risk. The interest cost must be met before dividends can be paid to shareholders. If interest cannot be paid and there is a serious risk of the business not being able to repay the debt, funders will exercise rights in their loan agreements to force repayment from asset sales.

■ Cost. With enhanced risk to debt providers the cost of the loans is likely to rise in the form of increased interest rates.

If there is too little debt, shareholders lose out through dilution of earnings which limits their return owing to:

■ Greater WACC. As equity is more expensive than debt, the business can lower its WACC by replacing equity with cheaper debt; the enhanced earnings can then be passed back to shareholders.

■ Restrained growth. With too little borrowing the business may
be operating sub-optimally as it could borrow more to fund
expansion and achieve greater growth.

For example, three businesses have the same total funds and
the same operating income. The difference is in the mix of debt and
equity in each business. The interest rate is 10% for each business. The
return to the equity investors is as follows:

Business	A	B	C
Debt	750	500	250
Equity	250	500	750
Total funds	1,000	1,000	1,000
Operating income	200	200	200
Interest (10%)	75	50	25
Income before tax	125	150	175
Tax (30%)	38	45	53
Earnings	87	105	122
Rate of return for equity investors	87 ÷ 250 = 34.8%	105 ÷ 500 = 21%	122 ÷ 750 = 16.3%
Leverage: debt ÷ total funds	750 ÷ 1,000 = 75%	500 ÷ 1,000 = 50%	250 ÷ 1,000 = 25%

Business A is highly leveraged. Should profits fall, earnings will
be quickly eroded and potentially jeopardise its ability to service its
interest obligations. Business B has what is generally accepted as the
maximum proportion of debt before funders impose constraints –
50% of the business is funded by debt. In business C, the low debt has
significantly reduced the rate of return for shareholders.

In practice, the figures in the example would be different because
as the proportion of debt rises, debt providers increase their interest
rates to cover themselves for the increased risk. The interest rate for
business A might rise from 10% to 18% to cover the risk, with the result
that the profits for the shareholders would erode as follows:

Business	A
Debt	750
Equity	250
Total funds	1,000
Operating profit	200
Interest (18%)	135
Profit before tax	65
Tax (30%)	20
Earnings	45

Rate of return for equity investors $45 \div 250 = 18\%$
Leverage: debt ÷ total funds $750 \div 1{,}000 = 75\%$

To prevent businesses from borrowing too much there are often covenants in a loan agreement that constrain the business. A common covenant is that a loan becomes immediately repayable if a certain debt to equity ratio is exceeded.

The optimum leverage for a business is seen to be around 50% of total funds. At this level the interest rate on debt is optimised and the return on equity is maximised.

Using the same profit data as in the examples above, Figure 6.2

FIG 6.2 **Leverage and return on equity compared**

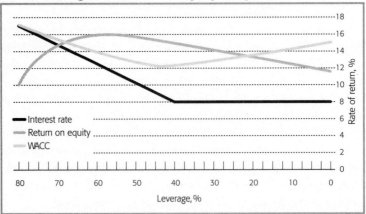

indicates that at high levels of leverage the punitive interest rate significantly reduces the earnings potential for equity investors. As the leverage level drops, the risk to debt providers falls and consequently the interest rate charged will also drop. With less profit being allocated to debt providers, the return to equity investors will rise. At low levels of leverage the return on equity falls as the advantage of using low rate debt diminishes. The optimum leverage is around 50% of total funds.

There can be scenarios where a higher level of leverage can be tolerated without the interest rate rising. This might be for businesses that have significant infrastructure which has a potential tradable value, such as the assets in property businesses or hotels where the quality of the assets will enable them to take on greater debt. Assets in the form of specialist machinery are less tradable and therefore provide lower-quality security.

There are many methods of calculating leverage and debt to equity ratios. Options are whether to include or exclude items such as payables, pension deficits and other liabilities.

One of the best methods is to compare interest-bearing debt to equity. This focuses on pure funding and excludes the operational aspects of the business such as payables. The calculation is as follows:

$$\text{Debt : equity}$$

However, this ratio is more easily expressed as a percentage by taking the interest-bearing debt as a proportion of total funds, which is calculated as follows:

$$\frac{\text{Interest-bearing debt}}{\text{Equity + interest-bearing debt}} \, \%$$

Note: Equity = share capital + returns (retained profit)

The higher the ratio the more highly leveraged is the business, and the closer the attention the lending banks will pay to its ability to cover its interest payments, and the more control they will exercise over the business.

In calculating this ratio it is common for lease obligations to be added to the debt amount. If a leased asset of $1,000,000 involved a business making ten annual payments of $150,000 (including interest at 8%), this obligation is similar to having debt equal to the asset value.

Where a business has a significant amount of cash as well as debt it can be sensible to calculate this ratio using net rather than gross debt. For example, a business may have borrowings and cash in different currencies and decide to keep the borrowing as a hedge against adverse currency movements rather than appear to operate with sub-optimal cash management. The measure is known as net leverage (or net gearing) and is calculated as follows:

$$\frac{\text{Interest-bearing debt} - \text{cash}}{\text{Equity} + \text{interest-bearing debt} - \text{cash}}\ \%$$

Interest cover

Although the level of leverage forms a crucial part of the analysis of risk carried out by debt providers, they are also interested in a business's ability to meet its interest payments. This is known as interest cover and is expressed as the number of times the business could pay the interest out of its operating income:

$$\frac{\text{Operating income}}{\text{Interest}}$$

If the measure is less than a value of 3 the risk to debt providers is high, as below this value there is little room to absorb any downturn in business performance or interest rate rises before interest payments can no longer be met.

In choosing the appropriate funding source, it is necessary to consider not only the impact that the additional funding will have on the current debt to equity ratio, but also the constraints that may be put on the business's taking on more funding in subsequent years.

Events that change the debt/equity mix
Profit generation

As a business makes profits or losses the level of equity in the business will rise or fall. It therefore needs to monitor the effect on the leverage.

Profits will reduce leverage and provide the business with capacity to take on further borrowings and vice versa.

If a business is making high profits, not growing significantly and using surplus cash to repay debt, its leverage will reduce to a sub-optimal level. This was the case for oil companies between 2005 and 2010 when large profits were generated from the hike in global oil prices. To avoid sub-optimal gearing, it may be preferable to distribute excess profits and cash through share buy-backs or special dividends, thus returning money to equity investors and maintaining leverage at a more advantageous level.

Marks & Spencer, a food and clothing retailer, took this principle still further. In 2002 it undertook a rare transaction when it returned £1.5 billion to shareholders, funded by raising debt. Its leverage changed as follows:

£m	2002	2001
Debt	3,000	1,694
Equity	3,081	4,566
Total funds	6,081	6,260
Leverage (debt ÷ total funds)	49.3%	27.1%

The effect of this is to reduce the company's WACC and enhance the return on equity.

Although many large companies have undertaken share buy-backs since 2002, there are no examples where this has been funded purely by new debt. Rather than cancelling any shares that are bought back, companies can hold them as treasury stock, which is shown as a negative value under shareholders' equity. Buying back and reselling shares provides an efficient tool to control leverage and keep WACC at the optimum point.

Pension fund deficits

In recent years many businesses that had established their own company pension schemes with defined employee benefits have found them to be underfunded, in that the net present value of the liabilities to current and future pensioners exceed the value of investments and contributions. Typically, the reason for this is a combination of increasing life expectancy and lower investment returns than were originally expected.

Where a deficit has occurred in a fund, there is a potential liability for the business to top up the pension fund should future fund performance fail to create the necessary amounts to meet those future liabilities. Investment analysts characterise these deficits as debt when assessing the leverage. Where companies are able to borrow to fund a deficit, it generally makes sense to do so because the interest on the borrowings is tax deductible in the company, whereas the interest earned on the funds deposited in the pension scheme is tax free.

Convertibles

Sometimes a funding instrument can be difficult to classify as debt or equity. An example is convertibles, which typically start by paying a low interest rate. At one or more future dates they can be converted to equity at a predetermined price. The normal rule is to include this type of item as debt up to the point of conversion and equity thereafter.

Maturity ladders

As a business grows it is likely to use a variety of debt instruments and start to create cash flows that have a predictable element (sales revenue) and an unpredictable element (asset purchases and disposals). It would be unwise for a business to lock itself into long-term debt and then find that it had started generating a substantial cash surplus. Thus a portfolio of debt should be structured with a series of loans that mature over a range of dates. This should also include a small amount of short-term debt (or overdraft) to balance out day-to-day cash receipts and payments. As each part of the debt portfolio matures, any cash that has accumulated can be used to offset the debt, with the net funding requirement carried into a new debt instrument.

For example, when Unilever acquired Best Foods in 2000 it paid around $20 billion, most of which was funded by debt. However, the debt was constructed with a portfolio of over 20 separate instruments, each with different maturity dates. In the years following the acquisition Unilever has made disposals of businesses with the cash received being used to repay debt. The original debt structure enabled the company to minimise its cash surpluses.

Cost of funding

So far notional figures have been used to illustrate the cost of each funding source and show how these combine to calculate WACC. It is possible to determine these more precisely.

Debt

International credit agencies such as Moody's and Standard & Poor's assess the risk of companies and allocate them a credit rating. A rating of AAA is very low risk and companies in this category pay low rates for their funding. However, a speculative mining company in a politically unstable country is a much greater risk and will expect to pay a much higher cost for its funding. The credit rating typically has an exponential correlation to a premium over a central bank or prime rate of interest. For example, AAA might correlate to 0.25% over the central bank rate, so if the central bank rate is 5%, the debt cost would be 5.25%. However, a rating of BB might be 1.5% over the central bank rate with a debt cost of 6.5%; and a rating of CCC might be 4.5% over the central bank rate with a debt cost of 9.5%. The increments, while remaining exponential, can widen and contract depending on the availability of debt. An illustrative profile of the credit increments is shown in Figure 6.3.

Credit-rating agencies use a range of measures and attributes to calculate their ratings. Ironically, the lower the leverage, the higher is the likely credit rating and the lower the interest rate charged on debt. Using this credit rating advantage to borrow more funds will push up the leverage, reduce the credit rating and increase the interest rate.

Standard & Poor's, an American credit-rating agency that is part of McGraw-Hill, uses the following system for its long-term credit ratings:

■ AAA – extremely strong capacity to meet its financial commitments. This is the highest rating assigned by Standard & Poor's.

FIG 6.3 **Illustrative profile of credit rating interest increments**

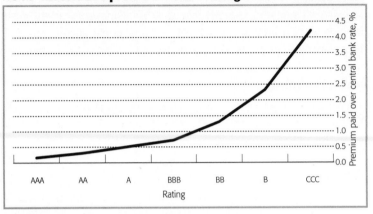

- AA – very strong capacity to meet its financial commitments.

- A – strong capacity to meet its financial commitments but somewhat more susceptible to the adverse effects of changes in circumstances and economic conditions than those in higher-rated categories.

- BBB – adequate capacity to meet its financial commitments. However, adverse economic conditions or changing circumstances are more likely to lead to a weakened capacity of the business to meet its financial commitments.

- BB, B, CCC and CC – businesses regarded as having significant speculative characteristics. BB indicates the least degree of speculation and CC the highest. Although such companies are likely to have some quality and protective characteristics, these may be outweighed by large uncertainties or major exposures to adverse conditions.

- D – in default and will fail to pay all or substantially all of its obligations as they come due.

- R – under regulatory supervision owing to its financial condition.

A reduction of one level on this scale reduces the interest rate payable. Therefore protecting and even improving a credit rating is a critical part of financial management.

Equity

To calculate the return required by investors the capital asset pricing model (CAPM) is used. This compares the return made on a risk-free investment with two factors: the overall return that is expected from the market and how well the business will be able to match the market.

Required return = risk-free return + beta (expected market return − risk-free return)

- A risk-free return is usually deemed to be a government bond where the investor is totally confident of both the interest and capital repayment.
- The market return is calculated by reference to one of the composite stockmarket indexes, which provides the average return from investing in, say, the top 100 companies.
- Beta is a coefficient that is used to quantify the risk of this investment compared with the risk-free return and the average market return. If the risk is greater than the average market risk, a higher than average market return will be demanded and vice versa.

A beta is calculated using regression analysis to measure how well aligned the company's performance will be to movement in the market as a whole:

- A beta of 1 indicates that a business's performance will be synchronised with the market.
- A beta of less than 1 indicates that a business's performance will be less volatile than the market.
- A beta greater than 1 indicates that a business's performance will be more volatile than the market.

For example, if a company has a beta of 1.1, it is theoretically 10% more volatile than the market.

Defensive companies, such as utility companies and some food manufacturers, typically have a beta of less than 1. High-tech companies typically have a more volatile return, more risk and a beta greater than 1.

Using the CAPM model and some assumptions the required return can be calculated:

Risk-free rate	5%
Expected market return	9%
Beta for the investment	1.2

Therefore the required return to the equity holders is:

$$5\% + 1.2\ (9\% - 5\%)\ \text{which equates to } 9.8\%$$

The implication of the theory is that the more a business performs like the market the lower is the required return. Consequently, the more unique and radical a business becomes the higher is the return that investors will require. This perhaps dissuades entrepreneurship in favour of the tried and tested.

Dividend policy

A dividend policy sets out the basis for when and how much of a business's earnings should be paid to the shareholders. This is crucial in managing investor expectations and in attracting equity. However, dividends that are paid out cannot be used for reinvestment or to provide the capacity for matching additional borrowings in maintaining an optimal leverage. Therefore payment of a dividend reduces the equity in a business, which may have an impact on potential growth and value creation.

If a business has a range of potential projects that all need investment and are likely to be value enhancing, why pay a dividend? Microsoft, which was founded in 1975, reinvested all its profits in the business until 2003, when it paid a dividend for the first time. Richard Brealey and Stewart Myers, the authors of many books and articles on corporate finance, list a dividend policy as one of the "10 unresolved problems in finance".

Institutional investors such as pension funds (which hold the majority of shares in most listed companies) want a regular income stream from their investments and are rarely content just to rely on the value of their equity rising. This gives them greater certainty that they will be able to meet their pension payment obligations.

A dividend stream signals either management confidence in the cash generation of the company or that the maintaining of the dividend will help to keep investors on board. This is because:

- reductions in the level of the dividend often imply that the business is facing financial difficulties and will lead to a fall in the share price;
- increases in the level of the dividend may imply that the business can continue to pay higher dividends long into the future, and this therefore leads to a rise in the share price.

Any decision on the payment of a dividend needs to take into account a number of factors:

- Payment constraints – such as available distributable reserves, cash availability or debt covenants.
- Public perception – what would a change of dividend imply?
- Sustainability – how long into the future can the dividend be maintained?
- Tax – what is the tax effect of a payment for both the business and investors (individual and corporate)?
- Investment requirements – the amount of cash required for investment projects or acquisitions.
- Weighted average cost of capital – the impact on the WACC in the business.

The dividend policy of Telecom, a New Zealand telecommunications company, states that it is "the company's intention to target an ordinary dividend payout ratio of approximately 90% of net adjusted earnings subject to there being no material adverse changes in circumstances or operating outlook. Dividends will continue to be paid on a semi-annual basis."

A dividend policy is only relevant to a business once it has established a track record of sufficient profitability or to a publicly quoted company because in the early years it is either necessary

FIG 6.4 **The factors affecting weighted average cost of capital**

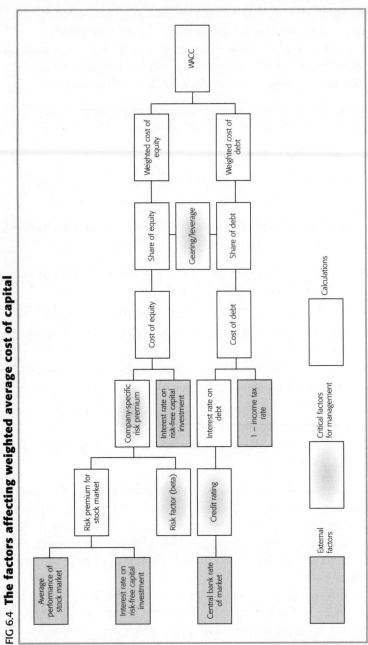

or desirable to retain cash in the business rather than distribute it. A dividend policy should be declared only if it can be seen to be sustainable for the foreseeable future.

Weighted average cost of capital

The WACC is the average funding rate across all the sources of finance. The weighted part refers to the way it is calculated with reference to the amount each source of finance contributes to the total.

The WACC is calculated from each type of investor's required returns, which in turn are based on factors such as credit rating, leverage, risk-free rates and the way the company's shares correlate to the market as a whole.

One other factor that will affect equity investors is tax. Interest costs on debt are chargeable against profits for tax calculation purposes and can therefore be used to reduce the tax paid by a business. So although debt may have a stated rate of, say, 8%, the actual cost to the equity holders is 8% $\times$ (1 – the tax rate). If tax is chargeable at 30% the actual cost of debt is as follows:

$$8\% \times (1 - 30\%) = 5.6\%$$

Multiplying the cost of debt by 1 minus the tax rate gives the tax benefit of debt financing to equity investors. This effect is called the tax shield of debt financing.

All the factors affecting WACC are summarised in Figure 6.4.

The formula to calculate WACC can be summarised as follows:

$$\text{WACC} = \frac{(E \times RE)}{(E + D)} + \frac{(D \times RD \times (1 - TR))}{(E + D)}$$

E = market value of equity
RE = return required for equity
D = market value of debt
RD = return required for debt
TR = tax rate

The above formula is too simple for businesses with several

sources of debt covering bonds, loans, and so on. To complete the calculation each type of debt would be included separately with its own applicable rate. The weighted part is important to ensure that each element added to the formula is included in proportion to the market value of all sources of finance. A way of representing this might be:

$$\text{WACC} = \frac{(E \times RE)}{TF} + \frac{(D_1 \times RD_1 \times (1 - TR))}{TF} + \frac{(D_2 \times RD_2 \times (1 - TR))}{TF}$$
$$+ \frac{(D_3 \times RD_3 \times (1 - TR))}{TF}$$

TF = total market value of all sources of finance
D_1 = debt type 1
D_2 = debt type 2
D_3 = debt type 3

For example, if a company is funded as follows:

Funding source	Amount ($m)	Cost of funding (%)
Market value of equity	50	12
Market value of bonds	14	9
Market value of an overdraft	1	15
Total	65	

Tax rate is 30%

The WACC is calculated as:

$$(50 \div 65 \times 12\%) + (14 \div 65 \times (9\% \times 70\%)) + (1 \div 65 \times (15\% \times 70\%))$$
$$= 10.75\%$$

A business's WACC is normally kept confidential for commercial reasons. For example, if two companies are seeking to acquire a business, with all other aspects being equal, the one with the lowest cost of capital will be able to afford to pay the higher price.

One company to break this tradition was Coca-Cola, which estimated its WACC to be between 8% and 10% (see page 11). However, even this is vague as the WACC range is broad and is not one that would have surprised any analyst who kept an eye on the company's financial statements. The company states the WACC was calculated on a "book basis", meaning that it used the value of debt and equity on the statement of financial position rather than a market value.

The WACC is crucial in any investment appraisal as it defines the minimum return required from projects to keep the investors satisfied. This is explained in Chapter 10.

Accounting for the funding cost

Once the funding source and cost have been identified they need to be accounted for in the financial statements.

Income statement

In the income statement the cost of servicing the funding will be shown. The principle of matching covered in Chapter 4 requires that the cost must be calculated with reference to the period for which the funding was taken and not simply the physical payments. For example, if a loan on which interest is paid quarterly is taken one month before the end of a company's financial year, no physical interest payment will be made before the year end, but the income statement should include the accrual of one month's interest.

For more complex debt instruments that defer the payment of interest until the end of the funding period, the interest should be allocated at a constant rate on the carrying value of the debt.

For example, a €100m zero-coupon five-year bond is redeemed at a premium of 61% (zero-coupon means at an interest rate of 0%). The true yield of the bond is 10% (calculated using the internal rate of return or IRR of the cash flows of the bond – see Chapter 10). The income statement and cash flows would be as follows:

Year	Interest charge in income statement	Cash flow	Carrying value	Yield on opening carrying value (%)
0		100	100	
1	10	0	110	10
2	11	0	121	10
3	12	0	133	10
4	13	0	146	10
5	15	−161	0	10

Statement of financial position

The statement of financial position will show the amount of debt or equity separately for each type of funding instrument. The amounts will be the value of the funding. There may also be an accrual shown under payables for the interest charged in the income statement but not yet paid.

Cash flow

The cash flow statement will show the cash received from and paid to investors. This will include the cash flow of the principle as well as the interest and dividends.

Private equity transactions

Private equity firms look for businesses that have substantial unrealised potential either in being managed better or by breaking them up where the sum of the parts is worth more than the total. They buy businesses (even leading companies) largely using debt, drive rapid growth in free cash flow and then sell their investment within 3–5 years. In many ways these deals break conventional long-term strategic development and financing principles.

Typically, such deals will be funded with 60–70% debt, a leverage proportion that would be feared in many businesses. However, if the value of the business can be made to double over the subsequent five years, the return to equity holders is four or five times their initial investment.

	At acquisition, $m	5 years later, $m
Debt	70	70
Equity	30	130
Company value	100	200

The company value is also known as enterprise value (EV), which is explained in more detail in Chapter 13.

The debt providers are prepared to accept this amount of leverage and risk primarily because of the management capability in the private equity firm. A manager's track record in spotting businesses with unrealised potential, hiring excellent operational management and driving cash returns is crucial. Should any of these fail, a change of management is usually swift and if necessary assets will be sold to reduce debt.

Private equity takeovers aim to be debt funded with an EBITDA (see Chapter 4) multiple of up to six – that is, the amount of debt is six times the cash flow generated over the past 12 months. Multiples of up to 11 have been seen in the market for exceptional opportunities that arose before the 2007 financial crisis.

To manage the risk for such high amounts, the debt is likely to be structured in several tranches with the lower-risk elements (or senior debt) on smaller interest increments over the central bank rate than the higher-risk (or junior debt) elements. An example interest increment profile is as follows:

Leverage element	Premium over central bank rate
Low-risk (senior) debt that has priority over other lenders – leverage up to 50%	2.5%
Higher-risk debt – leverage between 50% and 60%	4.5%
Highest-risk (junior) debt that is unlikely to have any security – leverage over 60%	9.0%

Should the management of the business add significant value in, say, two years, the deal can be refinanced. With increased equity value from the increased profits the leverage will have fallen, enabling the higher-risk debt elements to be replaced with further lower-rate funding.

While the business is in the hands of the private equity firm there will be a focus on limiting cash outflows. There will be no dividends and no scheduled capital repayments of debt, and new assets may well be leased rather than purchased.

If this process is so lucrative, it may seem that this should be a model for all businesses to follow, but it must be remembered that it only works for established businesses that have substantial unrealised potential. A successful business in strong hands will leave little opportunity for private equity investors to add value.

7 Cost to serve

A BUSINESS WILL MAKE A PROFIT only if it earns more revenue from its products or services than it spends on providing them. This may be an obvious statement, but it can be difficult to capture the true cost of provision.

An example is a company that manufactures and sells an electrical product such as a television. The cost of its manufacture is only a small part of the full cost of provision, which starts with research and finishes with any warranty claims. Along the way will be tooling, marketing, distribution and financing costs. The cost of provision should also include a contribution towards the business's administration and management (information technology, human resources and finance department) costs. In the long run, the revenue earned at the point of sale must be greater than all these costs taken together if the business is to be viable.

Knowing the cost of a product or service will enable judgments to be made as to whether it can be sold at a price that makes it worth developing or continuing to sell; Chapter 8 covers pricing.

Cost behaviour

To work out the full cost of a product or service, the first stage is to understand how the two main types of costs, fixed and variable, behave.

Fixed costs

Fixed costs are those that, in the short term, stay constant as changes in sales volume occur. An example would be the rent paid for premises.

FIG 7.1 **Fixed costs**

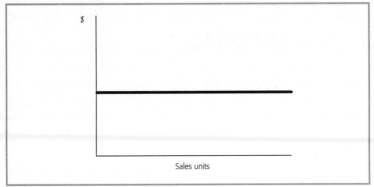

A small increase in a business's activity is likely to be able to be accommodated within its existing premises and hence the cost will not rise as volume rises. It is important to note that the "fixed" aspect is relative only to volume of activity and not price. The cost may still be subject to the impact of inflation and periodic rent reviews. A graph of a fixed cost is shown in Figure 7.1.

If this graph showed the annual depreciation charge of a machine, it would be valid for the production of any number of sales units up to the machine's capacity. However, if sales volume continued to rise, the business would need an additional machine, and the graph would become stepped as shown in Figure 7.2.

FIG 7.2 **Stepped fixed costs**

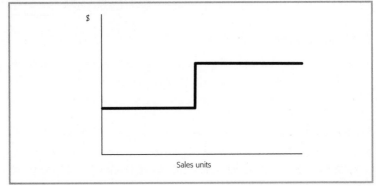

The most difficult point at which to operate is just before the step rises. In the example, the machine would be working at maximum capacity to meet demand. The pressure to deliver may compromise planned maintenance and cause work to be prioritised so the machine can be used optimally. Once a second machine is brought in there will be plenty of idle capacity across the two machines yet twice the depreciation cost. Although this provides a good opportunity to test and calibrate the new machine, the profitability will decline until volume rises and both machines are appropriately utilised.

A crude operational optimum for many such fixed costs will be at 75–85% utilisation of available capacity. This allows for the handling of uneven work patterns and a proper maintenance schedule to be operated.

It is often difficult to decide when and how to expand capacity without causing too much operational disruption. Putting in an additional machine may require temporary outsourcing until the new machine is fully tested. One way of helping to ensure that the transition goes smoothly would be to use price to manage sales demand, either by putting the price up to stem demand (to keep one machine) or by lowering the price to create demand (that justifies the second machine). The danger with this strategy is that it can undermine the longer-term price positioning for the product.

An example of where this strategy used is the airline industry. The seat price is set and flexed to try to fill each aircraft. Thus on a Friday night seats on short-haul flights rise in price compared with earlier in the day because there is a captive demand from business travellers going home for the weekend. Depending on the popularity of the route, the airline can change the type of aircraft it uses to increase or reduce available capacity. Again the price will be used to ensure that as much of the capacity is sold as possible.

Variable costs

Variable costs are the costs that will increase as volume increases or will decrease as volume decreases. They are sometimes referred to as incremental costs. An example would be components used in manufacturing because the more products that are made the greater is the total cost of components.

FIG 7.3 **Variable costs**

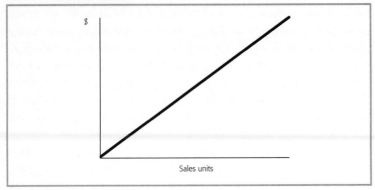

For low-level volumes, a graph of a variable cost looks like the one in Figure 7.3, reflecting a linear relationship.

As volumes rise there is greater purchasing leverage as volume discounts can be negotiated. The volume discounts cause the cost to rise more slowly, which brings down the unit cost. A graph of this effect is shown in Figure 7.4.

An example of this profile would be $1 per unit for the first 2,000 units, 80 cents per unit for quantities up to 4,000 units and 60 cents per unit for more than 4,000 units.

Customers are obviously attracted by the low price for placing large orders. However, if the high quantity of 4,000 units represented

FIG 7.4 **Volume discounts**

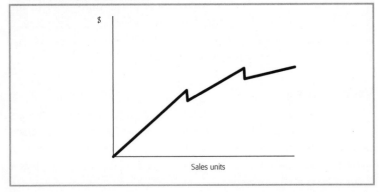

their annual consumption of a product, they would have the problem of both storage and perhaps more significantly cash being tied up in inventory. A solution is to have a "call-off order", whereby a business contracts to take a high quantity of a product over 12 months, thus benefiting from the lower unit price, but the product is called off in smaller quantities as required during the year. This keeps the inventory low as well as minimising the cash tied up. Suppliers also like this type of order as they can plan production and use slack time to build inventory required to fulfil the call-off orders.

Semi-fixed and semi-variable costs

In reality many costs are a combination of both fixed and variable elements. An example would be salaries, which are typically fixed, but overtime and bonus payments are usually variable. Similarly, electricity is a mixture of the two. In a manufacturing environment the electricity for lighting and heating a factory would be fixed, but the electricity to run the machines would be variable.

In such cases, where a cost exhibits both behaviours, it is normal to categorise the cost for planning and costing purposes by the most predominant behaviour it exhibits.

The importance of understanding cost behaviour

The operation of a business involves a combination of fixed and variable costs. For example, a supermarket's premises costs would be largely fixed, whereas the cost of buying in the groceries for sale would be variable. Its income statement might be simply stated (see Table 7.1).

TABLE 7.1 **Fixed and variable costs: a supermarket ($)**

Revenue	10,000
Variable cost	(7,000)
Contribution	3,000
Fixed cost	(2,000)
Profit	1,000

A business's "contribution" is its revenue less the variable costs – or the contribution that products make to fixed costs and ultimately profit. From contribution deduct the fixed costs to arrive at the profit.

If the supermarket is compared with a business that has a high fixed costs, such as a theme park, the cost structure would look very different. A theme park has high fixed costs because the cost of looking after the facilities and the rides is more or less the same however many people visit it.

TABLE 7.2 **Fixed and variable costs: a theme park ($)**

Revenue	10,000
Variable cost	(3,000)
Contribution	7,000
Fixed cost	(6,000)
Profit	1,000

These two businesses have the same levels of revenue and profit, but different cost structures. So which is the better business structure? In the context of costs the theme park, with its higher fixed costs (which it would find difficult to cut), will be more vulnerable if sales drop than will the supermarket, with its lower fixed costs. Conversely, if its sales rose by, say, 25%, the theme park would find itself making a bigger profit than the supermarket. Tables 7.3 and 7.4 show the effect of an increase and a decrease of 25% in sales on the two businesses.

TABLE 7.3 **A volume increase of 25%**

	Supermarket ($)	Theme park ($)
Revenue	12,500	12,500
Variable cost	(8,750)	(3,750)
Contribution	3,750	8,750
Fixed cost	(2,000)	(6,000)
Profit	1,750	2,750

TABLE 7.4 **A volume decrease of 25%**

	Supermarket ($)	Theme park ($)
Sales	7,500	7,500
Variable cost	(5,250)	(2,250)
Contribution	2,250	5,250
Fixed cost	(2,000)	(6,000)
Profit	250	(750)

The proportion of fixed to variable costs in the cost base is known as the operational leverage or gearing. The higher the operational leverage of a business, the more exposed it is to adverse trading. Therefore high-fixed-cost businesses, such as airlines or hotels, need a volume-based strategy in order to succeed. In short, they depend on high occupancy rates. However, businesses with high variable costs, such as high-volume wholesalers and retailers, depend on the margins (the contribution as a percentage of sales) they make. If they can save just 1% on their variable costs, this can translate into substantial incremental profit.

Of course, for any business, whatever its cost structure, the higher the margin and the higher the volume of sales it makes the better, but for most businesses the strategic priority will be volume or margin.

Business optimisation

Businesses typically have fixed or variable costs that are symptomatic of their industry, but this does not mean that they cannot make changes that reduce (or raise) their risk profile and their ability to respond to changes in volume.

A business can be positioned on a matrix as shown in Figure 7.5. The ideal zone is highly profitable. The fixed costs are low and the contribution is high. An example would be a drug like Zantac, developed by GlaxoSmithKline, which for many years was a substantial profit earner for the business. However, any successful pharmaceutical product will lose market share when the patent runs out and competitors launch generic versions. When this happens a common defensive strategy is to cut the price and spend more on

FIG 7.5 **Business optimisation matrix**

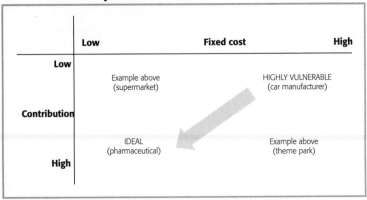

marketing, which has the effect of moving the product upwards and to the right on the matrix. Other products which can become ideal are fashion goods, where demand for them exceeds supply and allows high pricing, until demand drops, supply increases, or a competitive threat emerges, and what was once ideal becomes ordinary.

Highly vulnerable businesses are those such as big carmakers which have high fixed costs and a low contribution. Big rises in oil prices, the financial crisis, changing fashions, overcapacity and strategic errors (mainly in mergers and acquisitions) have led to a number of the biggest firms racking up huge losses. As a way to reduce their fixed costs there has been an increase in outsourcing of much of the manufacturing process, from components to subassemblies, with car firms completing only the final assembly.

The danger for businesses on the right-hand side of the matrix is that they are vulnerable to volume declines – as airlines found following the September 11th 2001 attacks on New York and Washington; Sabena and Swissair went bust and many airlines are still struggling. Subsequent terrorism events or natural disasters (hurricanes and ash clouds) that suspend travel reveal their continued vulnerability.

To reduce their fixed-costs base, many such businesses have moved into outsourcing by selling off fixed-cost elements and buying them on a unit basis. For airlines, such activities include baggage handling, catering, cleaning, ground handling and engineering, leaving them with direct control of the aircraft and crew and, most importantly, the customer relationship. Most airlines have a much lower fixed-cost base today than they had 10–20 years ago.

Actions to reduce fixed costs (potentially reducing contribution)

- Increase volume such that the fixed costs become a smaller proportion of the cost base.

- Derive value from sweating the assets by working them as much as is safely and practically possible. For example, airlines plan their schedules to maximise night-time flying between 11pm and 6am when there are often legal restrictions on landings and take-offs.

- Outsource on a unit cost basis, thus making the cost variable rather than fixed. For example, buying in a component at a cost per unit rather than paying for a machine and staff to make them yourself.

- Use standard platforms (such as one type of asset), thus minimising the amounts of spares that need to be held. For example, logistics companies generally have only one manufacturer of trucks, and airlines select either Boeing or Airbus.

- Use temporary staff to manage peaks in demand and thus avoid carrying the cost of staff throughout the year when demand is lower. For example, hotels often call in temporary banqueting staff for large functions.

- Use an element of profit-related pay rather than a fixed salary, thus aligning the employment cost to the performance of the business. Similarly, sales commission not only provides a sales incentive but also makes the cost variable.

- Assess the full life-cycle cost of an asset. A cheaper asset may over its useful life involve higher maintenance and ultimately faster replacement than a more expensive version. For example, a cheap printer may do the job, but soon its quality deteriorates and within a short time a new one is required.

■ Develop products that can use the waste from manufacturing the primary product. For example, Marmite, a yeast extract spread, is made from the residue from brewing beer, thus making the brewing waste a revenue earner rather than a disposal cost.

Actions to increase contribution (potentially increasing fixed costs)

■ Standardise components and consumables to enable bulk buying discounts.

■ Employ staff with accountable hours contracts rather than standard hours and overtime. The process is that the staff work the hours they are required, but only 1,600 hours in a year. Operationally, this requires one-twelfth of the staff to have their accountable hours year ending each month. This ensures that all the staff do not run out of hours at the same time.

■ Simplify the product or service. Cut out a stage in the process that reduces costs but does not result in customers perceiving any loss in quality. For example, KitKat, a chocolate bar, used to be wrapped in foil with a paper sleeve. The packaging now is just a single outer wrapper. Some organisations describe this action as "squeeze", which is the process of reducing the unit cost of production with no discernible loss in quality.

■ Get things right first time. Products that are made correctly reduce rework, returns and warranty claims. In most instances, there is a balance between the cost of perfection and the cost of rectification in that 100% quality is an aspiration but unlikely to be commercially achievable. An exception to this is the manufacture of satellite components, which must be 100% reliable as repair is not an option.

Other cost restructuring actions

■ Outsource or offshore to a low-cost country. This has been popular for the non-customer-facing parts of a business, including manufacturing, accounting and information technology. The cost of facilities is cheaper, but the biggest savings are often in labour costs.

■ Centralise. This has benefits in providing economies of scale (cutting out duplication of activity across many sites) but it can have the drawback that the central functions become impersonal and bureaucratic, and fail to understand the operational parts of the business they are there to serve. Success in centralisation can be achieved by the use of "common processes" that are applied at the point of customer interface; for example, a bank that maintains a branch network with staff that can have a relationship with their customers rather than a bank with a central impersonal call centre.

None of these actions on their own will make a business successful, but understanding where the business sits on the matrix and how it can be moved to a more sustainable place for the expected demand is crucial to success.

Break-even

Fixed and variable costs can be combined on one graph to illustrate the cost structure for a product, service or whole business as volumes change (see Figure 7.6). This is the start of a business model that can be used to understand the profit expectations at various volume levels.

The graph is constructed as follows:

■ The fixed costs are put on the graph first and are represented by the horizontal line parallel with the horizontal axis.

■ The variable costs are added on top of the fixed costs, touching the vertical axis at the same point as the fixed costs. The total area under the variable cost line represents total costs.

■ The sales line is shown last and goes diagonally up to the right starting at the origin.

A crucial point on the graph is where the business breaks even, which is where the sales line crosses the total cost line. Break-even is the point at which sales equals costs and the business makes neither

FIG 7.6 **Cost structure for a product**

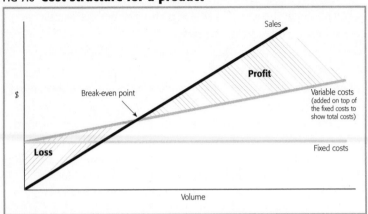

a profit nor a loss. A sales level above this point will yield a profit. A sales level below this point will yield a loss.

The formula for calculating the level of sales needed for break-even is:

$$\text{Break-even sales level} = \text{sales} \times \frac{\text{fixed cost}}{\text{contribution}}$$

Contribution being sales less variable costs

If this is applied to the supermarket and theme park example above, the following levels will be found:

Supermarket $10,000 \times \dfrac{2,000}{3,000} = \$6,667$ (break-even sales level)

Theme park $10,000 \times \dfrac{6,000}{7,000} = \$8,571$ (break-even sales level)

As you would expect, the calculations show that the business with the higher fixed-cost base has the higher break-even point and therefore the higher risk. Hence the strategies outlined above to reduce fixed costs can be effective in reducing the break-even point.

Break-even points provide operational information and are rarely published except in the airline industry. Cathay Pacific publishes a figure called "break-even load factor", which is defined as "a theoretical revenue load factor required at which the traffic revenue equates to the net operating costs". Load factor is the number of fare-paying passengers as a proportion of seats available. In its 2012 accounts, Cathay Pacific's break-even load factor was 76.0% and its achieved load factor was 76.2%, so if it had carried 0.2% fewer passengers, it would not have made a profit. This narrow gap meant that it made only $118m operating profit on revenues of $12,741m.

While a higher load factor may be more profitable, pushing it above 80% may affect customer service; for example, business travellers who book late and find the route is fully booked may shift their loyalty to another airline.

Product break-even points

The break-even concept is particularly useful for evaluating new product launches where it is helpful to understand the sales volume required to make the product profitable.

For example, a business plans to make and sell a new range of homemade bread. The ingredients are flour, yeast and water. Each loaf of bread will need electricity to cook it and a plastic bag for packaging. Collectively, these variable costs are $2.20. To make bread requires a dough machine and an oven. The depreciation of these two items amounts to $3,000 a year. If each loaf sells for $3, how many will need to be sold before a profit is made?

Contribution per loaf is the revenue less the variable costs which is:

$$\$3.00 - \$2.20 = \$0.80$$

With fixed costs of $3,000, it will take $\dfrac{\$3,000}{\$0.80}$ units to cover the costs

Therefore 3,750 loaves need to be sold before a profit is realised.

This minimum volume needs to be compared with the market

expectation for sales. A viable business is dependent on comfortably exceeding break-even and delivering the success defined in Chapter 1.

A reduction in fixed costs will reduce the break-even point and make the business viable at a lower level of sales. For example, the manufacture of the bread could be subcontracted on a unit-cost basis until the volumes were proven and the investment in equipment justified.

For a product launch, a business structure with low fixed costs is advantageous. Once volumes are sustained, some of the variable costs can be turned into fixed costs and thus deliver greater profits. An example would be bringing outsourced manufacture in-house, buying equipment and employing permanent labour.

Margin of safety

The margin of safety is the volume of expected sales that exceeds the break-even sales. For example, if the business planned to sell 5,000 loaves a year its margin of safety would be:

Budgeted sales − actual sales = 5,000 − 3,750 = 1,250 loaves

This can also be expressed as a percentage with the margin of safety shown as a percentage of the budgeted sales as follows:

Margin of safety ÷ budgeted sales × 100 = 1,250 ÷ 5,000 × 100 = 25%

Direct and indirect costs

Having explored the relationship between fixed and variable costs, it is necessary to understand the difference between two other classifications of cost in order to work out the full cost of a product. These are direct and indirect costs.

Direct costs

Costs that are specific to the provision of a product or service. Examples would be components and packaging for a manufacturing business. The cost of these items is specifically identifiable as constituents of the finished product. The majority of variable costs are direct. An exception would be sales commission, which is an indirect cost that is dependent on volume.

Indirect costs

Costs that do not have a connection with the provision of a product or service. An example would be the cost of running a reception desk or site security. These costs are necessary to running a business as a whole, but cannot be broken down easily to identify the amount attributable to an individual product.

These costs are sometimes called overheads and typically cover human resources, information technology and the finance department. Although they are difficult to link to a product or service, it is important that the product or service generates sufficient revenue not only to pay the indirect costs, but also to produce a profit.

Many indirect costs are typically fixed; for example, rent and the staff costs of those within the overhead departments.

The full cost of a product or service

The full cost of a product or service will consist of three elements: variable costs, direct fixed costs and indirect fixed costs. Each of these becomes increasingly difficult to calculate as the fixed costs need to be fairly shared or apportioned across the products and services that benefit from their use. A "fair share" is a judgment that provokes arguments in businesses as the method of apportionment used can make a significant difference to the perceived profitability of a product (see example below).

At this point it is important to note that the cost of the product or service does not determine its price (except in some cost plus type contracts in businesses such as construction or engineering). As Chapter 8 explains, price is normally determined by the position of a product or service in the market. The cost information is required to evaluate whether the market is attractive and profitable.

The cost of a tub of fruit-flavoured ice cream will be used to illustrate the process of calculating a full cost. The components of the full cost are shown in Figure 7.7.

FIG 7.7 **Components of a full product cost**

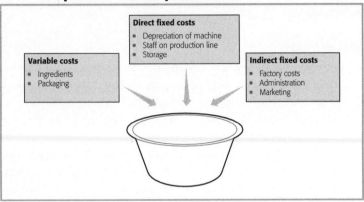

To produce 1 litre of ice cream the variable costs are:

Cream	0.75 litres at $1 per litre	= $0.75
Fruit puree	0.25 litres at $2 per litre	= $0.50
Sugar	100gm at $0.30 per kg	= $0.03
Packaging	One tub and lid	= $0.04

At this stage there is imprecision for items such as:

■ Wastage – 100 litres of ingredients put into a manufacturing process will not yield 100 litres of saleable product. For example, there will be product left on the side of the mixer or tubs may be overfilled. Therefore it is common to gross up the variable cost by a wastage element such as 3% or 5%. Driving these wastage levels down is a profit opportunity.

■ Price – which price for the ingredients should be used, the original cost price or the replacement price? The former is useful for calculating historic profitability and the latter for negotiating price increases for future deliveries to customers.

The direct fixed costs are:

Depreciation	Cost per year	$12,000
Staff	One person (including employment benefits per year)	$30,000

| Storage | Freezer depreciation and running costs per year | $8,000 |

The direct fixed costs total $50,000. But how much of this relates to one product? There are three issues:

1 Basis of allocation. A method of allocation should be used to divide the total cost fairly across the products produced. If production consisted of one flavour that was manufactured in one size, the cost could be simply divided by the number of tubs produced.

However, if two different sizes of ice cream were made, a 1 litre tub and a 2 litre tub, should the cost be split by litres rather than tubs? A further complication might be that two flavours are made, a cheap basic vanilla and a luxury double chocolate. If the luxury version can command a 50% price premium, there is an argument that the fixed costs should be split by a product's ability to pay.

In a service industry the amount of staff time taken on a job can be used as a basis of allocation – see job costing (page 125).

There is no correct answer here as a split per tub will charge both the 1 litre tub and the 2 litre tub with the same amount of direct fixed cost. This will clearly give an advantage to the larger size. Allocating by weight will give each size the same cost per litre, which will not reflect any economy of scale in producing the product in larger sizes.

Ultimately, the method of apportionment chosen is a management judgment that needs to be fair to the products and is preferably simple and clear to apply. Trying to capture data to make the process more precise will often only add complexity and potentially add even more cost in recording and using the information. This is the process of activity-based costing (see page 124).

2 Volume denominator. In dividing the cost by, say, volume there is a question about which volume. The options are last year's volume (which is historic), budget (which can be significantly at variance with reality) or actual (which can be known only in arrears). Ironically, the value chosen can be self-fulfilling.

For example, if the denominator were based on an optimistically high budget of 100,000 tubs, the cost per tub would be $50,000 ÷

100,000 or $0.50 per tub. This might make the product seem cheap to produce and perhaps enable better discounts to be offered to customers, leading to higher sales. The opposite is also true; if a cautious estimate of volume is used of 25,000 tubs, the cost per tub would be $50,000 ÷ 25,000 or $2.00 per tub. This higher value may make the unit cost uncompetitive and leave little or no room for discounts, and thus low sales may be achieved.

A realistic budget is the most common method used.

3 Seasonality. Ice cream has seasonal demand and thus it would seem unhelpful to have a volatile cost that moved between being low in the volume season and high in the slow season. Therefore the fixed costs would typically be calculated over an annual period to provide some stability to the product analysis.

With an allocation method selected and a volume basis the amount of direct fixed cost per unit can be calculated.

The indirect fixed costs are:

Factory costs	$215,000
Administration	$128,000
Marketing	$132,000

The total cost of the indirect fixed costs amounts to $475,000. These are the costs for the whole factory, which may produce many products and sizes of product. The difficulty here is not only in identifying how much of it relates to one product but also, as has to be done with direct fixed costs, in deciding the volume denominator.

Cost apportionment

The overheads need to be split across all the products made by a business. Failure to do this could result in a business not understanding the true cost of each product and hence its viability in a competitive market. The difficulty is to attribute costs to products where the link is indeterminable, such as the cost of site security.

The simplest method is to add up all the indirect fixed costs and allocate them by one of the bases mentioned under direct fixed costs, such as volume, units, machine time and labour hours. Although this is a clearly identifiable method, it can dictate thinking and ultimately behaviour. For example, if costs are allocated on labour hours, products that require fewer labour hours will be deemed to have lower costs. This may encourage efficiency, but it may also encourage managers to have labour-intensive work, such as component manufacture, done outside the business to reduce their overhead charge.

If the labour hours method were applied to the ice-cream example, the $475,000 of indirect fixed costs would be split over the number of direct production labour hours. If these are 9,500, then for every hour there would be a cost of:

$$\$475{,}000 \div 9{,}500 = \$50 \text{ of indirect fixed cost to be recovered}$$

If a member of staff earns $20 per hour, from the data above the ice-cream staff cost of $30,000 equates to 1,500 hours.

Ice cream would need to be responsible for $1{,}500 \times \$50 = \$75{,}000$ of indirect fixed costs. Cutting the number of staff hours on the product to reduce the allocation of indirect costs becomes a temptation for the product's management, but this could result in reducing quality and, in turn, long-term brand value.

A more sophisticated method of allocating indirect costs is to apportion them to production departments (design, manufacture, quality, warehouse, despatch, and so on). These departments then charge their costs to a product according to how much it draws on their facilities in terms of time and resources, thus helping make sure that each product is charged for the true cost of its manufacture.

The more refined the process becomes, the more data are required and the more cost is incurred in identifying, capturing and calculating the product cost. Therefore investing in costing detail should only be done to rationalise the portfolio. For day-to-day management it may be interesting information, but a focus on driving value for money from each cost is often more effective.

Assuming that 100,000 tubs of ice cream are to be made, the cost of one tub is shown in Table 7.5.

TABLE 7.5 **The cost of a tub of ice cream**

			$
Variable cost	Uplift by 5% for wastage	$1.32 per unit ÷ 0.95	1.39
Direct fixed cost	Assume 100,000 units	$50,000 ÷ 100,000	0.50
Indirect fixed costs	Assume allocated on labour hours	$75,000 ÷ 100,000	0.75
Total			2.64

This total cost is of course valid only for the allocation method applied and the volume of 100,000. For higher volumes the cost per unit reduces and vice versa.

Activity-based costing

The traditional methods described above allocate overhead costs to products or services based on factors about them such as volume. Activity-based costing was developed with the aim of more accurately reflecting cost by focusing on the activity or "driver" that caused the cost to be incurred.

For example, in running a warehouse the storage costs are determined by storage time, and forklift truck costs are determined by amount of product movement. Therefore products are charged for the time they are in the warehouse and for the number of pallet movements.

By understanding the drivers of cost, a strategy to reduce them can commence. Hence a reduction in storage time and pallet movements enhances efficiency in the business and the cost allocated to the product. The spare capacity released can then be used to support growth in the business without the need for additional warehouse space.

Pursuit of imperfection

The pursuit of better methods of costing may provide better management information on the profitability of products, but costing is an imprecise science and it should always be borne in mind that there is no such thing as a truly accurate cost of provision. Ultimately a "cake" of indirect cost has to be sliced between products. The slicing method will always advantage some and disadvantage others; the total size of the cake is not changed by the method of slicing used.

When ascertaining the cost of products the main issue to identify is what decisions are to be made using the data. The answer to this will determine the level of accuracy required. See Chapter 9 for decisions on the commercial viability of products in a portfolio.

Marginal costing

This is a process of making decisions based on the contribution of products regardless of the fixed costs and the arbitrary method used for apportionment. According to this principle, contribution is good and any contribution will help pay for the fixed costs and ultimately yield a profit.

The problem with this approach is that it can lead to underpricing such that insufficient contribution is generated to cover fixed costs. For example, if a hotel had a room empty at 9pm, what would be the minimum price it should accept to fill it?

As the fixed costs are being incurred whether the room is filled or not, the room charge must cover the variable costs, which comprise cleaning, changing the linen, consumables such as soap and maybe the provision of breakfast. Therefore as long as the hotel charges more than, say, $10 it will be making a contribution. However, if a hotel took this approach to selling, it might gain a reputation that after 9pm rooms are only $10. This would encourage more customers to delay their booking and arrival time to obtain this better price. Why pay $150 by arriving early? As more rooms are sold through this model, the fixed costs of the hotel infrastructure will not be covered, leading to losses. Realising this, hotels will refuse to offer deep discounts.

Job costing

In the ice-cream example above a product cost can be built up because the product is homogeneous. A problem arises when each product or service is different, such as in an engineering company, a law firm or a car repairer. To cost these "jobs" they have to be broken into standard units that can be costed, such as hours. Each hour of labour would be costed to cover not only the direct cost of the person doing the work, but also a share of fixed-cost overheads for running the business.

For example, a car repairer has one mechanic who is employed for 1,500 hours a year at $30,000. The business also has overheads of $12,000 a year. Based on this information, the mechanic costs $30,000 ÷ 1,500 or $20 per hour. To recover the overheads the hourly rate should be increased by $12,000 ÷ 1,500 or $8 per hour.

When quoting for work the hourly cost of the staff would be $28 per hour. Add to this a profit element and the mechanic has a charge-out rate of $30 per hour. However, this method assumes that the mechanic will be able to charge a customer for every hour worked. In practice, the mechanic will need to prepare quotations, complete administration, clear up and so on, which would mean that the income from customers might be insufficient to cover business costs.

An alternative way to calculate the hourly cost is shown below based on the business costs in Table 7.6.

TABLE 7.6 **Business costs ($)**

Salary	30,000
Overheads	12,000
Profit	3,000
Total costs	45,000

Instead of dividing the total costs by the number of available hours, an assumption needs to be made on the "utilisation rate" for the mechanic. This is the proportion of available hours that will be chargeable to customers.

If the assumption is that 1,000 hours will be charged to customers out of the 1,500 available hours, the hourly cost would be:

$$\$45,000 \div 1,000 = \$45 \text{ per hour}$$

In practice, the car repairer will have an over- or under-recovery of hours where the number of hours actually charged to customers is different from the assumed utilisation rate.

There are other ways of completing job costings apart from hours. Typical elements would be as follows:

- Direct materials. The cost of the actual components and materials used would be charged on to each job.
- Material handling. It is common to spread the cost of managing materials – ordering, collecting, storing and so on – among each component. The total cost of these management activities would be added up and spread over the expected value of materials handled in a year such that each component has a handling charge, perhaps 5%.
- Machine hours. Where a business has specialist (typically high-cost) equipment it is appropriate to charge jobs for the specific utilisation. To calculate an hourly charge the total cost of running the machine is forecast and then spread over the expected hours of utilisation in a year.
- Labour hours. As in the car repairer example above, the labour hours would be loaded with an overhead recovery rate to cover business costs that were not specifically covered by other recovery mechanisms listed above.

This is the basis of standard costing where jobs or activities are divided into separable costed activities for which a standard amount of time and materials are allocated and form the components of a job quotation. Most car repairers use this method for costing an annual car service, knowing the expected amount of time and materials required to complete the job.

With experience comes a learning-curve effect, whereby staff are able to achieve outputs in a decreasing amount of time, often based on familiarity and repetition. Therefore the standard times for activities should be reviewed to reflect experience and enable job costings to be completed competitively.

When managing standard costs it is important to understand the variances from standard and not jump to conclusions. If staff take longer than expected, this may be because someone is slower than standard (typical for new staff), or because the raw material they are working with is of poor quality and they took time to deal with it.

Life-cycle costing

Where products and services are not one-time purchases it may be appropriate to complete a life-cycle costing. For example, in the mobile phone industry a customer may sign up for a package and receive a new phone and free minutes and data in return for agreeing to pay an amount for a contracted number of months (see Figure 7.8).

In this example, the upfront costs of the handset, dealer commission and establishing the new contract will be far more than the revenue derived from the first payment.

Building up a profile of the full costing, including carrying the communication activities, managing billing and a share of overheads, will show the total cost of serving customers over their expected life with the business.

By ensuring that break-even is reached during the contract's life the business will know that, although it will have losses in the early months, the contract will be profitable overall. The costing principle here is to look beyond the boundaries of one financial year to understand the product costs over the life cycle of customer transactions. What mobile telecoms providers do is similar to the way that magazines attract people to take out subscriptions by initially offering a number of free or cheap issues. And in the pension business the commissions paid to financial advisers, who act as intermediaries in selling pensions to their clients, can take several years to earn back through management charges.

FIG 7.8 **Mobile phone packages**

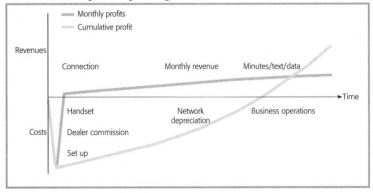

The uncertainty of costs

It is difficult to calculate the true cost of a product as there are so many variables and judgments involved in the process. Product or service contribution is the most accurate attribute as variable costs can be determined with relative ease. Therefore in some businesses managers are saved from becoming embroiled in the debates about allocating fixed costs by being given a product volume and percentage contribution. This could be, for example, 50,000 units at an average minimum contribution of 40%. In the budget process, the finance department can make sure that when these attributes are added for all products there is enough contribution to pay for all overheads and deliver the required level of return to investors.

8 Product pricing and profitability

IN CHAPTER 7 the cost of a product or service was built up. However, the cost may have little to do with the price at which it is sold. This can be illustrated by comparing a pair of Giorgio Armani jeans with a pair of Gap jeans. Although both pairs may be similar in their cost to manufacture, the Giorgio Armani jeans will typically sell for over four times more than the Gap jeans. They are both jeans and they both serve the same function, but the difference is in the cut and most importantly the brand name. The brand name (or label) – and what it says to others about the owner – is all. The target customer of each brand is different; customers of Giorgio Armani are prepared to pay for a degree of exclusivity and a feeling of being special.

To achieve financial success in a business it is crucial to understand what the target customers of a product or service want and what they perceive provides them with value. Value here does not mean cheap: value is where customers' desires or needs for a product or service are greater than the price being asked. This is all to do with a complex set of conscious and unconscious thought processes and judgments, together with the circumstances of the purchaser. For example, people are often content to pay much more for canned drinks on the beach than they would in a supermarket. The vendor has a captive market and is selling at a point of high consumer need. With foreign customers the vendor may also trade on them not really understanding the true cost as the price is in a foreign currency.

Pricing is of paramount importance to any business. Setting prices too high will depress sales, and under-pricing will increase sales but lower profitability. Successful pricing optimises sales volume, revenue and profitability.

As seen in Chapter 7, the calculation of cost is a science that requires mathematics to combine variable costs and allocate fixed costs. Pricing is more of an art for which there is no mathematics, just a compelling requirement to understand customers and their perception of value.

Defining value

Perceived value is complicated to define as it is a combination of needs and costs that are:

- tangible – relating to the physical product, such as quantity, style, price and so on;

- intangible – relating to feelings, such as impressing others or being indulgent; and

- timely – being able to deliver at the point of greatest need, such as selling umbrellas just as it starts to rain.

The value equation in Figure 8.1 sets out some examples of value for customers. The top line identifies the collection of needs and the bottom line the costs. On the left are the functional needs for which the value is often low. On the right are the aspirational elements for which the value will be higher. There is some similarity here to

FIG 8.1 **The value equation**

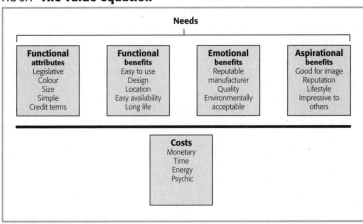

Maslow's hierarchy of needs, with the basic or physiological needs on the left and those of enhancing self-esteem or lifestyle on the right.

Maslow's theory suggests that individuals will focus on their basic needs, such as food or shelter, first. As their income grows their basic needs are taken for granted and their objectives change as they look for more indulgence and luxury.

The four levels of need are described below.

Functional attributes

These are items, often commodities, for which little differentiation can be offered. For example, since people stopped believing that different brands of fuel were significantly different, oil companies know that customers will buy fuel on price alone unless they provide other functional benefits that help attract customers to their filling stations, such as a shop or small supermarket.

Functional benefits

A benefit is an advantage, a point of difference that is worth more to a customer than its attributes. For example, a battery provides power, which is an attribute. To provide power for longer than any other battery is a benefit. Customers are prepared to pay more for this longer-lasting benefit than they would for a normal battery.

To distinguish between a benefit and an attribute the following link phrase is helpful:

Attribute   *which means that*   Benefit

This principle was illustrated by Theodore Levitt, a leading management thinker, who said: "People don't want to buy a quarter-inch drill. They want a quarter-inch hole."

Attribute: quarter-inch *which means that* Benefit: quarter-inch hole
          drill bit

Therefore customers want the benefit of the hole not the ownership of a drill bit.

Emotional benefits

Emotional benefits are about conveying or conjuring up feelings in customers. The feelings can be of contentment such as those expressed about reliability or safety. They can also be of exhilaration or those for improving health or fitness.

To distinguish between emotions and benefits the following linking phrase is helpful:

Benefit   *which makes you feel that*   Emotion

For example, with an electronic circuit breaker:

Benefit: to avoid being electrocuted, power is immediately cut from an appliance when there is a short circuit	*which makes you feel that*	Emotion: you can use power tools confidently

In building a customer proposition the emotional benefits can be more than just product based. They may involve trust in the product brand or in the retailer of the product.

Brand names are managed to create a personification of a word or logo that consumers can feel they have a relationship with. The key to strong brand management is the continuous reinforcement of what the brand promises. This is what will gain recognition and trust among customers and will earn their emotional attachment and loyalty.

Aspirational benefits

Aspirational benefits are about fulfilling beliefs or dreams. Celebrity cookbooks are often said to show "aspirational photographs", in that they entice you into believing that you can cook wonderful food and present it in a professional manner.

In fulfilling their aspirations consumers will pay premium prices for perceived value. Many aspirations are to do with beauty, desire, adulation and indulgence. This is where Giorgio Armani jeans justify their price as a brand – they have a reputation which enhances the status of the owner.

To distinguish between aspirations and emotions the following linking phrase is useful:

Emotion   *which makes you believe that*   Aspiration

For example, in the case of a fashionable brand of perfume:

Emotion: feeling of being special and confident	*which makes you believe that*	Aspiration: you will be more attractive to others

A strong part of aspiration is to be more attractive. In recent years some clothing manufacturers have taken to "vanity sizing", whereby they add an extra 2 inches to trouser waists and other clothes so that customers believe they are slimmer than they really are.

Costs

The costs to the buyer may not be only price, but can extend to much more in the value proposition. Some examples are as follows:

■ Flat pack furniture may well be cheap, but the effort and inconvenience of putting it together, combined with the risk of it not working out well, can make it worth paying more for ready assembled furniture.

■ Having a sofa covered in the fabric of your choice that can be selected from an infinite range sounds ideal except it can take three months to be completed and delivered. Compromising by choosing from a limited range of already covered items in a store makes it instantly available.

■ Expiry dates on such things as food and prepaid mobile phone minutes can dissuade customers, particularly when they will not last long.

The combination of a variety of factors builds up the value

proposition of a product or service. Comparing the alternatives and substitutes in the market makes it possible to position the price appropriately.

An example is the pricing of carrots. In their wholesale form they will be sold unwashed in large sacks. Most consumers will want them washed and some will be prepared to pay for them being chopped. The value proposition of different options in order of price is shown in Table 8.1.

TABLE 8.1 **Value proposition of different options**

Carrot type	Value proposition
Chopped into batons ready to cook	Convenience and impressive to others to serve for dinner
Organic version	Feeling that it is better for you
Bagged in 1kg packs	Convenience
Wholesale washed 25kg sacks	Benefit of being cleaned
Wholesale unwashed 25kg sacks	Commodity

By moving the value proposition up the value chain, a bag of ready chopped carrots may sell at nearly ten times the amount of the unwashed commodity. However, the market size at the premium end of the market will be smaller than at the cheaper end. The size of the business will dictate where it should position itself, and if it is large enough it may offer products at a number of positions. An example is Toyota, a Japanese vehicle maker, which makes cars in the volume sectors as well as in the premium sector under the brand Lexus.

It is possible that a service can have high perceived value and cost virtually nothing to provide. For example, many families who want to make sure they are seated together on a flight are happy to pay their travel firm a small surcharge to be able to reserve their seating positions when they buy the tickets. This also means that they do not have to arrive at the airport early to make sure of getting seats together. Once the necessary software is in place, this service can be provided at almost no cost, but this does not mean it is worth nothing. Smart businesses will capitalise on these opportunities as a highly lucrative way to generate revenue. These "golden eggs" are often unsustainable but valuable while they last.

The value proposition may need to work across a range of customers. For example, a children's food product such as potato smiley faces has three potential customers:

- Retailers (or customers) who buy the product believing that they can sell it easily and make money from doing so.
- Parents (or consumers) who will buy the product believing or knowing that their children will like it.
- Children (or end users) who will eat it and enjoy doing so.

Hidden value

For customers to make a proper value judgment about a product they need the important facts concerning what is on offer. The difficulty is to identify the right level of information, as research suggests that customers often read little or none of the information about what they purchase. Therefore the critical points of value and differentiation need to be displayed or described.

A similar problem arises when the value offered is not identifiable or appreciated by the customer, such as when a car is serviced. Thus many car repairers will also valet the car as part of the service so there is a visible benefit for the cost of the service and a feeling of satisfaction when driving away after paying the invoice.

Basis of proposition

The reason a customer will purchase a product or service will fall into one of two categories: to provide a solution to a problem; or to fulfil a desire or aspiration. Unless a product meets one of these criteria a business will struggle to create a market that is significant enough (see Figure 8.2).

Examples of an aspiration are clothing or audio-visual products. The marketing of these products plays a crucial role in increasing the desire of potential customers for them.

A solution is items such as medicines or cleaning products. The

FIG 8.2 **Meeting needs**

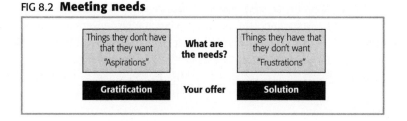

customer does not necessarily want to own these products but they want the benefits that they will provide.

Customer journey

In setting prices it is essential to position the value correctly to attract not only an initial sale but also repeat purchases. Finding the right balance will help customers become advocates of your products or services such that they will become your most effective form of marketing. Failing to get the balance right will do the reverse.

The way to get the balance right is to understand the customer decision points at each stage of their journey, from product ignorance through purchase and then onto potential repeat purchase. Figure 8.3 illustrates the process.

FIG 8.3 **Customer journey**

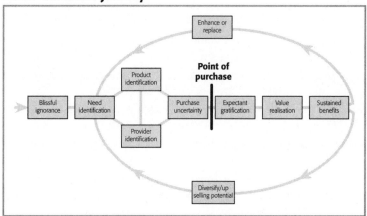

The start point is a customer who is in a state of blissful ignorance of both the product and the provider. Marketing is required to move customers to the stage of realising that they have a need for either gratification or a solution (as described above). This marketing will take many forms, ranging from the media (such as television, newspapers and the internet) to activation (such as an encounter by free sampling).

The next stage is to identify the right product and the right provider. Mobile phone retailers have a difficult task in trying to help customers identify the right handset and tariff structure without the process becoming too complicated and deterring them.

Once a decision to purchase is made there is a moment of uncertainty when the customer is not sure about the choice made. The more expensive the item, the greater the anxiety is likely to be. Many businesses help customers through this stage and give themselves a competitive advantage by providing an option to return items or a cooling-off period (such as 14 days) during which customers can change their mind and a contract can be cancelled with a full refund. The cost of fulfilling such an option needs to be included in the product costing.

The stage of expectant gratification is the customer demand for an instant benefit. It can also become the moment of instant disappointment, as when a child opens a battery-operated toy on their birthday only to find the batteries are not included. The technique is to make it easy and quick for the new customer to derive benefit. For example, most providers of IT equipment include a single sheet entitled "quick set-up guide". Upon opening the box the customer can quickly start to make progress without having to read a hefty manual.

Value realisation is when the product has to live up to the expectations promised. This is critical in customer perception of whether the product or service provides value. An example is when a hotel promises sea views and all that can be seen is a large construction site for a new hotel being built in front. It is this stage, above all, that will determine whether a customer becomes an advocate or a critic.

The last stage is sustained benefits, which are particularly relevant for long-life products such as cars, although they can apply to food items through their shelf life. Sustained benefits are the basis on which a repurchase will be made, and people are not going to repurchase products that break, wear out or fall apart in no time. Saving costs in manufacturing may lead to short-term enhanced profits, but it will create customer disappointment at this stage and lower customer retention.

Success right through this process will lead to two opportunities:

- Enhance/replace – when customers will make a repeat purchase or even upgrade to a superior product in the range. Loyalty will keep them with the same provider.
- Diversification – where customers so valued their purchase that they have trust in the provider and will willingly buy other products or services it offers.

Competition

Imagine the scenario of two identical retail businesses trading side by side. To gain market share the temptation would be to cut prices and draw customers away from the competitor. Very quickly the competitor can retaliate and similarly cut prices. Soon a price war develops which may lead to both businesses making losses. The business that can afford to carry the losses the longest will survive.

A more effective strategy, however, might be to add value rather than cut price by, for example, providing a higher-quality service that will make customers more likely to be loyal.

The product life cycle

The product life cycle depicts the profile of a product from its development through to its withdrawal (see Figure 8.4). Although the theory is perhaps flawed for commodities or generic products such as basic clothes, individual products or brands do conform to the profile with the main variable being the length of time it takes to go through each stage. The relevance of the model is for the alternative pricing strategies that need to be adopted at each stage.

The characteristics of the market and the product at each stage of the life cycle are explained in Table 8.2 and the appropriate pricing strategy in Table 8.3.

FIG 8.4 **The product life cycle**

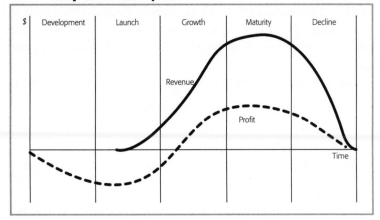

TABLE 8.2 **Characteristics in the product life cycle**

Development	Launch	Growth	Maturity	Decline
Investment, often substantial in the case of pharmaceutical companies, in a potential product with market expectations	Build market awareness through the media, aiming at early adopters or innovators who are keen to try new products	A process of building brand preference and market share with a focus on reducing the unit cost of production	Competition is intense with little differentiation between providers; customers churn between providers	New technology, substitutes or fashion reduce demand and volume declines, such as CDs and DVDs being superseded by downloads

Pricing strategies

Similar products can comfortably coexist at a range of prices provided they offer appropriate perceived value to their customers.

For example, you might find at least 12 brands of strawberry preserve in a supermarket with the cheapest selling for one-tenth of the price of the most expensive. The most expensive brand has twice the fruit and beautifully describes the care taken in the harvesting and cooking to a traditional recipe. The cheapest brand creates a wonderful benefit out of its inferiority – with less fruit it can be spread more easily.

TABLE 8.3 **Pricing strategy in the product life cycle**

Development	Launch	Growth	Maturity	Decline
Not yet launched	Either low penetration pricing to attract market share and fuel growth, as used for food products; or skim pricing to charge a high price to help recover the investment cost and create the perception of superiority, as used for electrical goods	Price begins to fade to make the product available to a wider market or the imitators. Value pricing is used and even parity pricing to similar products as the "new" becomes "old"	Price continues to fade and promotional pricing becomes more common to extend the life of the product and offer more value to customers	High discounts and stock reductions using clearance pricing prior to product deletion

The axis of success is illustrated in Figure 8.5 and pricing strategies are summarised in Table 8.4.

FIG 8.5 **Price versus perceived value**

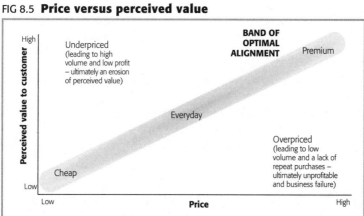

TABLE 8.4 **Summary of pricing strategies**

Strategy	Description
Penetration pricing	A temporary discounted price to enter a market and attract new customers. Often used at a product launch to gain quick market share
Skim pricing	A high price to enhance perceived value of latest technology and exclusivity of early adopters. Often used for short life-cycle products such as electronics
Value pricing	Using the value matrix to identify the differentiating factors for positioning the relative perceived value against competitors. This is the most common method of pricing
Promotional pricing	A short-run discount or extra value variant to create interest in the product and rekindle loyalty. Often used for mature products
Clearance pricing	A deep discount to clear products in decline from shelves, sometimes at a price that is below cost
Parity pricing	Matching prices to other businesses selling similar products but not illegally colluding in a cartel to keep prices artificially high. Governments have laws against cartels to encourage free trade and competition
Psychological pricing	Setting the price at a point such as $9.99 rather than $10.25 where it seems significantly better value than the 26 cents difference
Price discrimination	Setting prices at different levels for different customers. This is done in different countries for motor cars or for market segments such as hotels which have a corporate rate and a retail rate. The internet has made such price differences more transparent
Predatory pricing	Deliberate discounting to an unprofitable level with the intention of driving out competition. This is illegal in some countries
Life-cycle pricing	Taking a product and its consumables and pricing them over their life cycle; for example, inkjet printers and their cartridges or razors and their blades. The dispenser (printer or razor) is often priced cheaply to encourage an initial purchase. The consumables are priced expensively to recover the discounted cost. Making the consumables of unique design prevents alternative manufactures cashing in on the more lucrative part of the deal
Tender pricing	Typical in the construction or defence industry where bespoke production will be completed to a customer specification. Prices are often based on cost with a margin added. The contract is often awarded to the lowest bidder which can lead to a compromise in the quality of materials used and the profitability of the transaction
Cost-plus pricing	A variation on tender pricing based on the cost incurred plus a percentage margin. Such pricing is rare as it encourages contractors to spend as much as possible with no incentive to be economical

The attitude towards the customer

Without customers there would be no revenue and no business. A quote attributed to Mahatma Gandhi summarises this perfectly:

> *A customer is the most important visitor on our premises. He is not dependent on us. We are dependent on him. He is not an interruption of our work. He is the purpose of it. He is not an outsider to our business. He is part of it. We are not doing him a favour by serving him. He is doing us a favour by giving us the opportunity to do so.*

9   Portfolio management

CHAPTER 7 LOOKED at the products and services being offered to calculate the cost of their provision. This chapter looks at how to optimise the financial potential of a portfolio of products.

To understand the benefit of portfolio optimisation you have to look at historic examples, where strategic change came about as a result of poor financial performance. British Airways (BA) provides a good example. In the year to March 31st 2000 it earned a pre-tax profit of just £5m on sales of £8.9 billion and the carriage of 46.6m passengers. Dividing the profit by the number of passengers carried revealed that the airline earned just 10.7 pence per passenger.

BA then set out to identify where it made money and, more importantly, where it lost money. In its published accounts this was referred to as the airline's "future size and shape" review, which focused on removing unprofitable capacity, reducing costs and stripping complexity out of the business. To do this, detailed information about costs was required across the portfolio.

The results for the year to March 31st 2006 showed a vast improvement, not through growth, but through focusing on profitable activities. Pre-tax profit was £620m, even though revenue was down to £8.5 billion and passenger numbers were down to 35.6m. Profit per passenger was £17.41, an increase of 16,300% compared with the 2000 figure. Since then profits have been buffeted by events such as the 2010 ash cloud and staff strikes, but if it had not made the changes, its performance over the past few years would have been very different.

A similar turnaround took place at Sprint Nextel, an American telecommunications company, which in 2007 suffered a huge loss of customers and profit, reporting losses of $30 billion (including a goodwill write-off). In 2008 it embarked on a new strategy: "We continue to assess the portfolio of services provided by our Wireline segment and are focusing our efforts on IP-based services and de-emphasising stand-alone voice services and non-IP-based data services." By 2011 customer numbers had risen by 50% and profits – the first for four years – had just about returned, at $108m.

Techniques can be used to analyse a portfolio and improve long-term product profitability.

Focusing the portfolio

Among the many reasons a company may build up a portfolio of businesses, products or services are:

■ economies of scale – for example, having a single head office for all business units to avoid overhead duplication and to derive economies of scale in funding each business (a lower weighted average cost of capital – see Chapter 6);

■ diversified risk – selling ice cream and umbrellas to ensure that sales are less vulnerable to weather;

■ vertical integration – owning different parts of the supply chain, such as oil companies owning the oilfields, platforms, pipelines, refineries and gas stations;

■ purchasing power – the ability to obtain better prices from suppliers by being able to offer them more business;

■ life-cycle stages – for example, car companies will typically have several models that they relaunch in rotation. The cash generated from the new models provides the resources to invest in development to replace the old models;

■ common customers – a strong brand to which customers are attracted and loyal can be exploited by expanding into different product or service areas. There can also be an economy of scale in the marketing that supports the separate businesses.

Optimising a portfolio can involve fundamental changes that might include deleting products, launching new products, and relocating and laying off staff. The decisions made need to be objective and based on long-term value creation, not on sentimentality.

The management of a portfolio and its complexities involves consideration of the following:

- Heritage – the relevance of maintaining the accumulated legacy of past acquisitions, including products, services and operating sites, while respecting crucial cultural factors.
- Resources – whether the human and other resources such as equipment and systems currently in place are appropriate.
- Product life cycle – changes in technology or customer needs that create opportunities as well as close them.
- Market dynamics – changes in the operating landscape caused by new competitors, dominance of suppliers or customers, regulation and trends.

From the interpretation of these factors medium-term to long-term projections are needed to evaluate the potential of any business, product or service. Using discounted cash flow techniques (as explained in Chapter 10), each part of the portfolio can be appraised.

The first stage in this process is to be clear about the strategic purpose or vision of the organisation. What does the business make money out of today and what will it make money out of in the future?

A good product or service that meets a consumer need and is well managed should be able to make money. Therefore a business should collect together those products and services over which it can create synergy and market leadership, dispensing with those that detract from the core.

Predicting the area of focus for the future is no easy task. Business history is littered with companies that seemed to have broken the mould but later turned out to be flawed. Nokia's "inspirational" move out of timber products into telecoms resulted in the company earning a return on investment of almost 50% in 2006, but these returns evaporated as the company became complacent and failed to identify the change in handsets led by Apple. Even Enron was considered to have achieved success in the somewhat undynamic energy sector, but this turned out to have been down to "creative accounting".

FIG 9.1 **The McKinsey matrix**

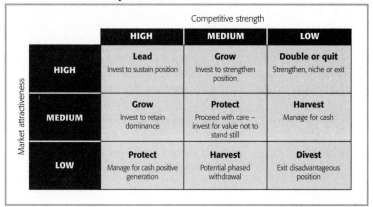

Source: McKinsey and Company

Portfolio strategy

A tool to help explore product and service potential is a portfolio matrix, of which several have been developed: the McKinsey matrix, the GE matrix and Shell's directional policy matrix. The concept is a more sophisticated version of the matrix originally developed by the Boston Consulting Group, known as the BCG matrix, which is famous for its question marks, stars, cash cows and dogs.

A portfolio matrix plots a business's competitive strength on one axis and its market attractiveness on the other (see Figure 9.1). The optimal place is to be a dominant player in an attractive market – for example, Microsoft for computer software or Nestlé for instant coffee.

The opposite is the least attractive place to be, a minor player in an unattractive market – for example, a family grocery store in a town dominated by global retailers. The options for the business are change or exit, perhaps becoming an upmarket deli to create a market position of its own. Trying to compete with the major retail brands on price and range will inevitably fail.

TABLE 9.1 **Factors affecting market attractiveness**

	Attractive	Unattractive
Market characteristics		
Market size	Large potential market	Small disparate market
Market growth rate	Growing and will continue to do so	Growth slowing, flat or declining
Pricing trends	Holding steady and moving up with inflation	Prices falling and becoming more competitive
Profitability trends	Changes in costs can be passed on to customers and margins maintained	Margins shrinking and pressure to squeeze out cost
Direct forces		
Intensity of direct competition	Fragmented with no competitor having significant market share	Market dominated by a few customers with high market shares
Customer purchasing pressure	Plenty of customers and low dependency upon any one customer	Few dominant customers with long-term supply contracts
Limiting forces		
Intensity of indirect competition (through substitutes)	No significant or viable alternatives	Plenty of alternative ways to derive the product or service benefit
New competitors entering the market and barriers to entry	High barriers to entry deterring new entrants	Low barriers to entry and new players can easily enter the market
Supplier dominance	Plenty of suppliers with oversupply and few that have any significant market share	Few suppliers or oligopoly
Regulatory restrictions	Deregulated market	Highly regulated and imminent restrictive changes awaited

Market attractiveness

Factors that affect the market attractiveness of a product or service can be summarised in three parts: market characteristics, direct forces and limiting forces (see Table 9.1).

The factors listed in Table 9.1 can be used to identify where on the vertical axis the market is positioned.

Competitive strength

This is a judgment on how well the business can compete against its competitors. It is important to find the critical points of differentiation or advantage:

- asset base or cost advantage;
- management strength;
- lower cost of capital;
- unique and protected (patent) offering;
- brand strength;
- customer loyalty;
- distribution channels.

The sustainability of each attribute needs to be assessed as the factors which are easily mimicked will quickly erode any perceived advantage. Investment in maintaining differentiation is crucial.

Plotting product or services on the matrix

Having assessed where each product should lie on the matrix, the plotting involves three stages:

- The location is plotted as a circle, the size of the circle representing the potential market size.
- Within the circle the current market share is indicated as a segment.
- An arrow is used to show how the market attractiveness and competitive strength are anticipated to develop as product strategies are implemented.

See Figure 9.2 for an example plotting of two products.

If a product is positioned in the square with high competitive strength and low market attractiveness and two competitors agree to merge, the market will become less attractive and competitive strength will be substantially reduced. The challenge is to respond with better differentiation and customer advantage for the product over others in the market.

FIG 9.2 **Plotting products or services**

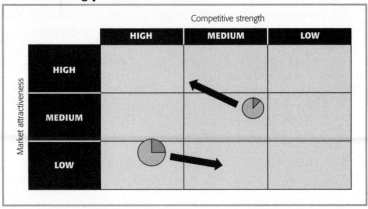

Having completed the analysis and positioning of each product and service in the portfolio, the actions identified in Figure 9.1 (see page 147) dictate the strategy to adopt for the medium to long term.

Although the strategic design of a portfolio is typically the domain of senior executives, often with the assistance of consultants, the effective management of the portfolio is the primary way to deliver a sustainable superior return on investment.

A product portfolio

The following scenario will be used to illustrate some of the tactical principles and analysis. Northern Cable is a fictitious business that manufactures and sells copper cable, primarily in its domestic market. There are three product lines:

- electric cable, the original product and the largest part of the portfolio;
- television (coaxial) cable, a product that grew in the 1980s and 1990s but since the advent of digital television has been fairly static and now shows a small loss;
- telephone cable, a product that grew rapidly as broadband and domestic networks were being installed but is vulnerable to the growing fibre-optic cable used in some domestic installations.

The business consists of three departments, one for each of the products. Each department is responsible for a machine that manufactures the cable by a process of copper extrusion and plastic insulation wrap.

The overheads for running the business are managed centrally and then charged to each department. They are allocated in proportion to the revenue earned by each department. This method does not reflect actual usage of the central services but just a simple share determined by the ability of each department to pay.

The information in Table 9.2 is presented as follows:

- Revenue – the income from selling each product.
- Variable costs – the components needed to manufacture each product.
- Contribution – the revenue less the variable costs.
- Contribution percentage – the contribution expressed as a percentage of revenue.
- Direct fixed costs – the fixed costs that are specific to each department, so if one product was dropped these direct fixed costs would be saved.
- Gross profit – the contribution less direct fixed costs (or revenue less variable costs and direct fixed costs).
- Indirect fixed costs – the overheads that have been split across the three products in proportion to the revenue that each has earned.
- Total fixed costs – the sum of the direct and indirect fixed costs.
- Profit/loss – the overall profit or loss of the product.

The importance of contribution

In Chapter 7, contribution was described as being revenue less variable costs. It is the contribution towards fixed costs and ultimately operating profit.

Contribution is important because in the short term most fixed costs are constant. Items such as rent or depreciation will not change substantially without changes in the business infrastructure. The

TABLE 9.2 **Northern Cable's three products ($ '000)**

	Electric	Television	Telephone	Total
Revenue	33,721	11,424	5,527	50,672
Variable costs				
Raw materials	13,688	3,427	1,348	18,463
Packaging	3,016	2,621	701	6,338
Energy	699	526	110	1,335
Total variable costs	17,403	6,574	2,159	26,136
Contribution	16,318	4,850	3,368	24,536
Contribution percentage	48%	42%	61%	48%
Direct fixed costs				
Labour	2,806	1,091	460	4,357
Depreciation	2,175	1,510	948	4,633
Maintenance	473	286	73	832
Total direct fixed costs	5,454	2,887	1,481	9,822
Gross profit	10,864	1,963	1,887	14,714
Indirect fixed costs				
Selling and marketing	1,600	542	262	2,404
Warehouse and distribution	3,147	1,066	516	4,729
Accounting, IT and HR	1,344	455	220	2,020
Executive office	685	232	112	1,029
Total indirect fixed costs	6,776	2,295	1,110	10,182
Total fixed costs	12,230	5,182	2,591	20,004
Profit/(loss)	4,088	(332)	777	4,532

maximisation of contribution is therefore a priority. However, the actions taken should be for the long-term benefit of the business and not for a quick increase in profit which may achieve a monthly target. For example, a discount offered to secure a quick sale may undermine longer-term pricing and the ability to sustain profit from a customer.

If contribution is the key to profitability in the short term, selling the products with the higher contributions would be preferable to selling those with lower contributions. The contribution percentage (which expresses contribution as a percentage of revenue) can be used to rank the products.

Table 9.2 shows that selling more telephone cable at a contribution of 61% will be more beneficial than selling television cable at a contribution of 42%. In other words, for every $1 of telephone cable sales there will be 61 cents of profit, whereas television cable will yield 42 cents of profit.

Ranking products by contribution is a way of focusing selling activities on the products that will provide the highest returns.

Closing down a product

Television cable shows a loss of $332,000, which is destroying value, so the instant reaction might be to consider its closure. However, a decision on a product deletion should always be based on long-term strategy, not a response to one year of poor performance. A clear understanding of market expectations and future potential should be the first part of any product review.

Three tests should be completed to determine a product's profit potential. These are shown in the decision tree in Figure 9.3.

Test 1 Does the product make a contribution?

Does the product make more money than the variable costs spent on its manufacture, let alone covering the overheads of running the business?

For a product that lacks contribution the likely conclusion is to exit fast. However, there may be other reasons to support a product that fails this test:

■ Does the business need to be active in all the product areas to be credible to customers? For example, would customers stop buying the other cables if the business no longer provided the full range? The product becomes known as a loss leader.

■ Would a competitor become stronger as a consequence and therefore undermine the remaining business?

FIG 9.3 **Three tests for a product**

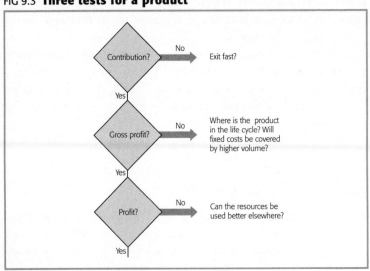

- Are raw material prices temporarily high, enabling a contribution to be made when they return to a more typical level?
- Can the product be reformulated to strip out cost and make it more viable?

Test 2 Does the product make a gross profit?

Achieving a gross profit would imply that a product can cover its own cost of production and contribute towards business overheads and ultimately profit. Failure at this level shows that the product cannot cover its own direct costs. However, this needs to be looked at in the context of the product life cycle (see Chapter 8), which shows the typical profile of sales volume after a product launch. Volume starts slowly, grows, reaches a plateau at maturity and then fades as other products take its market.

If substantial infrastructure is in place to handle future volume, a product is unlikely to make a gross profit until it is well into its growth phase. Therefore continued support is required until the product reaches its required volumes. However, a product in decline that does not make a gross profit should be closed down. Projections of anticipated sales volumes are critical to understand the product's potential, as a product closure decision based on one year's results would be somewhat hasty.

Test 3 Does the product make a profit?

What would happen to the rest of the business if it did not have the product? There is one immediate effect: the gross profit will be lost and it is the gross profit that helps cover a proportion of the business overheads. In the example, television cable makes a gross profit of $1,963,000 but is charged $2,295,000 as its share of the group overheads.

The loss that television cable makes is therefore $2,295,000 – $1,963,000 = $332,000. The business as a whole makes a profit of $4,532,000. Without the gross profit from television cable to help cover the group overheads, the business would have a profit of only $2,569,000. To make the close-down of television cable a viable option, the business would need to reduce its total overheads by more than $1,963,000. This is difficult when savings are required across several departments and economies of scale are destroyed.

The more effective conclusion is whether the business would be more profitable by diverting the central resources to focus activity on either of the other two products to derive better value.

Finally, the decision to delete a product should be made only after the completion of a business case which evaluates the expected future cash flows that would be lost (see Chapter 10). The cash flow approach will bring into account inventory levels for which sales revenue can be derived without cash expenditure. Using up inventory is significant in deciding the timing of a deletion.

Launching a new product

As with a product deletion, a product launch should be evaluated using a business case that is built around the future expected cash flows. However, from a portfolio perspective there are some factors that must be considered in forecasting the future expected cash flows.

Cannibalisation

As new products arrive, the revenue and costs involved should not be looked at in isolation. There can be ripple effects across the business where a new product cannibalises sales from existing products. For example, the launch of a new car in a range can take sales away from existing models. The loss of revenue from the other products needs to be included in the calculation of the benefits derived from the new one.

In some scenarios, the launch or enhancement of a product in a range can require at least five revenue considerations. An example is an improvement in mid-class seating in an aircraft:

- Upgrade – people who would have bought an economy-class seat trade up and buy the new mid-class one as it is so good.

- Spill – people who would have bought a premium first-class seat trade down as the mid-class one is "good enough".

- Steal – the new mid-class seating wins customers from competitors, as it is a better product than the alternatives.

- Retain – the mid-class improvement stops customers moving to competitors that previously had better mid-class seating.

- Loyal – customers who were happy with the previous mid-class seating and whose purchasing behaviour is unaffected by the changes.

Creeping fixed costs

With an established portfolio of products it might be reasonable to expect that new products will be accommodated within the existing head-office infrastructure and that economies of scale will result in extra gross profit without any extra indirect fixed costs. For small increments in scale this may be true, but for substantial changes head-office functions will also need to grow, which will mean higher indirect costs. Although some economies of scale are likely to occur, an allowance for costs creeping up should be made in calculating the viability of a new product.

Contribution ratios

In building a product range it can be a mistake to bring in cheaper or lower grades of product to widen the appeal to a greater number of customers. The danger is that the cheaper product may have lower margins, resulting in a lower profit from customers who would have happily purchased the premium version but switched to the cheaper one when it became available. Attempting to keep the contribution value constant across a range reduces the impact, but may make price positioning difficult in comparison to competitors and substitutes.

Scarce resources

In a production environment there can be instances of a component or an ingredient being in short supply and causing production to be constrained. Where these components are used across a range of products it is helpful to know how the production should be prioritised to use any scarce resources effectively. These constraints are typically short term so the fixed costs and allocations are unlikely to change significantly for the duration of the shortage. As a consequence it is not the profit that needs to be maximised but the contribution.

Priority should be given to the product that generates the highest contribution per unit of limiting factor. For example, if raw materials were in short supply, the product with the highest contribution per unit of raw material would be prioritised. In practice, it is unlikely that all raw materials will be in short supply at the same time so the analysis would have to be done more specifically than is illustrated here.

$$\text{Prioritisation factor} = \frac{\text{Contribution}}{\text{Raw materials}}$$

TABLE 9.3 **Prioritisation factor for the three products**

	Electric cable	Television cable	Telephone cable
Contribution	16,318	4,850	3,368
Raw materials	13,688	3,427	1,348
Contribution per unit of raw materials	1.192	1.415	2.498

It is apparent that the greatest return is derived from assigning the raw materials to manufacturing telephone cable in priority to the others. Telephone cable will yield almost $2.50 for every $1 of raw material consumed compared with a much lower return from either of the other two. Once customer demand for telephone cable is satisfied, the product generating the highest contribution per unit of raw materials is television cable with electric cable coming third.

The raw materials may be in short supply for only a few weeks so this prioritisation needs to be balanced against managing longer-term customer relationships, which may require electric cable to be produced sub-optimally. Retention of longer-term profitable business should normally be put ahead of short-term profit optimisation.

The prioritisation principle can be applied to all types of bottlenecks that occur in manufacturing or operations, not just components. Shortage of capacity in a particular process or a shortage of skilled labour can be managed with a similar calculation.

Prices and volumes

In selling products or services to customers price usually dominates the negotiation. Offering discounts makes customers feel they have struck a good deal though it will erode the supplier's margins and profit. To make the discounts attractive to both parties they can be based on volumes, such that an increase in the size of the order justifies the discount per unit. However, the relationship between price, volume and profit is not straightforward, as variable costs will change with movement in volumes but not with movement in prices.

For example, a customer offers a supplier 50% more volume if it can have a 10% discount. If the product had a 20% profit margin, would the supplier accept? At first glance the deal looks attractive: only 10% off to get 50% more business. The discount may be a small percentage in proportion to the revenue, but it is half the profit. The result is shown in Table 9.4.

TABLE 9.4 **Calculating the effect of volume discounts**

	Original deal	Customer offer of 10% discount for 50% more volume
Revenue	100 units @ $1.00 = $100	150 units @ $0.90 = $135
Variable costs	100 units @ $0.80 = $80	150 units @ $0.80 = $120
Margin	$20	$15
Margin percentage	20%	11%

Therefore the deal would make the supplier worse off, reducing overall profit from $20 to $15.

Figure 9.4 calculates the relationship between discounts and gross margin to derive the volume uplift requirements to maintain profit. The numbers show, for 100 original units, how many units would need to be sold at the discounted price to leave profit unchanged.

Applying Figure 9.4 to the example shows that with the 100 original units at a 20% margin, 200 units would be needed to make the 10% discount as profitable.

The formula for the calculation is:

$$\frac{\text{Margin}}{(\text{Margin} - \text{Discount})} = \text{Volume uplift required at new margin percentage to leave profit unchanged}$$

FIG 9.4 **Volume to discount effects**

					Discount offered (%)						
Gross margin (%)		0	5	10	15	20	25	30	35	40	45	50
	5	100										
	10	100	200									
	15	100	150	300								
	20	100	133	200	400							
	25	100	125	167	250	500						
	30	100	120	150	200	300	600					
	35	100	117	140	175	233	350	700				
	40	100	114	133	160	200	267	400	800			
	45	100	113	129	150	180	225	300	450	900		
	50	100	111	125	143	167	200	250	333	500	1000	

Applied to the example with 20% expressed as 0.2:

$$\frac{0.2}{(0.2 - 0.1)} = 2$$

Therefore twice as much volume is required.

The same uplift logic can be applied to a range of price- or volume-based promotions. Deep-discounted products that are offered in supermarkets on buy-one-get-one-free (BOGOF) or three-for-two deals require substantial volume increases to make them viable.

For a BOGOF to be viable the original profit margin percentage needs to be over 50%, as twice as much variable cost will be incurred for each sale made. For example, a product with 60% margin will have variable costs of 40%. If this is offered on a BOGOF, the variable costs for each sale will become 80% and the margin will fall to 20%. The uplift required is therefore:

$$\frac{0.6}{(0.6 - 0.4)} = 3$$

Therefore three times as much sales volume is required, which as it is a BOGOF means six times as many units are sold.

This calculation can be easily applied to show the volume targets for a promotion, but the reality is that consumers will stockpile the product, and sales in the weeks following the promotion will slow as consumers use up their purchases. This effect is known as the post-promotion dip. The benefit of this type of promotion is to clear excess inventory or to attract new consumers to try and use the product. In the absence of either of these two impacts, the promotion gives products away to consumers that are already loyal and would have been highly likely to pay the full price.

Summary

To manage a portfolio effectively requires a combination of strategic engineering and excellent operational effectiveness. Decisions need to be made for the long-term benefit of the product, service and business, not just as a response to short-term targets and pressures.

10   **Investment appraisal**

FOR A BUSINESS TO BE SUCCESSFUL it must, as was outlined in Chapter 1, invest in projects that yield a greater return on investment (ROI) than the average cost of an investment dollar, defined as the weighted average cost of capital (WACC). For example, if the WACC is 10%, projects generating returns that exceed this rate will be creating value for the investors.

The term "project" covers a range of activities from the purchase of a piece of equipment through to the acquisition of another company. The common feature is that they all involve an initial outlay of funds with an expectation of future benefits. The uncertainty of the future benefits requires detailed analysis to ensure that the investment risk is worthwhile.

A typical cumulative cash flow profile over the life of a project can be represented by the graph in Figure 10.1 which is known as a "J" curve:

FIG 10.1 **J curve**

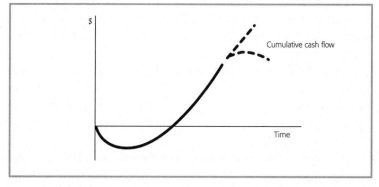

At the outset money is spent taking the project cash flow into a deficit. As revenues increase and costs decrease the bottom of the trough is reached. The increasing revenue eventually turns the cumulative cash flow positive and the project starts to yield benefits. However, these benefits may not be sustainable because of competitive pressures or technology changes and the cash flows can reach a plateau or even fall.

As projects can involve substantial investment in proportion to the size of a business, it is important that the right investments are made at the right time and at the right price, and then managed effectively. The ability to exit a project halfway through can be limited (particularly if the investment is in specialist or bespoke assets), which reinforces the need to evaluate the potential returns on any investment robustly before funds are committed.

Organisations use the business case process to structure project proposals, evaluate their potential and seek approval from a range of sponsors and executives. The decision becomes collective, shared among functions and people with experience to make sure that risk is minimised and that there is confidence in the anticipated return.

The point of greatest risk is when the cumulative cash flow has reached the bottom of the trough. Turning the corner is critical, and once there is a net surplus the project has paid back all the investment made. The business case process is effectively asking permission to take the organisation to the bottom of the trough on the justification of the upside return. Publicly listed organisations prefer not to be at the bottom of the trough at their year end, so timing of the investment is an important aspect of the decision.

As mentioned in Chapter 1, a business is simply a collection of business cases. However, they are all starting and delivering returns at different times (see Figure 10.2).

The outflows at the inception of each project will build the asset base and the inflows from later years form the basis of the cash flow and income statement. Therefore the financial performance of any one year represents the combined results from project investments in the current and preceding years.

To deliver a superior ROI every year means there is a limit to the amount of outflow that can be tolerated when compared with the

FIG 10.2 **Summary of projects**

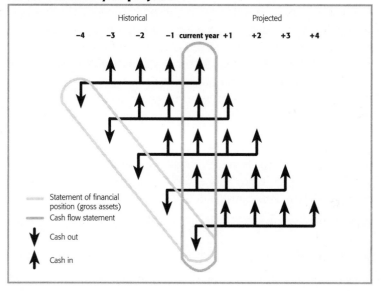

projected inflows. This leads to capital being rationed and a budget for investment. Projects need to compete on merit to have a share of that budget. Merit can be that a project will produce the desired financial returns or it may come down to operational necessities such as complying with legislation on health, safety and the environment.

This chapter explores the business case process and the techniques used to complete a financial evaluation. Unlike some of the other chapters, which report and analyse transactions that have taken place, the project appraisal process is about quantifying future expectations with assumptions and then exploring the implications of the uncertainty implicit in those assumptions.

The business case process
Approval in concept

To evaluate a project properly can take considerable time and resources. It may include proving technical feasibility, exploring market potential, building a cost model and analysing risks. A business will not want to spend time or money on these activities without a belief that the project is likely to be worthwhile. Therefore the first stage of a project is its "approval in concept". This is where an investment committee sanctions the project idea and commissions development of a detailed business case. In effect, the committee is authorising the investment of time and money in producing the detailed documentation and evaluation.

An approval in concept is a short briefing paper consisting of the following sections:

- Project concept.
- Strategic justification (which includes nil return projects that may be required for legal compliance with new laws such as health and safety or emissions).
- Competitive advantage, which will provide differentiation in the market.
- Perceived risks.
- Project team. This can be one of the most important attributes of a successful project – people seen as a "safe pairs of hands" and who have proven track records in the business find it easier to gain approval than those who are unknown to management.

Other items can also be included, but the approval document should not seek to make the detailed business case.

The purpose of the approval in concept stage is to elicit one of two answers: "We like the idea; please investigate it further" or "We think this is not right for us."

The business case document

Typical questions the detailed business case document needs to answer are as follows:

- What determines the value in this proposal – what factors will deliver and sustain the success/competitive advantage that is offered?
- What is the evidence – in terms of surveys, past history or success of similar ventures in other places – that these factors will deliver the projected results?

- Does the management understand the business, its markets, its customers and its competition?

- What options have been considered to achieve the same aim? Why wouldn't it be better to do nothing?

- What are the likely and the possible returns and rewards if the venture should prove successful?

- What is the experience of the people involved and have they the skills to realise the potential in the project?

- What are the financial and other risks of backing the project and what is the worst possible scenario?

The business case will be a comprehensive document topped with an executive summary and tailed with a set of appendices backing up the assumptions made in the evaluation.

The most important ingredients in the success of any venture are usually the managers who are responsible for it. Therefore most investors or investment committees need to believe in and trust the managers. The rigour and quality of the business case play a crucial role, but equally if not more important are interpersonal factors such as interaction at meetings, the ability to answer questions and harmony of thinking.

The business case will open the door to a project being heard; the meeting and presentation have to bring it alive and convince management. The typical contents of a business case are listed in Table 10.1 and explained in more detail below.

TABLE 10.1 **Typical contents of a business case**

Topic	Contents
Executive summary	■ Succinct summary of critical factors to enable a quick assimilation of the business case

Topic	Contents
Proposition	■ The business case concept and scope ■ Alignment to business strategy ■ Alignment to branding and corporate image ■ Why is the business best placed to capitalise on this opportunity? ■ Market analysis of where the product or service will be positioned ■ Customer response – what is the evidence that the target segment will buy this product or service? ■ Research, feasibility, patentability and protection ■ Competitor response and time frames ■ Regulatory and legal compliance issues ■ Sustainability and life cycle of benefit ■ Impact on other projects (interdependencies, synergies and potential cannibalisation of existing revenues) ■ What is our experience of delivering this type of project? ■ Management involved and experience ■ Approval of stakeholder departments such as purchasing, technical, sales, etc.
Options	■ How else can the benefit be derived? ■ Options for outside party involvement (partner, subcontracting, renting, etc.) ■ What is the best timing for implementation? ■ Ability to scale up ■ Why isn't do nothing a better option?
Financial case	■ Cash flow projections for future capital expenditure (capex), revenue and operating expenditure (opex) ■ Validation for key assumptions, particularly growth rates ■ Are any of the benefits available without this project? ■ Verification of completeness of costs and contingencies ■ Valuation with key measures – payback, net present value (NPV) and internal rate of return (IRR)/modified internal rate of return (MIRR) ■ Impact on financial reports and measures – income statement, statement of financial position and return on investment (ROI) measures ■ What options are there to reduce costs? ■ Consultation with treasury for funding and purchase options (buy or rent, etc.) ■ Any significant tax implications ■ Intangible benefits that cannot be financially quantified

Topic	Contents
Implementation	■ Project plan and key milestones ■ Roll-out and deployment criteria ■ Safety, health and environmental (SHE) issues ■ Resources required in terms of people, skills and equipment ■ Synergy benefits available
Risks	■ External, operational and assumption ■ Scenario and sensitivity analysis ■ Mitigation plans ■ Exit options
Post investment appraisal (PIA)	■ Requirements to be able to track progress and achievement of benefits

Executive summary

At the beginning of the business case document there should be an executive summary. Typically, this should be a one-page or at the most two-page overview of the opportunity, providing a succinct summary of the salient points so that these can be easily assimilated.

Five Cs can be used to capture the crucial information:

■ Concept – an overview of the proposition.

■ Customer – the market research that validates the potential revenue.

■ Competitor – anticipated responses in the market by competitors.

■ Cash flow – the financial evaluation and key measures.

■ Challenges – an overview of the risks that have been considered.

With suitable references to the relevant pages in the full document, senior managers will find it easier to review the business case.

The proposition

The extent of the concept analysis and supporting research to prove its worth will depend on the nature of the project, and the requirements for justifying a new product launch will be hugely different from those for justifying the purchase of a new software package.

The main purpose of this section is to identify the factors that justify the investment, including why this project can create and sustain better value for the business than others. A COWS (challenges, opportunities, weaknesses and strengths) analysis may be suitable. This is also known as a SWOT analysis (the T standing for threats). The first part of a COWS analysis is to list the challenges and opportunities, which are both market-based external factors. The market potential must be strong for the project to be viable. The second part is the weaknesses and threats, which are internal reviews of the business's capability to carry out the project to its full potential.

Options

A proposal does not provide a valid choice for an investment committee unless all the potential routes to implementation have been explored in selecting the chosen option – examples are scale, sourcing of asset (buy, rent, joint venture, outsource), timing, and so on. A thorough analysis in this section will often avert much of the challenge that can arise at the approval stage.

A robust proposition, presented with the most suitable option for implementation, can provide an overwhelmingly convincing case to proceed.

Financial case

Most of the remainder of this chapter covers the principles behind building the financial projections for the project and valuing the benefits. The most effective approach is often to build a spreadsheet model that represents how the project will develop. To understand the real potential a model should be constructed allowing for the impact of alternative assumptions and scenarios to be explored. The flexing of assumptions (for example, an increase or decrease in the growth of customer numbers) and the methodical examination of alternatives (for example, making or buying in a component) will then reveal the range of potential outcomes.

The approval or rejection of the overall business case can be made with the knowledge of the expected outcome and in the light of the financial risks that lie ahead.

For large investment projects a member of the business's treasury function will also need to be consulted to identify sources of finance and deal with any foreign currency transactions that may be required.

Implementation

Although a project plan provides the structure for this section, the critical question to answer at this stage is: What are the resources required to deliver the project benefits, on time and in full?

The people, skills and other parties required for each stage of the project need careful consideration. Setting milestones by which activities need to have been done will make the full extent of what is involved clear and will help in managing the project, assuming it goes ahead.

Examples of common problems are as follows:

- Suppliers are not geared up to provide the volume of product at the right time.
- Skilled contractors or consultants are not available on specific dates.
- Inflexibility in resources should the project implementation plan become deferred.

Risk assessment

The risk assessment covers three categories of exposure:

- **External risk** – the exposure of the project to factors outside the control of the business, such as exchange rates, tax rates and energy prices. The response to these risks may well be an exit, so the options to limit losses and abandon a project should be identified. If the costs of exit are likely to be high compared with the deteriorating potential of a project, continuance may be a less unattractive option.
- **Operational risk** – unforeseen events that will reduce or delay the value of the opportunity, such as construction delays, a substitute product produced by competitors or a shortage of resources. Although a further investment of cash will usually resolve the problem, it will reduce the benefits anticipated from

the project. Insurance cover, performance bonds or supplier fixed-price guarantees can be used to limit such risks.

■ **Assumption risk** – this is to do with the judgments made for the capital expenditure (capex), revenue and operating expenditure (opex). If these are significantly flawed (revenues are lower or costs higher than anticipated), it is important to understand what degree of loss can be absorbed before the project is deemed to have failed. Scenario and sensitivity analysis can be used to explore possible outcomes. This is explained in more detail below.

Post-investment appraisal

Should the project gain approval, it is important the business can not only validate that the promised benefits are derived, but also gain any insights that would help with future projects. Therefore the measures and information required to monitor implementation should be identified at the approval stage. Appropriate data can be captured to enable reviews to be completed during implementation and after fixed periods of time, such as six months, a year or three years.

The approval process

The size of investment and nature of a project will dictate the level of management required to give it approval. Typically, authority levels are based on financial criteria, for example as in Table 10.2.

TABLE 10.2 **Illustrative criteria for approving a business case**

Project investment	Approval level
Under $25,000 for projects already planned in the budget	Budget-holder
Under $100,000 for planned and unplanned projects	Divisional director
Under $1m for all projects	Country director
Under $5m for all projects	Country board
Over $5m for all projects	Group board

Before a case is submitted for formal approval it may well have to be circulated among a number of relevant stakeholders such as human resources, information technology, technical, safety, purchasing and taxation. Obtaining a list of signatures of those who have reviewed the case is the first stage in gaining credibility. A list of well-respected and experienced senior managers will give those who have to complete the final approval confidence in the proposal. A list of less-respected and relatively inexperienced managers will prompt deeper investigation and challenge. In short, there is an influencing strategy required to ensure a smooth approval.

Ultimately, management want to know that the project is the best use of limited cash and that responsibility for the project is in safe hands.

The financial case

The aim of the financial case is to build a detailed projection of all the future cash receipts and payments that will occur as a project unfolds. These cash flows can then be valued to ascertain whether the profile is attractive enough to justify approval. The cash flows are normally split into three categories:

- Capex – short for capital expenditure, which is the purchase of assets, such as property, plant and equipment.
- Revenue – this will be the cash receipts from the sale of products or services.
- Opex – short for operating expenditure, which includes items typically found on an income statement such as payroll or utilities.

Table 10.3 gives an example of a cash flow analysis.

TABLE 10.3 **Cash flow analysis**

	0 2013	1 2014	2 2015	3 2016	4 2017	5 2018
Capex	(1,000)					
Revenue		100	300	700	1,200	1,500
Opex		(210)	(240)	(300)	(390)	(430)
Net cash flow	(1,000)	(110)	60	400	810	1,070

The example represents a small manufacturing business where a machine is purchased for $1,000 at the outset. Revenue starts being earned and grows as the product is marketed. The opex costs are a combination of fixed costs (salaries) and variable costs (raw materials). Overall, the net cash flow received or paid each year is the data required to value the opportunity.

The cash flows are just the future receipts and payments. Any costs that have already been spent, such as on research, are excluded as they have already been sunk into the project. Regardless of the approval outcome this cost cannot be recovered.

The rules for assembling this analysis are as follows.

1 Cash flow

The analysis is based exclusively on cash flows rather than profit flows. Cash flows include the receipts and payments for a project's revenues, costs, capital expenditure and taxation. The first step is to distinguish between profit flows and cash flows. Some of the principal areas of difference are summarised in Table 10.4.

TABLE 10.4 **Differences between profit flow and cash flow**

Type of data	Profit flow	Cash flow
Revenue	Recognised when the product or service is delivered	Recognised when the receivable is paid
Cost of sales	Recognised when the product or service is delivered	Recognised when cash is paid out to suppliers

Type of data	Profit flow	Cash flow
Overheads	Spread evenly over the period of benefit using the concepts of accruals and prepayments	Recognised when the cash is paid for each item (typically in arrears)
Taxation	Based on profits earned in a year	Typically paid by instalments or in the year after it has been earned
Fixed assets	Cost is spread over the period of use by way of depreciation	Recognised in total at the time of purchase (unless paid by instalments)

Relevant revenues

Only incremental revenues that will be generated as a direct result of the business decision should be included. Existing or anticipated revenue streams resulting from earlier decisions should be excluded.

Incremental revenues may be the result of events such as the launch of a new product or service or a successful advertising campaign. If the launch of a new product is likely to reduce sales of an existing product, this should be shown as lost revenue as a consequence of the project.

Relevant costs and capital expenditure

These are costs and capital expenditure that arise solely as a result of the project; any costs that are subject to pre-existing, legally binding contracts should be excluded. The costs and capital expenditure must also be cash items. Any that do not include incremental cash should be excluded, so depreciation charges, notional rents and internal cross-charges should all be excluded from the project's appraisal.

To evaluate a proposal, the project appraisal techniques should be applied only to the cash flows that result from the operation of the project. These cash flows are distinct from the cash flows required to finance the project. This separation is necessary to determine whether the project is worthwhile as a venture in its own right. If it is viable, the funding of the project will involve a separate set of decisions, and may require its own cash flow evaluation. Consequently, any finance-related cash flows such as interest payments and repayments of money borrowed to finance the project should be excluded.

Relevant taxes

Businesses pay tax on their profits and this represents a cash cost to the business. However, tax is calculated after the charging of interest, and as finance charges are not relevant costs the tax paid should normally be calculated as if the business paid no interest.

Table 10.5 lists the main types of cash flow to include and exclude.

TABLE 10.5 **Cash flows to include and exclude**

Cash flows to include	Cash flows to exclude
Cash generated from revenue	Equity or loan finance (received or repaid)
Cash paid for purchases	Dividend or interest on the finance
Cash paid for running costs	Lease payments (see below)
Cash paid and received on the purchase or sale of assets	Interest received on surplus deposits
The equivalent cash purchase cost for assets that would otherwise have been leased (see below)	
Tax payments or receipts	

Assets that are leased have a special treatment in the cash flows. There are two types of lease and each has its own treatment:

- Operating lease – usually a short-term rent and would be treated in the same way as other opex costs.

- Finance lease – typically spans the life of the asset and is similar to purchasing by instalments. The lease payments are calculated not only to pay for the cost of the asset but also interest on funding the lessor's investment in the asset. As cash flow models should exclude funding costs, any asset subject to a finance lease should be shown as an equivalent purchase cost at the point of first use. The equivalent purchase cost can be found by discounting the lease payments at the implicit rate of interest in the transaction (see discounting below).

2 The cash effect of change

It can be difficult to know where to start when building the cash flows for a project. For example, in assessing the impact on manufacturing costs of introducing new product packaging, it is possible to evaluate the current packaging cost and the new packaging cost and compare the results.

A more efficient way to assess the project is to evaluate the effect of changing from the current situation to the proposed one. Assume that production with the old packaging will continue and then identify any receipts and payments that will be different when switching to the new packaging. The benefits of this approach are that there is only one cash flow analysis, and that it focuses exclusively on those aspects of manufacturing that will be affected by the change. Anything that is unaffected by the change is ignored.

This approach can be applied to any project – an acquisition, a product launch, a closure or capital expenditure. The important point is to focus on the cash effect of the changes that will take place as a consequence of the project.

3 Dealing with allocated overheads

In compiling the project cash flows, there can often be a conflict between assessing the project on its own and assessing it as part of the business. In Table 10.5 one of the items is "cash paid for running costs". This can include central overheads that are allocated to a product or department.

For example, a factory that already makes several products launches a new one. The costs of the factory (rent, heat, light, and so on) are allocated to products on a dollar per tonne basis. On the launch of this new product the organisation is unlikely to be spending much more on the factory, yet part of the cost is now being attributed to the new product.

If the costs of the factory were ignored in the analysis of the new product, the financial evaluation would show unrealistically low manufacturing costs. The implication could be that the new product would be viable only if the other products in the factory were able to cover the factory costs. This is the principle (and danger) of marginal costing. To deal with this problem, some companies have developed a principle that they apply to all projects: treat the project as part of the company and not stand-alone, and develop the cash flows for overheads as follows:

■ If the project is to add business to the company, then assume its share of allocated overheads is a real cash flow cost. This is typically charged on a revenue or unit basis.

■ If the project is to remove business from the company, then assume there will be no cash flow saving in the allocated overheads.

This principle is perhaps prudent in the impact it can have on projects and may be seen as negating the economy of scale effect. In any proposal it is worth stating clearly the way overheads have been treated. Some businesses ask for the financial analysis of their new product proposals to be calculated twice – once including allocated overheads and once excluding them – as this provides a more rounded picture of the project.

4 Sign convention

In building the cash flow forecasts it is important to be disciplined about the sign convention. The standard convention is that a cash receipt is positive and a cash payment is negative.

FIG 10.3 **Cash flow timing**

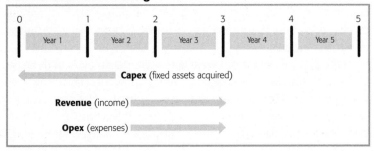

5 Cash flow timing

Most project cash flows are forecast with annual time intervals. The standard layout is shown in Figure 10.3.

Time 0 is the moment the first cash flow takes place. Time 1 is one year after the first cash flow takes place; time 2 is two years after the first cash flow takes place, and so on. Under these assumptions all cash inflows and outflows during any particular year are assumed to take place at either the beginning or the end of the year. With these annual intervals it can be difficult to identify the appropriate point at which to place a cash flow. An overriding principle is to be prudent and if necessary accelerate payments and defer receipts. Therefore the following general rules apply:

- Capex. These outflows should be placed at the start of a year. A large capital spend may be spread over the first few years of the project and thus the expenditure in any year would be put at the start of that year.

- Revenue. This is typically shown at the end of the year in which it has been received.

- Opex. Caution would suggest these costs should be shown at the beginning of the year in which they are paid out, but the principle of matching overrules. Therefore opex costs are normally shown being matched against the revenue they support. By applying this treatment the profit in any year is deferred to the end of the year in which it is earned.

The effect of these prudent timings is to make the project appear marginally less financially attractive than it actually is.

6 Time periods

There are two dimensions to time periods:

- How far into the future should cash flows be predicted?

- What unit of time should be used – years, quarters or months?

There are no general rules, but there are often specific corporate guidelines that have to be complied with. On the basis that it is easier to predict cash flows for next year than for year 10, if the cash flows arising more than a decade ahead are critical to a project's success or failure, it is a high-risk project. Even dependency on cash flows beyond five years can be risky.

For many proposals the nature of the project will determine the duration of evaluation. For example:

- Advertising campaigns or promotions – up to three months by week.
- IT projects – up to four years by quarter.
- Manufacturing – up to ten years by year.
- Buildings or construction – up to 20 years by year.

The length of time over which projections are made is based on the potential life cycle of the product (see Chapter 8). Other factors such as fade in a product's appeal and competition will cause margins to erode over time and thus future years may have the benefit of higher volumes but at potentially lower prices. For electronic products the impact of destructive technology can also play a part. Destructive technologies are innovations which destroy others; for example, digital music downloads are killing CDs. Long-term production projections for these types of products are likely to be unrealistic.

7 Residual values

For capital expenditure it is often relatively easy to identify the upfront purchase or construction costs. It is more difficult to identify the end cash flows such as disposal proceeds or costs. For example, a proposal for a nuclear power station could include designs and tenders and therefore accurately identify construction cost. At the end of its useful life in 30 years' time, how much will the site will be worth and how much should be allowed for decommissioning and decontamination?

There are a few general principles:

- Cars. In evaluating car ownership it is reasonable to assume a resale value using second-hand value guides. It might be reasonable to assume that after four years a car is worth about 25% of the purchase cost.

- Plant. In companies, most equipment and machinery is not bought with an intention of resale. This is partly because there will be a limited second-hand market and partly because technology changes will cause obsolescence (for example, computers). With such items no residual value should be assumed, apart from scrap values for material.

- Buildings. For special purpose buildings it would be prudent to assume no residual value. For office buildings that have alternative uses a residual value is appropriate depending upon location.

- Land. In evaluating the residual value of land there are four main considerations:
  - Will the activity on the land contaminate or change its value (for example, a chemical storage facility)?
  - Is the value affected by its surroundings which may be subject to change (for example, a retail site that is reliant on passing trade that will decline should a bypass be built)?
  - Can the land be used for more than one purpose (for example, it could be sold for housing)?
  - How will inflation and market conditions change its value?

In addition to the estimation of residual value, consideration should be given to any significant tax consequence that may also arise from the receipt or payment in the final year. If the residual value is the factor that swings a project into viability, the business should consider whether the trading activities are really viable.

As well as identifying residual values and costs it is helpful to identify exit costs during the life of the project. If a 25-year project does not deliver the desired benefits, it is helpful to know the cost of exit after 5, 10, 15 and 20 years.

8 The effects of working capital

Working capital consists of inventory, receivables and payables. These are the items in the statement of financial position that tie up cash but normally turn over quite quickly. Their effect on the project cash flows is normally a timing delay of a month or two. In the case of a business whose customers normally pay their invoices within a month of receipt, any sales made in December will be recorded in the income statement that month but will not turn into cash until the following January. Table 10.6 shows the effect of timing delays from receivables. Table 10.7 illustrates the way this is often shown in cash flows.

TABLE 10.6 **The effect of timing delays from receivables**

Year	Revenue	Cash calculation		Total cash received	Receivables
1	1,200	$1,200 \times {}^{11}\!/_{12} =$	1,100	1,100	100
2	2,400	$1,200 \times {}^{1}\!/_{12} =$	100	2,300	200
		$2,400 \times {}^{11}\!/_{12} =$	2,200		
3	3,600	$2,400 \times {}^{1}\!/_{12} =$	200	3,500	300
		$3,600 \times {}^{11}\!/_{12} =$	3,300		
4	0	$3,600 \times {}^{1}\!/_{12} =$	300	300	0
Total	7,200			7,200	

TABLE 10.7 **Timing delays in cash flows from receivables**

Year	Revenue	Receivables	Net Cash
1	1,200	(100)	1,100
2	2,400	(100)	2,300
3	3,600	(100)	3,500
4	0	300	300
Total	7,200	0	7,200

The effect of receivables is not a loss of money, merely a delay in its receipt. However, in cash flows it is wrong to assume that working capital is never lost as there will or may be bad debts.

Foreign trade settlement times can be longer. Also movements in exchange rates may mean that less (or more) cash is received than anticipated – though the costs of hedging the exposure can be taken into account.

Similar principles apply for payables where cash payments lag behind the receipt of inventory and consumables. For inventory there needs to be a base quantity held. This can be shown as an investment arriving at time 0 and being released at the end of the project.

Valuation of the cash flow forecast

Once the cash flow projections for a project have been identified, the next stage is to complete a quantitative appraisal of those cash flows as a basis for deciding whether the anticipated benefits are sufficient compensation for the risk involved.

The techniques for completing the quantitative appraisal of an investment are:

- payback
- net present value (NPV)
- discounted payback
- internal rate of return (IRR) and modified internal rate of return (MIRR)

These are the generic names, but many organisations have developed their own terminology to describe these – for example, yield or DCFR (discounted cash flow return) instead of IRR.

Two projects are used below to illustrate the techniques. Both involve an investment of $10,000 now, but each has a different profile of cash returns over its five-year life.

TABLE 10.8 **Cash returns**

| | Project A | | Project B | |
	Cash out	Cash in	Cash out	Cash in
Year 0	(10,000)		(10,000)	
Year 1		1,000		5,000
Year 2		2,000		4,000
Year 3		3,000		3,000
Year 4		4,000		2,000
Year 5		5,000		
Total	(10,000)	15,000	(10,000)	14,000

At first glance project A appears to be the better option. Over the five years it achieves a return of $5,000 more than the money invested whereas project B achieves only $4,000 more. However, project B returns the money faster and deriving the return earlier will reduce the risk in the investment. The quantitative techniques help evaluate the risk and reward in the project to determine which would be preferable.

Payback

This is the simplest method of investment appraisal and provides a quantification of risk in terms of measuring how quickly the original investment is returned. The general principle is that projects which recoup their initial cash investment faster are more attractive. Risk here is defined as uncertainty, because predicting cash flows next year is likely to be more accurate than predicting those in five years' time. The measure is the time taken to reach the cash break-even point, when the total cash out equals the total cash in.

On the cumulative cash flow curve shown in Figure 10.4, the payback is the time it takes for the line to return back to zero. The effect on the two projects is shown in Table 10.9.

The payback for project A is four years and for project B it is two years and four months (if cash is earned evenly through each year).

Many companies use this measure to dismiss projects that do not

FIG 10.4 **Payback**

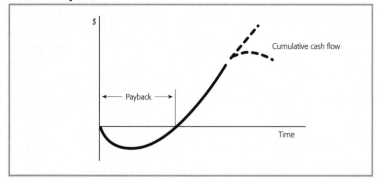

TABLE 10.9 **Payback**

	Project A		Project B	
	Cash movements	Net investment	Cash movements	Net investment
Year 0	(10,000)	(10,000)	(10,000)	(10,000)
Year 1	1,000	(9,000)	5,000	(5,000)
Year 2	2,000	(7,000)	4,000	(1,000)
Year 3	3,000	(4,000)	3,000	2,000
Year 4	4,000	0	2,000	4,000
Year 5	5,000	5,000		
Total	5,000		4,000	

pay back within a set period. If a project has a payback of over ten years, only governments and large corporations are likely to accept the risk and back it.

The problem with the payback principle is that it is short term. It fails to consider cash flows beyond the payback period (for example, project A could make $2m in year 6 and its payback would still be four years).

It should also be noted that payback makes no allowance for interest (for which a discounted payback is used, see below) and therefore does not measure the return made by a project.

Net present value

This measure shows the surplus cash made by an investment after funding costs have been deducted. It uses the principle of discounting cash flows. For example, if someone is offered $100 now or $100 in one year's time, they will choose to receive $100 today, because if interest rates are 10% and the $100 is invested, in one year it will have grown to $110. This is the concept of the time value of money. The future value of $100 at a 10% interest rate is shown in Table 10.10.

TABLE 10.10 **Future value of $100 at 10% interest rate**

Now	1 year	2 years	3 years	4 years	5 years
$100	$110	$121	$133.10	$146.41	$161.051

This uses the principle of compound interest. However, if someone is offered $110 in one year's time or $121 in two years' time, the choice becomes more difficult. From Table 10.10 it is clear that they are both worth $121 at the end of two years. The ability to compare depends on choosing the same point in time whether it is now, in two years' time or in ten years' time. Each cash flow needs to be either compounded to find a future value or discounted to find a present value.

The two options would both be the equivalent of receiving $100 today. The principle of working out what a future cash flow is worth now is the basis for all project appraisal and company valuations. The year 0 value of a future cash flow is known as its present value (PV). Adding together the PV of each cash flow in a project provides the net present value (NPV).

To find the NPV of the cash flows in project A the procedure is as follows: using a discount rate of 10%, each future cash flow can be multiplied by 100 and divided by the compound interest value from Table 10.10 (see Figure 10.5).

The NPV of project A is therefore $651, which is substantially less than the apparent surplus of $5,000 found by simply adding the series of cash flows. The reduction is caused by having to fund the investment in the early years of the project.

FIG 10.5 **NPV calculation**

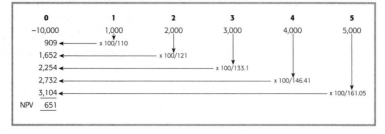

A better way to find the PV of a cash flow is to use the formula:

$$\text{Future value} \times \frac{1}{(1 + \text{interest rate}) \char`^ \text{number of years}} = \text{present value}$$

To apply the formula the interest rate is expressed as a fraction so 10% would be shown as 0.1. The ^ symbol means "to the power", for example if the number of years was two, the denominator would be squared.

TABLE 10.11 **Net present value**

Project A	Cash movements	10% discount factor	Present value
Year 0	(10,000)	1.0000	(10,000)
Year 1	1,000	0.9091	909
Year 2	2,000	0.8264	1,652
Year 3	3,000	0.7513	2,254
Year 4	4,000	0.6830	2,732
Year 5	5,000	0.6209	3,104
Net present value			651
Project B			
Year 0	(10,000)	1.0000	(10,000)
Year 1	5,000	0.9091	4,546
Year 2	4,000	0.8264	3,306
Year 3	3,000	0.7513	2,254
Year 4	2,000	0.6830	1,366
Net present value			1,472

The present value of \$2,000 received in two years' time when interest rates are 10% is:

$$2{,}000 \times \frac{1}{(1 + 0.1) \char`^ 2} = 1{,}652$$

Expressed another way, if $1,652 was put on deposit today at 10%, it would be worth $2,000 after two years.

Applying this formula to the two projects will have the effect shown in Table 10.11, assuming the cost of money is 10%.

Project B generates a much higher profit than project A. This could be expected because as shown in Table 10.9 project B requires no net investment after its payback in year 3.

When interpreting the NPV the simple rules are that positive is good – there is a surplus over and above the cost of funding; and that negative is bad – there is insufficient cash from the proposed project to pay for funding.

What discount rate should be applied?

The discount rate is not the current bank rate as this is volatile and could change significantly over the life of a project. Also it does not reflect the fact that a substantial proportion of investment funds is likely to be derived from shareholders. The more appropriate rate is the weighted average cost of capital (WACC) to a business as explained in Chapter 6. This is a longer-term rate that takes into account the mix of funding sources including equity, loans and overdrafts.

The WACC is the rate required to meet investors' expectations. Therefore if a project delivers a positive NPV at the WACC rate it will have achieved a surplus above the minimum required by the investors. However, the WACC does not allow room for risks that might create shortfalls in projects; so many businesses add a risk factor and use a risk-weighted WACC to evaluate projects. For example, a WACC rate could be around 10% but may be adjusted to 12–15% to allow for risk.

A multinational business might use a risk adjustment table as shown in Figure 10.6.

The left-hand side is the project risk. Low risk would be those projects that the business is experienced in running; for example, opening a new store for a supermarket. The risk rises for projects in which the business has less experience, such as a supermarket moving into selling mobile phones.

Along the top is the country risk. Low risk would be those countries that have political and economic stability, such as the

FIG 10.6 **WACC hurdle rates**

	Country risk			
	Low			High
Low	10%	15%	20%	25%
	15%	20%	25%	30%
	20%	25%	30%	35%
High	25%	30%	35%	40%

(Project risk — vertical axis label)

G8 countries. The highest-risk countries are those with conflict or unstable governments.

The hurdle rate table (which shows the minimum IRR – see below – a project must achieve for approval) implies that an unfamiliar project in a high-risk country needs to earn a substantial return to justify the risk.

Non-annual time intervals

If a project is prepared with time intervals that are not annual (such as quarterly or monthly), the discount rate needs to be converted mathematically; for example, a monthly interest rate is not one-twelfth of the annual rate. If the annual rate is 12%, the calculation of the monthly rate is as follows:

$$12\sqrt{(1 + 12\%)} - 1 = 0.9488\%$$

Discounted payback

Normally payback is calculated ignoring the time value of money. This can be misleading, so it is more realistic to use the discounted values calculated when producing the NPV because they reflect the funding cost that will have to be paid out as the project unfolds.

Table 10.12 shows that project A has a discounted payback approaching five years compared with project B, which has a discounted payback of just under three years.

TABLE 10.12 **Discounted payback**

	Project A		Project B	
	Discounted cash movements	Discounted net investment	Discounted cash movements	Discounted net investment
Year 0	(10,000)	(10,000)	(10,000)	(10,000)
Year 1	909	(9,091)	4,546	(5,454)
Year 2	1,652	(7,439)	3,306	(2,148)
Year 3	2,254	(5,185)	2,254	106
Year 4	2,732	(2,453)	1,366	1,472
Year 5	3,104	651		
Total	651		1,472	

Internal rate of return

Although the interpretation of NPV may be simple, with positive being good and negative bad, this does not provide an appreciation of the variations the project can absorb and still be viable. A good indicator is to know how high an interest rate can be tolerated before a project is rejected. With a WACC of 10%, if the highest rate at which the project can still be profitable is only 11%, there is little room for error before the project becomes value destroying. Compare this with a project that is value creating up to, say, 32% – there is plenty of room for error and delays, and a profit is still likely.

The interest rate at which a project makes neither a profit nor a loss is known as the internal rate of return (IRR). With a project of more than two years there is no formula to calculate this rate and iteration is the only technique that can be used. Spreadsheet software programs such as Excel also use iteration to find this value.

Calculating the NPV of a project at different discount rates will identify the rate at which it is zero. In Figure 10.7 the NPV of project A has been plotted for a range of discount rates. The graph is a curve and therefore any linear interpolation will only be an approximation of the actual rate.

The rate for project A is 12%, meaning that it has little tolerance for errors before it would make a loss. For project B the rate is much higher at 17.8% as illustrated by the calculations in Table 10.13.

FIG 10.7 **NPV for a range of discount rates**

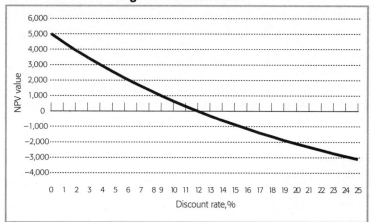

TABLE 10.13 **NPV of project B at 17% and 18% discount rate**

	Cash movements	Discount factor 17%	Present value	Discount factor 18%	Present value
Year 0	(10,000)	1.0000	(10,000)	1.0000	(10,000)
Year 1	5,000	0.8547	4,274	0.8475	4,237
Year 2	4,000	0.7305	2,922	0.7182	2,873
Year 3	3,000	0.6244	1,873	0.6086	1,826
Year 4	2,000	0.5337	1,067	0.5158	1,032
Net present value			136		(32)

Because cash flow data is a series of assumptions, there is little or no point in calculating the IRR more precisely than whole numbers.

The IRR is the primary method of investment appraisal, although most organisations use it in conjunction with the net present value to make sure that a large profitable project is not rejected in favour of a smaller project with a higher rate of return.

Modified internal rate of return

An IRR correctly identifies the annual return on investment for a project providing there are no interim cash flows being generated (an interim cash flow is one that arises other than in the first or last year of the project). Where interim cash flows exist the normal IRR calculation assumes they can be reinvested at the IRR rate, which may be unlikely. More realistically, especially in smaller businesses, interim cash flows are used to reduce investment capital and are therefore applied to avoid paying funding costs at the WACC rate. This actual reinvestment rate of interim cash flows is likely to be much lower than the IRR rate, making an IRR rate that is calculated on a project with interim cash flows overvalued.

The modified internal rate of return (MIRR) calculations start by taking the negative cash flows (payments) and discounting them all to time zero. The positive cash flows (receipts) are all compounded to the final period of the project using a reinvestment or WACC rate. The MIRR is the rate that discounts the total future value of all the positive flows to match the total present value of all the negative flows. Many believe this to be a more realistic expectation of value from a project or at least a quantification of the minimum return that can be expected.

With a WACC/reinvestment rate of 10%, the difference in the two projects would be as shown in Table 10.14.

TABLE 10.14 **IRR and MIRR compared**

	Project A	Project B
IRR	12.01%	17.80%
MIRR	11.40%	13.84%

The fall in rate when using MIRR, especially for project B, shows that the application of the high positive cash flows that arise in years 1 and 2 is critical to the overall return. If the cash flows are directed towards other projects that yield 17.8%, the IRR is valid. If the cash flows are used to repay investment capital, the project return is much lower.

Inflation

In preparing the cash flows for a project a decision must be made on whether to take inflation into account. A standard process used by many companies is to set an index, such as 2%, which will be applied to the cash flows each year.

The terminology used in preparing the cash flows is as follows:

- Nominal – cash flows include inflation.
- Real – cash flows exclude inflation.

Most businesses operating in economies with low levels of inflation prepare their cash flow forecasts in a nominal format (including inflation). This is because historic revenues and costs are often used as a basis for projecting trends into the future. These historic results are recorded in nominal terms and so forecasting on the same basis is usually easier.

In countries with high levels of inflation it is usually preferable to forecast in real terms as the nominal forecast soon becomes meaningless. The task of predicting consumer expenditure on a product ten years from now after taking into account the effects of high annual inflation is considerably harder than thinking about it in constant prices, or in real terms.

Impact on WACC

To value cash flow projections the discount or WACC rate must be on a consistent basis. A series of nominal cash flows must be discounted with a nominal WACC and a series of real cash flows must be discounted with a real WACC. The difference is illustrated in Figure 10.8.

As shown in Figure 10.8, if the quoted rate of interest for a deposit is 5%, this will be made up of two elements: a compensation for inflation, perhaps 2% (without this the spending power of the investment would reduce for the period of the deposit); and real interest, perhaps 3% (the actual gain in value of the deposit).

Therefore a nominal WACC would be calculated on quoted rates of interest for each investor and a real WACC would be calculated by deducting inflation from the quoted rates.

FIG 10.8 **Real and nominal**

Inflation	2%	
Real interest rate	3%	◀ Real
Quoted interest rate	5%	◀ Nominal

Taxation

To make sure that a project is appraised realistically the calculations should include the effect of taxation, which can take several forms as illustrated below. In unfamiliar jurisdictions expert advice should be sought when considering the tax effects of an investment project.

Income tax

This is likely to be the most significant of the taxes as it is charged on the profits made by the company, but it should be noted that taxable profits are not the same as the accounting profits in the statutory accounts.

Accounting profits are calculated in accordance with the law and agreed standards, and involve many judgments. The intention is that companies should present a true and fair view of their results. Judgments include the rate of asset depreciation and the amount of bad debt provisions (see Chapter 5).

Taxable profits are calculated in accordance with tax legislation which is prescriptive and has little room for judgment. The reason for detailed rules is to prevent businesses from being "too prudent" and using cautious judgments to reduce or even eliminate profits and pay little or no tax.

Depending on the country where the profits are earned, there are typically four main differences between profits for statutory accounts and taxable profits:

■ Depreciation calculated on a business's determination of asset life is not normally allowed as a cost to the business. Instead allowances are given which are a substitute, but at prescribed rates. For example, in the UK capital allowances are used on a 25% reducing-balance basis (see Chapter 5); in the United States depreciation allowances are given based on the Internal Revenue Service's depreciation schedule for any given class of asset.

■ General provisions are not normally allowed as a cost to the business. Only specific provisions are acceptable. For example, a firm cannot claim 10% of receivables as likely bad debts; it must specify which receivables are likely not to pay and by how much.

■ Only expenditure that is wholly and exclusively necessary to the business is allowed as a cost. In the UK the days of entertaining third parties and claiming the cost against tax are gone.

■ Capital associated expenses such as the legal fees to buy assets are sometimes not deductible expenses but may be able to be pooled with the assets for capital allowances.

As the project appraisal is constructed from cash flow projections the calculations for the tax payments can become lengthy. First the project cash flows have to be converted into profit flows, then the taxation calculated and finally the physical tax payments put back into the cash flow.

Capital gains tax

Tax charged on capital gains (the profit can be subject to reliefs) when assets are sold for more than they cost. For businesses this may be rare for items of equipment, but it is likely on land and buildings.

Payroll tax

Employment taxes levied on employers should be included in employee costs, not just the gross salary.

Sales tax and value-added tax

Taxes charged on sales are usually collected by businesses and paid to the government periodically. Sales tax or VAT paid on purchases is either tax deductible or recoverable.

The normal treatment is for the sales tax element to be excluded from the cash flow projections, as this cash will pass through the bank account but not be retained by the business. Only irrecoverable sales tax on supplies should be left in the cash flow so that the true cost of any purchases is fairly reflected.

Specialist areas

Industries are often subjected to their own taxation regimes; for example, oil and minerals companies pay extraction taxes and waste management companies pay landfill tax. Care is required to ensure any such taxation is included in the cash flow projections.

Impact on WACC

The section on inflation above showed that the discount or WACC rate had to match the cash flows in being either nominal or real. The same principle applies here. If the cash flows exclude taxation, the WACC rate should exclude taxation (see Chapter 6); and if the cash flows include taxation, the WACC should include taxation.

Consistency enables the cash flows to be valued with the correct discount rate. With inflation of several percent and income tax rates being typically between 20% and 50%, the valuations can be misleading if an incorrect WACC rate is used.

Using spreadsheets for project evaluation

The discounting process lends itself to being completed on a spreadsheet, for which there are commands available to speed up the calculation of the factors. This is a brief summary of their use in Excel as there is an important aspect to their application.

NPV

Returns the net present value of an investment based on a series of cash flows and a discount rate. The net present value of an investment is today's value of a series of future payments (negative values) and income (positive values).

Syntax

$$= NPV(rate, values)$$

- Rate. The rate of discount over the length of one period.
- Values. The range of cash flows from year 1 to year n, excluding year 0. They must be equally spaced in time, in the correct order and occur at the end of each period.

If the series of cash flows include a value at time 0, this should not be discounted and, importantly, it should be excluded from the NPV calculation and added to the answer as follows:

$$= \text{NPV(rate, values 1:n)} + \text{value0}$$

IRR

Returns the internal rate of return (IRR) for a series of cash flows represented by the numbers in values. The internal rate of return is the interest rate received for an investment consisting of payments (negative values) and income (positive values) that occur at regular periods.

Syntax

$$= \text{IRR(values 0:n, guess)}$$

- Values. The range of cash flows from year 0 to year n. It must contain at least one positive and one negative value. IRR uses the order of values to interpret the order of cash flows. Note that with this formula the value at time 0 is included within the array.
- Guess. A number that you guess is close to the result of IRR.

Excel uses an iterative technique for calculating IRR. Starting with the guessed number, IRR cycles through the calculation until the result is accurate within 0.00001%. If IRR can't find a result that works after 100 tries, the #NUM! error value is returned.

In most cases you do not need to provide guess for the IRR calculation. If guess is omitted, it is assumed to be 0.1 (10%).

MIRR

Returns the modified internal rate of return (MIRR) for a series of cash flows represented by the numbers in values. It is calculated considering both the cost of investment and interest on reinvestment of cash.

Syntax

MIRR(values 0:n, finance rate, reinvest rate)

- Values. The range of cash flows from year 0 to year n. It must contain at least one positive value and one negative value.
- Finance rate. The interest rate to fund the negative cash flows.
- Reinvest rate. The interest rate received on the positive cash flows.

Payback

There is no function in Excel for payback, though it can be automated using the IF statement to test when the cumulative cash flow changes from negative to positive.

Business modelling

The mathematics involved in the discounting calculations are more easily completed on a spreadsheet, which can also be used to build an entire cash flow model. Once built, the model can be used to test scenarios and sensitivities to determine a project's viability. To achieve this structure the model needs to have:

- flexible inputs;
- sequential logic (to enable others to see consequences of changed inputs);
- clear outputs that calculate the value of the investment, performance ratios and benchmark factors.

Details of how to build robust business models are given in *The Economist Guide to Business Modelling* by John Tennent and Graham Friend.

Sensitivity analysis

However carefully the cash flow assumptions are projected, it is unlikely that reality will yield the same result. Indeed, the further into the future the cash flow is projected the less accurate the result is likely to be. Therefore it is perhaps more relevant to identify the "arena of likely outcomes" than to rely on a specific numerical result for a project.

Each combination of realistic alternative assumptions will yield a different result. Being comfortable with the perimeter of this arena will give confidence that it is acceptable to implement this project. If the arena of likely outcomes is large and has negative potential, the approver of a project needs to focus on the risks and likelihood of failure.

The simplest and most common way to explore a project's potential is to have three sets of data:

■ An expected outcome comprising the most realistic set of assumptions.

■ A best case that illustrates the potential should the project exceed expectations.

■ A worst case should conditions be adverse and the project matures less fast.

This method is sometimes seen as simplistic and a more comprehensive process is required. Some companies like to see the separate impact of effects such as 10% increase on capital, 10% increase on operating costs, 10% decrease in revenue and one-year deferral of revenue commencement. This is perhaps more formal, but better still is to develop a dependency ranking to identify the most important assumptions.

Dependency ranking

This is the process of ranking all the assumptions in order of their importance to the final outcome or NPV. It can help focus attention on the assumptions that must be validated to ensure that a project should proceed.

To identify this ranking the project cash flows need to be modelled on a spreadsheet. Basing the model on the expected outcome that is anticipated from the project, each assumption can be tested one by one. A function in Excel called "Goal Seek" can be used to calculate the percentage amount that each assumption would need to change for the NPV to become zero.

Ranking the assumptions in order of the percentage change that can be tolerated (the smallest being the most critical to the project) will identify the assumptions that require validation.

Monte Carlo analysis

Monte Carlo analysis provides a way of exploring a huge number of scenarios through a model and being able to evaluate statistically the "arena of likely outcomes". Instead of setting one value for each assumption, the principle is based on setting a range within which the assumption value should lie. For example, the revenue growth rate may not be 4%, but it probably lies between 3% and 5%. Using a spreadsheet's random number generator, a model can be set up to randomly select an input value from each assumption range and then use this to derive a project result. By operating several hundred or more iterations, an expected value and standard deviation can be calculated.

The standard deviation enables the model result to be quoted with a confidence level. One standard deviation away from the expected value is 68% confidence, two standard deviations away is 95% confidence and three standard deviations away is 99% confidence. This enhanced statistical presentation of a project's results may seem helpful to the sanctioning and approval process, but the wider the range of input values, the larger is the standard deviation number and the bigger the arena of likely outcomes. Hence a narrow range of well-researched assumptions is still the way to derive a realistic result from the model.

The profile of a Monte Carlo analysis is a normal distribution curve which shows the expected value and confidence intervals (see Figure 10.9).

Setting up a Monte Carlo analysis requires a spreadsheet macro that is explained in *The Economist Guide to Business Modelling* in Chapter 20.

FIG 10.9 **Monte Carlo analysis**

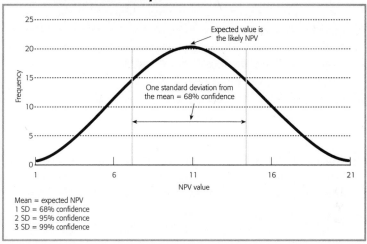

Mean = expected NPV
1 SD = 68% confidence
2 SD = 95% confidence
3 SD = 99% confidence

Summary of the financial section of the business case

A typical financial case for a project would contain the following schedules either in the main body of the proposal or as an appendix:

■ **Assumption table.** A data sheet of all the assumptions used in the project.

■ **Activity, volumes and resources.** A development of the assumptions over the life of the project to produce operational data including product or service volumes, headcount, prices, inflation indexes, and so on.

■ **Cash flow projections.** A cash flow analysis including capex, revenue, opex, working capital, residual values and taxation.

■ **Income statement and statement of financial position implications.** Statements showing the incremental effects over the life of the project. Typically, these show low asset values towards the end of the project as the asset values depreciate away.

■ **Tax computation.** Calculations based on profits and converted into a cash flow to be included in the cash flow projections.

- **Key measures.** A cash curve estimation to show the J curve effect. Also some operational measures based on the income statement and statement of financial position including ROI (this can be disproportionately high towards the end of the project because of the low asset values), percentage of revenue measures and asset turnover measures.

- **Valuations.** Payback, NPV, IRR and MIRR clearly stating whether they are nominal or real and pre-tax or post-tax.

- **Scenarios and sensitivities.** A range of alternative scenarios and assumptions together with their implications for valuation. Where appropriate a Monte Carlo analysis with confidence intervals to show the arena of possible outcomes.

- **Assumption dependencies and validations.** A dependency ranking table to identify critical assumptions. Appropriate evidence for the validity of those assumptions.

- **Impact on reported results.** For large projects the effect on the income statement, statement of financial position and key measures should be shown.

11 Business planning, budgeting and reporting

CHAPTER 1 DEFINED SUCCESS for the investors in a business. Budgeting and business planning is the process used by management to create the blueprint for achieving that success. It is a structured way of setting long-, medium- and short-term goals to which resources and staff can be oriented and aligned.

This is typically a three-stage process (see Figure 11.1).

The vertical axis is the degree of achievement of the long-term goals and the horizontal axis is time. Over time a business should become closer to realising its long-term plans and indeed may need to redefine those plans to respond to changes in the market and business.

The starting point for any budgeting process is the definition of the organisational mission and objectives. As described in Chapter 1, it

FIG 11.1 **Budgeting and business planning**

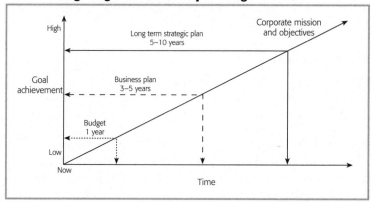

is the responsibility of senior management to create and achieve this in agreement with the investors. In the absence of a long-term goal it is difficult to have a frame of reference to provide the direction for originating the business plans and budgets.

For example, Procter & Gamble, a consumer goods company, has the following strategy (stated on its website in 2013):

> We are focused on strategies that we believe are right for the long-term health of the Company and will deliver total shareholder return in the top one-third of our peer group.
>
> The Company's long-term financial targets are:
>
> - Grow organic sales 1% to 2% faster than market growth in the categories and geographies in which we compete,
> - Deliver earnings per share (EPS) growth of high single digits to low double digits, and
> - Generate free cash flow productivity of 90% or greater.

The next stage for a business is a ten-year strategic plan that will aim to deliver the ambitions. A strategic plan defines the strategic objectives and the agenda for their fulfilment; it will be light on detail and only provide indicative timings. In contrast, a budget will be a financial plan for the year ahead and will define in detail the objectives that will be achieved as the first stage of the ten-year plan.

A business plan, with typically a three- or five-year horizon, falls between these two others in terms of financial detail and strategic imperatives. Though in sequence, it would be produced after the strategic plan and before the budget.

Strategic plan

The contents of a strategic plan would be derived from a detailed strategic analysis of the market, customers, competitors and resources.

The types of tools used for this process include the following:

- PESTEL (political, economic, sociological, technological, environmental and legal). The purpose is to identify changes taking place in the market under each of these headings and deduce what implications and opportunities arise. For example, completing this analysis in the 1990s would have awoken car companies to the trend in sports utility vehicles and encouraged BMW to enter a market segment it had not operated in before. Completing it in the 2000s would focus on the economic issues of high oil prices and encourage the design of more efficient models. Today it is about alternative fuels and low CO_2 emissions.

■ Structural forces. Michael Porter in *Competitive Strategy* identified various forces on the business that will inhibit the realisation of long-term profitability. They are the direct forces of competition and customers, and the indirect forces of suppliers, regulators, substitutes and new entrants. The changing strengths or weaknesses in these forces are the areas that need to be analysed to identify whether the market is becoming more or less attractive. For example, the globalisation of retailers makes it more difficult for food manufacturers to increase margins as their customers are relatively few in number and very powerful in negotiations.

There are many more tools which would fill a whole book in their own right. Individually none of them provide answers, just the stimulus to identify opportunities in a structured manner.

The output from this analysis would be summarised in a COWS (or SWOT) framework (as explained in Chapter 10). This forms the basis of the strategic agenda to address the findings in terms of:

■ what the business will provide by way of products or services;
■ the business model to provide the products or services;
■ the channels to market;
■ the resources required – covering people and investment.

Headline numbers for revenue, production, headcount and investment may also accompany this to provide a basis of prioritising the agenda and setting the base lines for the business plan and budgets that will follow.

Business plan

The origination of the business plan is the process for articulating the operational and financial imperatives that need to be achieved within 3–5 years. These business attributes will be used as the basis for managing investor expectations when the financial results are communicated. On a practical level the plan enables the business's resources to be appropriately allocated and aligned. Organisational design of departments and job roles can be a by-product of the process as the focus and co-ordination of functions are oriented towards achieving the deliverables.

As with a strategic plan, a business plan may be light on detail with only headline financial numbers identified for each of the years covered by the plan. The use of business modelling techniques can be a valuable support tool to explore scenarios and options as the plans evolve.

The output would be in the form of a confidential booklet setting out the primary objectives for functions and the people responsible for the achievement.

Typical contents are:

- Executive summary
- Current business situation
- Strategic analysis
- Strategic plan
- Marketing plan
- Operations/production
- Management and organisation
- Forecasts and financial data
- Financing
- Risk and analysis
- Business controls
- Appendices

For more information on this process see *The Economist Guide to Business Planning* by Graham Friend and Stefan Zehle and *The*

Economist Guide to Business Modelling by John Tennent and Graham Friend.

Budgeting

The third stage of the process is the creation of the annual budget which should cover the first year of the business plan and the strategic plan. This will be a highly detailed document allocating resources to individual departments, projects, managers and cost codes.

The budget will serve three purposes over the year of its operation: planning, control and motivation.

Planning

Before the year starts the budget will be the means of planning the way the business will achieve its aims according to its performance measures. Detailed revenue estimates by product, cost expectation by cost code and anticipated timing of investment will all be included.

It is common to find that what managers say they need in terms of resources exceeds what a business can afford. Thus a process needs to take place whereby requests for resources are pared back while retaining confidence that the plan can be achieved.

Contingency may be included to allow for uncertainty and to give executives confidence that they will not be put in the position of having to give investors a "profits warning" or tell them about a failure to meet expectations.

Control

As the actual results start to be reported month by month, the budget enables performance to be monitored and executives to know if they are on track for the expectations they have created. In effect, it provides the basis of an early warning signal of any need to initiate corrective action.

Over a whole company, those departments or divisions that are overachieving can help prop up the underachievers and keep the overall result on target.

Towards the end of the financial year soft areas of cost can be cut to fine tune the final result. Typically, these will be expenditures that can be delayed or costs where the benefit will not be seen in the same financial year. This might include areas such as marketing, training or travel.

Motivation

The budget combined with individual objectives or targets provides the basis on which employees are motivated and stretched. In the absence of such a structure, spending may become higher than necessary and the extra effort required to help bring in the required revenue may not be made.

Sometimes the budget can be seen as a constraint on a department's or an individual's activities, so it may not always be warmly embraced. Therefore the motivational aspect needs to be carefully managed. If people do not believe they have the resources to achieve the results desired, or if they believe that the targets set are far too ambitious to be achievable, both morale and management performance will be lower.

In theory, this all sounds workable. In practice, because the achievement of budgets is used as a measure of personal performance, managers will start to play political games to make sure that they have a budget that will enable them to shine. As the political games are played out, the objective of the budget process as well as its benefits can become lost.

Budget process

To be effective budgets need to be "owned" by the managers that have responsibility for their achievement. Ownership is not just authority to spend, but a feeling of individual commitment to the objectives and a willingness to deliver what is required with the resources allocated. To create the feeling of ownership, individual managers should be part of the budget-setting process so they can identify and justify the resources they need.

Budgets are usually constructed in one of two ways:

- **Top-down approach.** Senior managers state what they expect from their operational managers with respect to performance on revenue, profitability, cost savings and other dimensions.

The operational managers may then try to negotiate with senior managers on the budget targets they consider to be unreasonable or unrealistic. The benefit of this approach is that the budget will be based on the achievement of the organisational measures, though it can lack insight as to whether the resources allocated will be sufficient to deliver the numbers that are set. This approach is typical of highly focused organisations, such as those bought by private equity, which are on a mission and likely to run their budgets with specific expectation.

■ **Bottom-up approach.** Operational managers develop the budgets and submit them to their senior managers based on their perception of achievable goals and the resources needed to achieve those goals. Senior managers may (and usually do) review and revise these budgets through a process of negotiation with operational managers. The benefit of this approach is that it is likely to be in tune with the reality of day-to-day activities, though the initial budget will typically lack sufficient stretch or not add up to the required corporate measures, and so a process of boosting budgeted revenue and looking for cost savings takes place.

The process in many businesses is one of iteration whereby a bottom-up approach is used at the outset. Submissions are added and reviewed with top-down pressures seeking revisions to the numbers. A second draft is submitted and the process repeated until three or even four versions have been completed before being finally agreed.

The budget cycle

Some of the usual stages in a budget timetable are listed below. They are for a business that has a financial year that ends in December. In Figure 11.2 a clock face is used to represent the months in the year with December 31st at 12 o'clock, March 31st at 3 o'clock, June 30th at 6 o'clock and September 30th at 9 o'clock.

■ **Assemble.** The process starts in June of the year before with a first cut of the budget. This will typically be prepared using a bottom-up approach within a range of corporate guidelines

FIG 11.2 **The budget cycle**

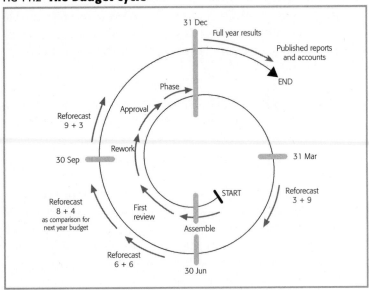

(such as standard values for anticipated payroll costs, pension contributions, inflation, and so on).

- **First review.** All the individual budgets are added up for the senior management or board to review and comment on.

- **Rework.** The iterative process (described above) takes place to refine initial budget submissions and align them with the corporate measures required by the investors.

- **Approval.** Overall approval of the budget by the board makes it the basis for managing financial performance for the year ahead. In theory this should be completed before the start of the year, though in some businesses the rework phase can take many months and continue into the budget year.

- **Phase.** This is the process of allocating an annual budget across the 12 months of the year so that as the actual results come through there is a valid comparison available to monitor progress (see below).

At this stage the process has reached the start of the financial year and each budget-holder should have been given their annual phased budget setting out their financial responsibilities.

■ **Reforecast.** Once the year is under way many businesses will reforecast the expected outturn for the whole year based on the experience of the year's activities to date and what is known or anticipated for the rest of the year. Some businesses will complete this quarterly, others half-yearly. The process involves taking the actual results to date and estimating the remaining months to predict the expected total for the year (see the details below).

This process does not change the original budget, which remains constant throughout the 12 months, but is crucial in determining the actions required to make sure the budget is achieved.

The numbers are as follows:

3 + 9: three months actual and nine months estimate
6 + 6: six months actual and six months estimate
9 + 3: nine months actual and three months estimate
8 + 4: eight months actual and four months estimate

The last set of reforecast data is sometimes completed by businesses to form a comparison for use when the following year's budget is assembled. It may also be prepared in the format of the following year's organisational structure to reflect any changes in budget areas and responsibilities.

■ **Full-year results.** This is the internal reporting of the final results after the end of the financial year as a basis for audit and the final published accounts.

■ **Published accounts.** The publication of the full audited accounts for investors and anyone else interested in the company's performance.

Businesses use many variations of this process, but the activities are broadly similar (with the exception of a rolling budget process – see below).

In any system there is often criticism of the amount of time and resources committed to setting and reviewing the budget and to later reforecasts. In total hours invested it is often the single most consuming activity within any business, and therefore efficiency, automation and simplicity in the budgeting process are critical if managers are to have time to deliver real results rather than constantly budget for them.

Rolling budgets

In the traditional budget process outlined above each financial year is treated separately, which contradicts the continuity of business across these artificial points in the growth of an organisation. Consequently, actions to enhance one year may well be to the detriment of a later year or even the speed at which the long-term goals are able to be achieved. For example, delaying a marketing initiative to save costs in the current year may enhance profits now, but it could reduce revenue (and profit) in the subsequent year.

To counteract this approach of looking at each year in isolation, some businesses (typically larger organisations) have moved to rolling budgets. Each quarter managers are asked to forecast the next 18 months. This not only keeps the horizon moving through financial year ends, but also takes into account shifts in expectations arising from any changes in the market. These quarterly reviews also break the business out of an annual crescendo of budget activity and make the focus on managing future results more routine.

This may be a more logical way of managing budgets, but it does not give any relief from the pressure of investors, who still want to see annual results improving year on year.

Setting a budget

Setting a budget is never easy as it involves predicting the future and therefore uncertainty. The process is not about getting the budget absolutely right; it is about not getting it too wrong.

In many organisations the budget process commences with the timetable, templates and guidance notes being issued by the finance department. Those in the finance department may be the stewards of the process, but they will often be too detached from the operations to be able to construct a valid budget themselves. Hence operational managers have to complete most of the templates. Headline budget values may be agreed for the whole business, and then parts of this will be allocated to divisions, departments and individual budget-holders.

There is logic in the way in which budgets are created within an organisation. For example, revenue attributes will often be at the start of the process by setting sales volumes and prices. Once volumes are known, production and purchasing can construct their budgets. The budgets of central departments such as finance, information technology and human resources can be drawn up in parallel to the operational budgets so that all departmental budgets can be completed within a short time frame.

For a budget-holder the stages in constructing a budget are as follows:

- **Objectives.** Having a clear understanding of what has to be achieved by the end of the financial year. This will be product, service or project related.

- **Volume driver.** What is the scale of activity required? For products this will be units; for services it may be activities or hours.

- **Resources.** What resources – people, components, costs, and so on – will be required to fulfil the objectives? Reference to previous years or similar projects can provide the details of the scope of these resources and a check for completeness.

- **Dependencies.** What will the resources be dependent upon? For example, a manufacturing budget will be dependent on forecast sales volume, which in turn will be dependent on forecast marketing activity and so on.

- **Assumptions.** The most difficult part of constructing a budget is arriving at sound assumptions for each of the resources required. Inevitably, as the budget year proceeds the actual results will be different, so it is important to keep a record of the budget assumptions in order to make it possible to compare, analyse and interpret the actual results with the budget.

The process of justifying each resource according to the benefit that will be derived is known as zero-based budgeting. Taking last year's value and adding an inflation assumption neither challenges the value of activities nor encourages alternative solutions to be explored.

In building the assumptions it is important to separate out the fixed and variable costs (see Chapter 7). The variable costs will be dependent on a volume assumption that is identified at stage two (volume driver) above.

For items that will be used across a business, such as payroll costs, pension contributions and inflation, standard assumptions should be given to every budget-holder.

Some contingency should be allowed for events such as staff being promoted, leaving and needing to be replaced. Contingency for external factors such as weather or transport interruptions should be taken at the whole company level rather than budget-holder level to avoid the total contingency amount becoming excessive.

■ **Budget validation.** Once the budget is complete the next stage is to validate the assumptions and total amounts by checking that they are reasonable and consistent with previous years and known factors. Using the techniques of horizontal and vertical analysis can help to identify inconsistencies that may require reworking or specific justification as part of the approval process (see below for an explanation of the techniques).

■ **Approval.** As described above this is the approval of the budget by senior management. In arriving at the approval stage, there will inevitably be some reworking of the initial budget in order to set higher revenue targets and to make cost savings.

■ **Phasing.** Once the budget is approved it should be phased across the 12 months of the year. The process is sometimes known as seasonalisation or calendarisation. For example, a budget of $120,000 could simply be divided by 12 and phased as $10,000 per month. However, if it was a revenue budget for a business manufacturing diaries, this would clearly misrepresent how the revenue would be earned. Accurate phasing makes budget reviews more effective, as differences (or variances) between actual and budget are performance related and not a result of poor phasing.

Accurate phasing also helps with cash flow management as the finance department then knows when cash inflows and cash outflows are likely to happen. Poor cash flow forecasting makes it difficult to manage debt drawdowns and repayments effectively and can therefore add costs in terms of unnecessary interest payments.

The easiest way to apply phasing is to mirror the profile of previous years. To do this take 100% and allocate it by month across the prior year's results and the proportions of the year's total will be revealed. For example, if costs in month 1 last year were $38,147 and the total for the year was $405,884, month 1 incurred 9.4% of the total. If each month is exactly one-twelfth of the total for the year, they will each be 8.33%. Repeat this process for the two previous years and indicative patterns emerge that may be suitable to apply to the forthcoming year. Consideration is required for known deviations or events such as Easter and Ramadan, which do not occur in the same month this year as they did last year.

This budget process may be applied to most revenue budgets that deal with income and costs, but there is also a requirement to produce a capital budget that covers the purchase, sale and replacement of fixed assets. There is normally an investment limit dictated by funding availability and depreciation costs. The actual expenditures will be decided on the submission of business cases (see Chapter 10). Capital items usually involve sizeable cash outflows so their timing is an important element of the cash flow budget.

Standard costs

In setting budgets it can be helpful to break down cost areas into component building blocks. For example, in a manufacturing environment the budget for cost of sales is wholly dependent upon sales volumes and the mix of products. Therefore knowing the budget cost (or standard cost) per unit will speed up the process.

If, for example, the manufactured product is "easy chairs", a typical process will start by setting standard quantities for the component parts such as wood, fabric and consumables. Using predicted prices the standard cost for each product can be calculated. Making the chairs will require labour and machine time. Standard durations for each process can be identified, such as carving the wood, assembling the frame and covering it with fabric. Knowing these times helps to predict the amount of labour required to construct the anticipated product volume and hence the overall headcount and the labour cost budget.

Setting the standards can be difficult, particularly for labour hours. Carefully timing individuals may encourage them to operate slowly so they are not set too high a production rate. Encouraging quicker speeds may affect quality. An efficient and sustainable standard enables the workforce to remain motivated, standards of quality to be upheld and budgeting to be more realistic.

Horizontal and vertical analysis

Looking at any set of financial results in isolation is fairly meaningless, so comparisons are needed to understand the quality of financial performance. These comparisons can be with the results for a prior period, with budgets, or with other divisions or competitors. However, among the factors that have to be taken into account are that inflation will affect comparison with prior periods, currency may affect comparison with other divisions and scale of operation will affect comparison with competitors.

There are two helpful techniques that make comparisons easier: horizontal and vertical analysis.

Horizontal analysis

This measures the consistency of growth of revenue and costs over time. Take the results for three years shown in Table 11.1.

At first glance there is a problem with the decline in income, but what are the main factors causing this?

Horizontal analysis keeps all figures in the oldest year as a constant 100% and then looks at the proportional change on 100%

for all figures in other years. For example:

	Year 1	Year 2	Year 3
Revenue (%)	100	$100 \times \dfrac{1{,}207}{1{,}107} = 109.0$	$100 \times \dfrac{1{,}326}{1{,}107} = 119.8$
Cost of sales (%)	100	$100 \times \dfrac{964}{841} = 114.6$	$100 \times \dfrac{1{,}056}{841} = 125.6$

TABLE 11.1 **Results for three years ($ '000)**

	Year 1	Year 2	Year 3
Revenue	1,107	1,207	1,326
Cost of sales	(841)	(964)	(1,056)
Gross profit	266	243	270
Employment	(125)	(136)	(154)
Transport	(23)	(36)	(38)
Other	(56)	(68)	(72)
Income	62	3	6

Table 11.2, which is built from the data, makes it much easier to see why the results have declined. Sales have grown at a rate of nearly 20% over two years, while costs have grown by far more than this

TABLE 11.2 **Horizontal analysis of results for three years (%)**

	Year 1	Year 2	Year 3
Revenue	100.0	109.0	119.8
Cost of sales	(100.0)	(114.6)	(125.6)
Gross profit	100.0	91.4	101.5
Employment	(100.0)	(108.8)	(123.2)
Transport	(100.0)	(156.5)	(165.2)
Other	(100.0)	(121.4)	(128.6)
Income	100.0	4.8	9.7

(particularly transport). Having a more detailed breakdown of cost categories in the table will help diagnose problems more specifically. Some of the causes might be the variable or fixed nature of the costs (variable being proportionate to revenue while fixed remain constant).

Vertical analysis

This measures the consistency of cost proportions for a given level of revenue. In Table 11.3 the size of the companies being compared is so different that it is not easy to make a quick evaluation of which company is performing better.

TABLE 11.3 **Two companies in the same business ($ '000)**

	Company A	Company B
Revenue	10,076	1,326
Cost of sales	(7,591)	(964)
Gross profit	2,485	362
Employment	(1,354)	(154)
Transport	(284)	(38)
Other	(265)	(78)
Income	582	92

This is when vertical analysis can help, as it keeps the revenue figures at a constant 100% and looks at the proportion of 100 that each cost represents. For example in company A:

$$\text{Revenue} = 100.0\%$$
$$\text{Cost of sales} \quad 100 \times \frac{7,591}{10,076} = 75.3\%$$
$$\text{Gross profit} \quad 100 \times \frac{2,485}{10,076} = 24.7\%$$

The comparison of the two companies in Table 11.4 shows that overall company B looks more profitable with higher margins and more efficient staff. However, its overheads are much higher than company A's and these should be areas for investigation.

If the department being compared does not have revenue, only costs, the same analysis can still be done by using total costs as 100%, with each cost item taken as a proportion of the total.

TABLE 11.4 **Vertical analysis of two companies in the same business (%)**

	Company A	Company B
Revenue	100.0	100.0
Cost of sales	(75.3)	(72.7)
Gross profit	24.7	27.3
Employment	(13.4)	(11.6)
Transport	(2.8)	(2.9)
Other	(2.6)	(5.9)
Income	5.8	6.9

Cash budgets

Although most businesses ask managers to be accountable for profit, it is the cash budget that will be most important in planning the funding of a business, particularly a start-up or one with large debts.

The format of a cash budget can easily be drawn up from the operating and capital budgets. Table 11.5 is a typical example.

The completion of a cash budget enables funding requirements and repayments to be planned, though this can only be done effectively if the budgeted timing and the amounts of cash flows are sufficiently accurate. A capital investment planned for quarter one that is delayed until quarter three will disrupt any cash drawdown that has been arranged for the original timing. Prompt communication of significant changes in cash timing will help those in the finance department reschedule funding arrangements.

For further understanding of cash flow forecasting, see *The Economist Guide to Cash Management* by John Tennent.

TABLE 11.5 **A cash budget ($'000)**

	Month 1	Month 2	Notes
Opening balance	1,000	3,264	The closing balance from the previous month
Receivables collected	28,439	29,302	Not revenue as there may be a period of debt collection of, say, 30–90 days
Payables paid	(12,876)	(14,286)	Not costs as purchases will not be paid for, say, 30–90 days after receipt
Expenses paid	(6,299)	(6,814)	These will be items such as payroll for which no credit period is taken
Capital expenditure	(42,000)	0	Purchase of assets (and any disposal proceeds)
Non-operating payments	0	(4,000)	Items such as corporation tax or dividends
Net cash before financing	(31,736)	7,466	
Payment or receipt of financing	35,000	(5,000)	Receipts and repayments of capital and interest
Closing balance	3,264	2,466	

Review of budget reports

Once the year is under way, monthly reports enable budget-holders and senior management to keep track of progress against amounts in the budget. Regular analysis of the results will help determine the need for any corrective action and reallocation of resources.

A typical report consists of three parts, each representing different time periods:

■ the month just completed;

■ year to date (the company year rather than the calendar year, although for many companies these are the same);

■ full year.

These three time periods are shown as vertical blocks in Figure 11.3. The year to date is usually the most informative about current performance as individual months are affected by factors such as the number of trading days, accruals and accrual reversals, which can show one-off variances that may be misleading. After month three or four these monthly variances usually become smoothed in the cumulative figures and genuine trends emerge.

Within each of the three time periods there is normally a comparison of actual performance with budget and prior year results. Without a comparative the actual numbers are almost meaningless and difficult to interpret in terms of success or failure. Typical columns in the management accounts that report progress against budget and the previous year's performance are as follows:

- Plan or budget (the budgeted result for this year)
- Actual (the actual results achieved for this month and year to date)
- Last year (the comparative for the same period in the last financial year)
- Variance to plan (the difference between plan and actual)
- Variance to last year (the difference between last year and actual)

The calculation and explanation of variances are given in the next section.

For the full year no actual results are available so two additional columns may be shown:

- Forecast (the expected year-end result based on mid-year estimation)
- Monthly run rate to hit plan (the amount that needs to be earned or can be spent in each of the remaining months of the year for the business to achieve plan); see section below for the calculation process

Figure 11.3 shows a report in September for a business with a December year end. The rows shown in the report are the main headings of an income statement. For operational management there would be reports for each item showing the component costs in far more detail, though in a similar style.

FIG 11.3 Example budget report

MONTHLY RESULTS

$'000	September Plan	Actual	Last year	Variance plan	Variance last year	YTD Plan	Actual	Last year	Variance plan	Variance last year	Full year Plan	Forecast	Last year	Variance plan	Monthly run rate to hit plan	Variance last year
Revenue	43	41	40	(2)	1	665	614	649	(51)	(35)	864	798	814	(66)	83	(16)
Cost of sales	(17)	(16)	(16)	1	0	(307)	(287)	(314)	20	27	(397)	(361)	(378)	36	(37)	17
Transportation	(2)	(3)	(2)	(1)	(1)	(40)	(40)	(48)	0	8	(52)	(51)	(63)	1	(4)	12
Other operating income	0	0	0	0	0	1	2	2	1	0	1	2	3	1	(0)	(1)
Gross profit	24	22	22	(2)	0	319	289	289	(30)	0	416	388	376	(28)	42	12
Advertising	(3)	(2)	(3)	1	1	(43)	(27)	(26)	16	(1)	(53)	(32)	(31)	21	(9)	(1)
Marketing	(1)	(2)	(2)	(1)	0	(17)	(18)	(17)	(1)	(1)	(24)	(24)	(24)	0	(2)	0
Market research	(1)	(1)	(1)	0	0	(10)	(9)	(9)	0	1	(13)	(13)	(12)	0	(1)	(1)
Administration	(11)	(11)	(10)	0	(1)	(107)	(99)	(104)	8	5	(136)	(128)	(131)	8	(12)	3
Other operating costs	(5)	(3)	(3)	2	0	(64)	(59)	(69)	5	10	(82)	(73)	(87)	9	(8)	14
Operating income	3	3	3	0	0	78	76	64	(2)	12	108	118	91	10	11	27
Interest	(2)	(1)	(2)	1	1	(19)	(19)	(20)	0	1	(25)	(26)	(28)	(1)	(2)	2
Tax	(1)	(1)	(1)	0	0	(26)	(22)	(23)	4	1	(36)	(39)	(38)	(3)	(5)	(1)
Net income	0	1	0	1	1	33	35	21	2	14	47	53	25	6	4	28

Ratios

	September Plan	Actual	Last year			YTD Plan	Actual	Last year			Full year Plan	Forecast	Last year		Monthly run rate	
GP%	56%	55%	55%			48%	47%	45%			48%	49%	46%		51%	
OI%	7%	8%	8%			12%	12%	10%			13%	15%	11%		13%	
NI%	0%	3%	0%			5%	6%	3%			5%	7%	3%		5%	

At the foot of the report are a set of performance measures that show each of the profit lines as a proportion of revenue (GP = gross profit, OI = operating income, NI = net income).

To those unfamiliar with this type of report the volume of information can be daunting, making it difficult to know where to start. The technique is to identify the most important number on the page and work outwards from there. In Figure 11.3 the most important row is operating income or the EBIT line. The most important column is the year to date variance to plan. The variance is the difference between the actual result and the budget, so on this sheet the most important number is the year to date variance in operating income which is minus 2. In other words, the profit to date is $2,000 below budget. This is worse than required, but not too far away; it could easily be made up in the remaining three months.

From this point look upwards in the variance column to identify why the difference has occurred. The main reason is the shortfall in revenue that is partially offset with a consequential saving in cost of sales. It is the variance column that provides the list of differences and hence can help identify in what areas actions are required to correct any shortfall in results.

Variance analysis

Variance or causal factor analysis compares an actual result with a budget to identify the specific causes of difference. Once the causes are known, action can be taken. Variance analysis will show only the effect of differences, not their cause. It is the role of management to investigate and respond.

Variances can be presented in one of two ways and it is important to understand which is being used before reading a report:

■ Positive is good and negative is bad – therefore positive or favourable variances are results that are better than budget and negative or adverse variances are results that are worse than budget; that is, sales in excess of budget is positive and costs in excess of budget is negative.

■ Positive is more than budget and negative is less than budget – therefore a positive variance for a revenue item is favourable whereas a positive variance for a cost item is adverse and is unfavourable.

Most businesses use the first method, which is easier to read (this is also the method used in the example report in Figure 11.3).

The variances in the example are presented as dollar values. Percentages can also be used. There are benefits in both methods and therefore some businesses will show both, but this extra information can make it difficult to fit into an already detailed report with, as in the case of the example, 17 columns.

The benefits of each method are as follows:

- Percentages show the proportionate gap between the actual result and the comparative. However, large percentage variances on small items may not matter much, whereas small percentage variances on big items can be critical. For example, a 1% negative variance on projected revenue of $100m comes to $1m, whereas a 20% overspend on an office supply cost budget of $100,000 comes to $20,000.

- Dollar values show the financial effect caused by each item for which the actual results are different from those budgeted. Therefore small costs that have large percentage variances are ignored, but large items with costly variances can be targeted for action.

Although simple differences can provide some insight into why results have not achieved the budget, a more investigative approach can help reveal better reasons. Take the results in Table 11.6.

TABLE 11.6 **Budget and actual results**

	Budget	**Actual**
Sales volume ('000)	100	90
Sales value ($ '000)	1,000	990
Variable costs ($ '000)	(500)	(495)
Fixed costs ($ '000)	(200)	(210)
Profit ($ '000)	300	285

Comparing actual with budget indicates that the only area to come in better than budget is variable costs. However, this is misleading because volume was down 10% and therefore variable costs should, by definition, be down as well. For a realistic comparison the effect of a volume difference needs to be eliminated. This can be achieved by comparing actual results with what is known as a flexed budget.

A flexed budget is a reworked budget based on the original budget assumptions but applied to actual volume. Therefore revenue and variable costs can be flexed using average "per unit" values (for example, sales were budgeted at an average $10 per unit and therefore for 90 units the revenue would be $900). For fixed costs there is no flexing required as they are constants, regardless of any changes in volume.

TABLE 11.7 **A flexed budget**

	Original budget	**Flexed budget**	**Actual**
Sales volume ('000)	100	90	90
Sales value ($ '000)	1,000	900	990
Variable costs ($ '000)	(500)	(450)	(495)
Fixed costs ($ '000)	(200)	(200)	(210)
Profit ($ '000)	300	250	285

The expected profit from selling 90 units would have been $250 and therefore the result of $285 shows some success.

Having calculated the flexed budget, a variance statement can be produced to reconcile budgeted profit to actual profit (see Table 11.8).

The sign convention in the variance statement is that a variance enhancing profit is positive and a variance reducing profit is negative and shown in brackets.

This variance statement would be more useful if the individual costs were analysed in greater detail. The level of detail is a judgment, but when it comes to actions the size of the variance dictates the priority.

TABLE 11.8 **Variance statement**

	($'000)
Original budget profit	300
Sales volume variance (the difference between original budget profit and flexed budget profit) 250 − 300 =	(50)
Sales price variance (the difference between actual sales value and flexed sales value) 990 − 900 =	90
Variable costs (the difference between actual variable costs and flexed variable costs) 450 − 495 =	(45)
Fixed costs (the difference between actual fixed costs and flexed fixed costs) 200 − 210 =	(10)
Actual profit	285

Further investigation can be completed for each cost. For example, a variable cost for materials could be analysed between price and usage, adding detail to the above example:

Variable cost budget per unit 2.00kg @ $2.50 each × 100 units =$500
Variable cost actual per unit 2.75kg @ $2.00 each × 90 units =$495

Materials usage variance:
For each unit: an extra 0.75kg was used at the budgeted price of
$2.50 per kg × 90 units
(change in material used × budget price × actual units)   = (169)

Price variance:
For each 2.75kg the price was 50¢ less than budget × 90 units
(actual materials used × change in price × actual units)   = 124

Net materials variance (as shown above)   = (45)

Mix and yield

In a production environment where raw materials are mixed together in standard proportions (the recipe), it is also possible to calculate further variances that analyse the mix (variances to the recipe) and yield (changes in output quantity) effects of each batch.

For example, if two ingredients are needed for producing a clear fruit juice (apple and orange) the two variances can be illustrated. The standard recipe is as follows:

Apple juice	51 litres	$0.30 per litre	$15.30
Orange juice	51 litres	$0.20 per litre	$10.20
Total	102 litres		$25.50

The standard cost of the juice is $25.50 per 102 litres, though once the pulp is removed there are 100 litres that are saleable. Therefore each litre costs $0.255 to produce ($25.50 ÷ 100).

If the mix is inaccurately prepared and the pulp is poorly controlled, the result could be as follows:

Apple juice	43 litres	$0.30 per litre	$12.90
Orange juice	59 litres	$0.20 per litre	$11.80
Total	102 litres		$24.70

The mix variance is therefore favourable as being $25.50 − $24.70 = $0.80. In this calculation the price per litre is the budget or standard price for which there may also be price variances.

If only 98 litres were produced once the pulp had been removed, there would also be a yield variance for the 2 litres of lower production output. It is calculated by taking the variation in output volume at the budgeted cost per litre of output:

100 litres − 98 litres @ $0.255 per litre = an adverse variance of $0.51

Mix and yield variances should not be confused with material usage and price variances as their causes are quite different:

- Usage variances may be caused by consumption greater than expected because of quality issues such as rejects.
- Price variances are a consequence of buying at a price that is different from the price in the plan.
- Mix variances relate to changes in proportions of input quantities that may be caused by shortages of an ingredient.

■ Yield variances relate to changes in output quantities through incorrect processing.

Validating the variances

Once the variance analysis has been produced it will provide the basis for identifying the appropriate actions to take. It is not a matter of cutting cost until profit is back on track or increasing expenditure to justify the original budget request. Several processes are required before a conclusion can be drawn.

Although substantial variances may show up, they may not be valid if the actual data is incorrect or the budget data is an inappropriate comparison. Examples of these are as follows:

■ The actual data may contain coding errors where amounts have been entered against the wrong account code such that a budget line is overstated in one area and equally understated in another. A check of the individual transactions posted to a budget code can reveal these errors.

■ Although a budget may appear under-spent there may be expenditure incurred but not yet recorded in the accounting system for which an accrual would help reconcile the difference. An analysis using the following headings may be helpful to reconcile any variances that are identified:

	$
Actual money spent and recorded in the accounting system	507
Expenditure incurred but not yet recorded (accruals)	71
Expenditure already committed for future months (purchase orders)	104
Unused portion of annual budget	392
Total annual budget	1,074

■ The phasing of the budget may not match the way the actual results are being achieved, although the budget for the year as a whole still remains valid.

FIG 11.4 **Five levels of analysis**

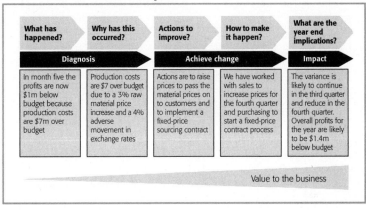

What has happened?	Why has this occurred?	Actions to improve?	How to make it happen?	What are the year end implications?
Diagnosis		Achieve change		Impact
In month five the profits are now $1m below budget because production costs are $7m over budget	Production costs are $7 over budget due to a 3% raw material price increase and a 4% adverse movement in exchange rates	Actions are to raise prices to pass the material prices on to customers and to implement a fixed-price sourcing contract	We have worked with sales to increase prices for the fourth quarter and purchasing to start a fixed-price contract process	The variance is likely to continue in the third quarter and reduce in the fourth quarter. Overall profits for the year are likely to be $1.4m below budget

Value to the business

Variance reporting

Calculating the variances in accordance with the methodology described above identifies only what has happened. This needs to be translated into why and what is to be done to build on positive variances and improve on negative variances. Figure 11.4 illustrates the typical five stages of commentary that should be made when reporting on variances.

As indicated by the triangle at the bottom of Figure 11.4, the value to the business is in action not information:

- The first two stages report the situation – what has happened and why it has occurred. This is history and summarises the causes of the problem.

- Stages three and four identify actions – what needs to happen to improve the situation and the progress that has been made on implementation.

- Stage five estimates the impact – what will be the implications for the business by the end of the year.

This type of report can show senior management that an emerging problem in the business is being handled effectively and practical actions are being implemented.

FIG 11.5 **Budget report for staff costs**

Month 6	Year to date		Full year			Variance
	Actual	Run rate spent	Budget	Budget remaining	Run rate to spend	lower / (higher)
	$	$	$	$	$	$
Salaries	50,302	8,384	104,045	53,743	8,957	574
Pension	4,200	700	8,270	4,070	678	(22)
Car lease	2,100	350	5,000	2,900	483	133
Mobile phones	2,072	345	3,016	944	157	(188)
Medical insurance	383	64	774	391	65	1
Accommodation	1,184	197	1,411	227	38	(160)
Meals	679	113	1,455	776	129	16
Mileage	2,107	351	2,385	278	46	(305)
Welfare	20	3	48	28	5	1
Other	2,867	478	4,982	2,115	353	(125)
Total	65,914	10,986	131,386	65,472	10,912	(74)

Run rates

Another technique to help managers interpret budget performance is run rates. It can be used to monitor the rate at which a budget is being used up during the year and the rate at which spend can continue for the remaining months of the year. It is particularly effective for analysing fixed costs or costs that have little phasing difference.

Figure 11.5 is an extract from a budget report for staff costs. The report is prepared in month six.

The details of the report are shown in Table 11.9.

Reforecasting

Reforecasting is necessary to see if the budgeted results are likely to be achieved and, if they are not, provides an opportunity for action to be taken. Variances on the year to date results may signal problems that are emerging, but the reforecasting shows whether any significant adverse variances will be turned around. The temptation for budget managers fearful of having to account to senior management for underperformance is to offer up reforecasts or predictions of probable outturns that show everything is under control. This clearly hides problems that, if left unresolved, are likely to get worse and be more shocking when they finally emerge.

TABLE 11.9 **Details of budget report**

Year to date actual	The actual results for the first six months of the year
Year to date run rate spent	The cumulative spend to date divided by the number of months elapsed. For example, salaries: $$\frac{50,302}{6} = 8,384$$
Full-year budget	The budget for 12 months
Budget remaining	The budget left to spend in the last six months. This is calculated as the full-year budget less the actual spend in the year to date
Run rate to spend	The maximum monthly rate that can be spent in the remaining months of the year to stay within budget. This is calculated as the budget remaining divided by the number of months left in the year, in this example six months
Variance	The difference between run rate to date and run rate to spend. A positive value means that future monthly expenditure can be higher than in the past and vice versa. It is the negative variances that need to be investigated and action taken to make sure problems do not build up for later in the year

TABLE 11.10 **Details of reforecast report**

Year to date (YTD) actual	The actual results for the completed months of the year
Full-year budget	The budget for the full 12 months
Projection based on actual run rate	Based on the actual run rate per month for the year so far, this column assumes the rate will continue for the full 12 months. For example salaries: $$\frac{50,302}{6} \times 12 = 100,604$$
Adjust for known events	Exceptional items known to be incurred in the remaining months that will affect the run rate or events that take place in the year to date that will not be repeated
Forecast result	The total of the run rate projection and known event adjustments
Variance	The difference between the full-year budget and the forecast result. It is the variances that will stimulate action to bring performance back in line with the budget. Such actions may include the delay in taking on new or replacement staff and a restriction on travel and mobile phone usage

FIG 11.6 **Reforecast report for staff costs**

Month 6	YTD Actual	Full year Budget	Projection				
			Projection based on actual run rate	Adjust for known events	Forecast result	Variance + / (-)	Known events
	$	$	$	$	$	$	
Salaries	50,302	104,045	100,604	12,000	112,604	(8,559)	New hire
Pension	4,200	8,270	8,400	500	8,900	(630)	New hire
Car lease	2,100	5,000	4,200		4,200	800	
Mobile phones	2,072	3,016	4,144	600	4,744	(1,728)	New hire
Medical insurance	383	774	766	50	816	(42)	New hire
Accommodation	1,184	1,411	2,368		2,368	(957)	
Meals	679	1,455	1,358	800	2,158	(703)	Xmas party
Mileage	2,107	2,385	4,214		4,214	(1,829)	
Welfare	20	48	40		40	8	
Other	2,867	4,982	5,734	4,800	10,534	(5,552)	Recruitment
Total	65,914	131,386	131,828	18,750	150,578	(19,192)	

There are three techniques for forecasting probable outturns:

■ **Revenue.** This will depend on market data, competitor activity and customer feedback. It is notoriously difficult to predict and relies as much on experience as on trend analysis.

■ **Variable costs.** These are most easily predicted using vertical analysis (explained above). If component costs are 28% of revenue for the year to date, in the absence of other price or usage information it would be reasonable to assume this ratio stays constant for the reminder of the year.

■ **Fixed costs.** As these should be broadly constant month to month, a prediction using run rates can be the most efficient.

The example in Figure 11.6 extends the analysis shown above and includes some new headings. The details of the report are shown in Table 11.10.

Making budgeting effective

Budgeting is often far easier to describe than it is to operate. Fundamentally, it is the planning of revenue and expenditure, followed by the monitoring of actual results as they emerge and introducing change when expectations are not met.

As mentioned previously, layered on top of the budgeting process are varying degrees of internal politics, implied performance assessment of budget-holders (including bonuses) and compromise in sharing limited resources. It is this behavioural aspect that lies at the heart of any adverse view on budgeting, not the financial mechanics. It is unlikely that anyone in any business will say: "I really enjoyed the last budget round." This type of attitude is not helpful and can fuel in-fighting within a business to the detriment of focus on business activities.

The following factors can make budgets more effective:

- There should be an emphasis from the top of the organisation on the importance of the budgeting process and the accountability of budget-holders.

- Managers should be accountable only for activities they can control or significantly influence.

- Managers should be included in the budget-setting process (the bottom-up approach, see page 207) so that they feel ownership and commitment.

- Budgets should be set to stretch, but they should be achievable so that commitment can be maintained.

- Variances should be reported, investigated and if necessary acted upon promptly (long delays mean opportunities will be missed).

- Managers with budget-holding responsibilities should be free to offset over- and under-budgeted items, providing their totals remain on track.

12 **Operational ratios and measures**

THIS CHAPTER LOOKS at the process of analysing and interpreting financial information, the measures that are used to monitor business performance and the indicators that are used to drive performance improvement.

Business measurement

Harrington, a past chairman of the International Academy for Quality, is credited with the following quotation which summarises his view on business measurement:

> *Measurement is the first step that leads to control and eventually to improvement. If you can't measure something, you can't understand it. If you can't understand it, you can't control it. If you can't control it, you can't improve it.*

With modern IT systems there is the ability and even a temptation to produce a profusion of measures to monitor every attribute of a business. The danger is that this can result in a lack of managerial focus and even confusion when the measures conflict. What is needed is a clear understanding of what defines success, a simple way of measuring progress towards achieving success and an organisational culture that is committed to improvement.

In selecting measures to monitor a business, an important aspect to consider is that their use will significantly influence management behaviour, particularly if managers' bonuses depend on their achievement. For example, if sales volume growth is used as a measure it may encourage the sales force to sell, but at what price? The measure ignores the profitability of each sale as well as the creditworthiness of the customer. Measuring the growth in the amount of cash profit received would discourage price discounts and give cash collection a higher priority.

For a comprehensive guide to company analysis, ratios and measures, see *The Economist Guide to Analysing Companies* by Bob Vause.

Which is the better business?

Table 12.1 sets out the income statement for three companies. Which is the better business?

TABLE 12.1 **Income statement ($'000)**

	Company A	Company B	Company C
Revenue	450	350	250
Cost of sales	(280)	(200)	(140)
Gross profit	170	150	110
Overheads	(50)	(40)	(30)
Profit	120	110	80

The difficulty is to decide what is meant by better. Clearly company A is the largest in terms of the amount of revenue and profit it generates, but does this mean it is better?

What may be more interesting is to know how much money is invested in each of these three businesses to derive this profit.

TABLE 12.2 **Statement of financial position ($'000)**

	Company A	Company B	Company C
Investment	1,500	1,200	800

Table 12.2 shows that company A requires almost twice as much capital as company C to operate. In Chapter 1 success was defined as

being able to: "Create a sustainable superior return on investment."

Return on investment (ROI) was calculated as:

$$\text{ROI} = \frac{\text{Profit}}{\text{Investment}} \ \%$$

Success requires the ROI to be better than a deposit rate to compensate investors for the risk of putting their money into the business. A return of 20% or more would be a good result for a top company.

Applying the calculation to each company shows that company C, although being smaller than the other two, generates the best return on investment (see Table 12.3) and this would be the main performance measure to judge operational effectiveness.

TABLE 12.3 **Return on investment**

	Company A	Company B	Company C
$\dfrac{\text{Profit}}{\text{Investment}} \times 100$	$\dfrac{120}{1,500} \times 100$	$\dfrac{110}{1,200} \times 100$	$\dfrac{80}{800} \times 100$
ROI	8%	9%	10%

Portfolio of performance measures

Although ROI is the main operational performance measure, it sits within a portfolio of measures used to evaluate a whole business. Depending on your relationship with the company, the other measures will have higher or lower importance. For example, shareholders will be interested in dividends and expectations for the future; and suppliers will be interested in when or whether they will be paid. The three main categories of performance measures are shown with examples in Table 12.4.

TABLE 12.4 **Investor, liquidity and operational measures**

Investor measures	Liquidity measures	Operational measures
Leverage/gearing	Current ratio	Margin
Interest cover	Acid test	Gross margin
Return on equity		EBITDA margin
Earnings per share		Asset turnover
Price/earnings		Reinvestment rate
Dividend cover		Costs as a percentage of
Dividend yield		revenue
		Inventory days
		Receivable days
		Payable days
		Industry-specific measures

Since the 1980s consultancies have been developing new measures that have supporting research to show they have found a better correlation between financial performance and share price than those mentioned above. These measures are more commonly cash flow based, removing the distortions that are sometimes created by accounting policies used in traditional profit measures. They also try to reflect risk more genuinely than simple ROI measures are able to. These are covered with the investor measures in Chapter 13.

The benefits of ratios

Ratios enable the performance of a business to be compared over time, in different currencies and in varying scales of operation. They are as valid for a small business based in the UK as for a large multinational based in Japan.

Although many of them are calculated in arrears and therefore show how well a business performed last month or last year, they can also be applied to business plans and budgets to set improvement targets and goals.

Not only can the use of ratios be applied to monitoring and managing trends within a business, but also industry sector benchmarks emerge such that comparisons to similar businesses become possible.

For example, if one major oil company spends 4.2% of its revenue on employment costs, how does another manage to spend only 3.6%? Although the answer does not lie in the ratios, the right question does. The company with the higher employment cost percentage must have one or more of the following: more staff, higher pay rates, better benefits, a top-heavy structure with more senior (and therefore more expensive) staff, less outsourcing or contractors. Whatever the reason for the difference, the information provides an opportunity to investigate whether the business is optimally structured. The lower percentage is not necessarily best, as fewer staff may jeopardise quality, customer service or even safety.

One point to bear in mind when using these measures to make comparisons across an industry sector is that because companies use different methodologies, the data may not have been produced in a consistent way, so the measures are only indicators of differences between firms rather than absolute truths.

The calculation of ratios may vary in practice, particularly by country. For example, there are over 14 common methods of calculating return on investment (some of which are explained below).

The financial statements, on which the ratios can be applied, are compiled in accordance with legal requirements and guidelines from accounting bodies. However, there is still room for judgment; for example, the depreciation policy for machinery may be to write off an asset over eight years in one company and ten years in another. Such differences in accounting policy will affect the ratios and need to be taken into account in comparisons.

East Coast Printers: an illustration of how ratios work

The fictitious East Coast Printers is in a highly competitive sector where technology moves fast and new equipment requires significant investment. A few years ago the company acquired a smaller printer in another state; a significant amount of goodwill arose on the acquisition which is recognised on the statement of financial position (goodwill is explained in Chapter 16).

Its income statement and statement of financial position are shown in Tables 12.5 and 12.6. For the rest of this chapter, the figures and tables that include numbers are based on East Coast Printers' income statement and statement of financial position.

TABLE 12.5 **East Coast Printers: income statement ($'000)**

	Current year	Previous year
Revenue	13,860	12,540
Cost of sales	(8,370)	(7,430)
Gross profit	5,490	5,110
Selling	(1,100)	(1,030)
Administration	(1,270)	(1,090)
EBITDA[a]	3,120	2,990
Depreciation	(1,380)	(1,290)
EBIT[b]	1,740	1,700
Interest	(810)	(650)
EBT[c]	930	1,050
Tax	(280)	(320)
Earnings	650	730
Notes		
Dividend	580	570
Employment cost	2,310	2,060
Research	400	480

a Earnings before interest, tax, depreciation and amortisation.
b Earnings before interest and tax.
c Earnings before tax.

The statement of financial position is set out so the top half includes the business assets and liabilities that total to the net assets and the bottom half includes all the funding that totals to the capital employed. This layout may differ in structure and order of items from layouts used in some countries, but the individual assets and liabilities have the same meaning regardless of where they appear on the page.

TABLE 12.6 **East Coast Printers: statement of financial position ($'000)**

	Current year	Previous year
Goodwill	4,020	4,020
Tangible fixed assets	8,520	7,190
Total fixed assets	12,540	11,210
Inventory	2,960	1,910
Trade receivables	2,830	2,040
Other receivables	960	830
Cash	120	1,020
Current assets	6,870	5,800
Trade payables	(2,050)	(1,090)
Other payables	(880)	(760)
Current liabilities	(2,930)	(1,850)
Provisions	(560)	(650)
Net assets	15,920	14,510
Shares	2,050	2,050
Retained profit	5,630	5,230
Equity	7,680	7,280
Short-term debt	2,290	1,280
Long-term debt	5,950	5,950
Total debt	8,240	7,230
Capital employed	15,920	14,510

Return on investment

As defined earlier, ROI is:

$$\text{ROI} = \frac{\text{Profit}}{\text{Investment}} \ \%$$

With a set of financial statements to refer to, the questions are: which profit should be used and what exactly is investment?

Profit

On the income statement there are five levels of profit. The purpose of each is as follows:

- Gross profit – measures how profitable the sales have been after deducting direct costs. In this example it would be the cost of items such as paper and inks.

- EBITDA – a relatively new measure of profit that has become popular because it is a good indicator of the cash generated by the business. Depreciation and amortisation are a book entry to reflect the usage of fixed assets rather than a cash cost (see Chapter 4).

- EBIT – the profit after all operating costs and before any financing costs or taxation. It is also known as operating income.

- EBT – the gross profit to shareholders before corporation tax is deducted.

- Earnings – the net income available for shareholders; a proportion of this will typically be distributed as a dividend with the rest being kept back in the business for reinvestment.

The profit for ROI calculations is EBIT as it reflects operational performance before funding. If two businesses have the same EBIT, but one is funded by debt and the other by equity, their operating results are the same. The difference lies in the funding mechanism, interest payments and WACC (see Chapter 6) not operations. Other investor measures are covered later in this chapter.

Investment

The money required to fund the business is the equity and debt. This is expressed on the statement of financial position as capital employed. Therefore one measure could be return on capital employed (ROCE). This is also known as return on invested capital (ROIC).

The calculation is shown in Table 12.7 and reveals that in the current year the return fell by almost 1%. If deposit rates offered by a bank are 5%, the business is generating a return over twice that of a risk-free investment.

As the top half of the statement of financial position (net assets) totals to the same value as capital employed, an identical calculation also gives another measure, return on net assets (RONA). Some companies prefer this measure because management can influence the components of net assets by actions that reduce investment in items such as inventory or receivables. A reduction in net assets will enable debt to be repaid and thus reduce capital employed.

TABLE 12.7 **Return on capital employed**

	Current year	Previous year
$\dfrac{\text{EBIT}}{\text{Capital employed}} \times 100$	$\dfrac{1,740}{15,920} \times 100$	$\dfrac{1,700}{14,510} \times 100$
ROCE	10.9%	11.7%

One anomaly in the calculation of RONA and ROCE is the inclusion of cash, as it is not employed in the business and did not contribute to the generation of the EBIT. Therefore an alternative measure is return on net capital employed (RONCE) where cash is deducted in the calculation.

TABLE 12.8 **Return on net capital employed**

	Current year	Previous year
$\dfrac{\text{EBIT}}{\text{Capital employed} - \text{cash}} \times 100$	$\dfrac{1,740}{(15,920 - 120)} \times 100$	$\dfrac{1,700}{(14,510 - 1,020)} \times 100$
RONCE	11.0%	12.6%

Averaging assets

In calculating the return, it seems strange to be using the year-end statement of financial position as the denominator in the calculation.

A fairer value that actually reflects the capital employed during the period the EBIT was earned would be an average value over the year. This is often taken as the average of the opening and closing statement of financial position, return on average capital employed (ROACE).

TABLE 12.9 **Return on average capital employed ($'000)**

	Current year	Previous year
$\dfrac{\text{EBIT}}{\text{Average capital employed}} \times 100$	$\dfrac{1,740}{15,215^a} \times 100$	$\dfrac{1,700}{14,245} \times 100$
ROACE	11.4%	11.9%

a (15,920 + 14,510) ÷ 2 = 15,215

The previous year's value for capital employed will require a value for capital employed at the end of the year before; for this purpose the number is $13,980. As mentioned above, cash could also be deducted from this calculation.

Total resources

To find a return based on the total amount of resources in a business a measure called return on total assets (ROTA) can be used. To find this number the total fixed assets need to be added to the total current assets. However, on statements of financial position that are laid out with assets on one side and liabilities on the other the number for total assets will already be shown.

TABLE 12.10 **Return on total assets**

	Current year	Previous year
$\dfrac{\text{EBIT}}{\text{Total assets}} \times 100$	$\dfrac{1,740}{19,410^a} \times 100$	$\dfrac{1,700}{17,010} \times 100$
ROTA	9.0%	10.0%

a 12,540 + 6,870 = 19,410

The principle of averaging (see above) can also be applied to this calculation.

Net operating assets

One of the most common methods used within companies to evaluate performance is to calculate a return on net operating assets (RONOA). This focuses on the statement of financial position items that management can influence.

The four items to include are: tangible fixed assets (on the basis that managers cannot influence goodwill and most other intangible assets), inventory, trade receivables and trade payables. All other items are ignored as they relate to such things as taxation or pension deficits, none of which are used in generating the EBIT.

TABLE 12.11 **Net operating assets ($'000)**

	Current year	Previous year
Tangible fixed assets	8,520	7,190
Inventory	2,960	1,910
Trade receivables	2,830	2,040
Trade payables	(2,050)	(1,090)
Net operating assets	12,260	10,050
Return on net operating assets		
$\dfrac{\text{EBIT}}{\text{Net operating assets}} \times 100$	$\dfrac{1,740}{12,260} \times 100$	$\dfrac{1,700}{10,050} \times 100$
RONOA	14.2%	16.9%

This method of calculating a return also forms the basis of the hierarchy of ratios, which analyses all the operational components of RONOA and links the changes in operational activity to the achievement of return on investment. This is explained below.

In conclusion, return on investment is a term that is used loosely. The range of alternatives in the examples above illustrates the need for one of the many options to be chosen and then applied consistently when making comparisons.

The advantages and disadvantages of RONOA are shown in Table 12.12.

TABLE 12.12 **Advantages and disadvantages of RONOA**

Advantages	Disadvantages
■ Easily understood by managers because the measure is similar to an interest rate on a savings account	■ There is no standard method of calculation
■ Does not reflect any growth in the business because the return is independent of the size of business	■ Start-ups will take a while to deliver returns and the measure does not take into account the long-term potential returns
■ The measure is an average of all assets regardless of their individual risks	■ The measure can dissuade from investment where assets are added before returns emerge leading to a decline in the rate of return
■ Ultimately a business or project must generate a return greater than WACC to justify its existence	■ A scenario with more costs and less capital can give better short-term returns
	■ Over time depreciation will reduce the value of fixed assets and enhance the return. Fixed assets should be revalued to a market value for a fair measure
	■ Excludes the value of intangible assets such as brands
	■ Unsuitable for use in businesses where there is negative operating capital (eg, retailers with rented fixed assets)

Operational measures

If return on net operating assets is expanded into its full form it would be expressed as follows:

$$\frac{\text{Revenue} - \text{costs (cost of sales and overhead costs)}}{\text{Tangible fixed assets} + \text{inventory} + \text{trade receivables} - \text{trade payables}} \times 100$$

To increase the rate of return there are six actions:

1 Maximise revenue.
2 Minimise costs.

FIG 12.1 **The hierarchy of ratios**

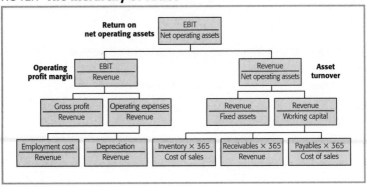

3 Maximise the utilisation of tangible fixed assets.
4 Minimise inventory levels.
5 Collect receivables faster.
6 Take credit on purchases whenever possible.

If these are the core six actions, it would be helpful to have performance measures to show how well each action is being managed. An adaptation of the hierarchy of ratios originally produced by Du Pont, a chemical company, is widely used for this purpose, as shown in Figure 12.1.

The top ratio is the return on net operating assets, explained earlier. The two ratios on the second level are known as operating profit margin and asset turnover. The operating profit margin looks at how effectively profit is generated from revenue and goes on to analyse the items in the income statement. The asset turnover looks at the volume of revenue produced from the investment in the business and goes on to look at each component of investment covering the items in the statement of financial position.

Operating profit margin

This ratio shows the amount of profit derived from each dollar of revenue. The objective is to increase the value of this measure as much as possible. It is a percentage that is calculated as follows:

$$\frac{\text{EBIT}}{\text{Revenue}} \%$$

EBIT is defined in the same way as RONOA and is the earnings (or profit) before interest and tax. Revenue should exclude any purchase taxes such as value-added tax (VAT).

TABLE 12.13 **Profit margin**

	Current year	Previous year
$\frac{\text{EBIT}}{\text{Revenue}} \times 100$	$\frac{1,740}{13,860} \times 100$	$\frac{1,700}{12,540} \times 100$
Profit margin	12.6%	13.6%

In reviewing this measure over a number of years, a business would want the percentage to be maintained or growing. As the volume of sales grows there can be economies of scale that will often help increase the margin. The economies of scale are derived from fixed costs such as accounting, information technology and human resources, which typically do not rise as fast as revenue. The costs of these departments are mainly payroll and the headcount may stay constant over a range of sales volume levels. Conversely, as a business reduces in size it is difficult to remove these fixed costs and a margin can therefore decline.

In the absence of product development or service improvement, it is likely that margins will decline (or fade) over time. What was new becomes old and starts to compete more on price than its previously superior or pre-eminent attributes.

The ROI can be compared with any business, as it is a uniform indicator. However, the profit margin is particular to an industry. For example, a food retailer typically has low margins compared with a telecommunications provider, which has high margins. This does not imply one business is better than another, only that the cost structure of each business is different. In food retailing, the majority of the costs are in the purchase of groceries in the cost of sales, whereas for a telecoms provider the costs are mainly in the network, which is capitalised as a fixed asset.

Asset turnover

Asset turnover measures the volume of sales achieved for every dollar invested in the business. It is a factor, not a percentage, and is calculated as follows:

$$\frac{\text{Revenue}}{\text{Net operating assets}}$$

The value of revenue is the same as that used for the profit margin. The net operating assets are the same as those used for the RONOA.

TABLE 12.14 **Asset turnover**

	Current year	**Previous year**
Revenue	13,860	12,540
Net operating assets	12,260	10,050
Asset turnover	1.13	1.25

The objective with the asset turnover is to achieve high asset utilisation. Therefore having invested in assets, they should be used to generate revenue. For an airline this is a fundamental: the greater the seat occupancy in an aircraft, the greater is the asset turnover. However, in pursuing strategies to enhance asset turnover it is important to allow for downtime and maintenance.

Like the profit margin, the asset turnover is specific to an industry as illustrated below.

Linking profit margin to asset turnover

You will see from the calculations for profit margin and asset turnover that revenue is a common factor. RONOA can be expressed as margin multiplied by asset turnover:

$$\text{RONOA} = \text{Margin} \times \text{Asset turnover}$$

$$\frac{\text{EBIT}}{\text{Net operating assets}} = \frac{\text{EBIT}}{\text{Revenue}} \times \frac{\text{Revenue}}{\text{Net operating assets}}$$

FIG 12.2 **Three business examples**

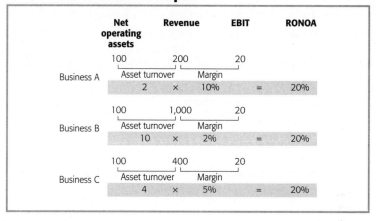

	Net operating assets	Revenue	EBIT	RONOA
Business A	100	200	20	
	Asset turnover	Margin		
	2	× 10%	=	20%
Business B	100	1,000	20	
	Asset turnover	Margin		
	10	× 2%	=	20%
Business C	100	400	20	
	Asset turnover	Margin		
	4	× 5%	=	20%

Figure 12.2 shows three example businesses. Which is the most successful?

All have the same performance as the RONOA is identical. However, business B would appear to have to work harder than either of the other two in that it needs to sell five times more than business A.

For example, this could be seen as follows:

- The RONOA of a food retailer might be 5% margin × 3 asset turnover = 15%.

- Compare this with the RONOA of a telecoms company, which might be 15% margin × 1 asset turnover = 15%.

These two companies achieve a similar RONOA, but because of the sectors they are in earn it in very different ways.

More importantly, the analysis of RONOA is used to evaluate the impact of business decisions. If a company invests significantly in assets, it is likely that its asset turnover will fall. To maintain the RONOA it has two choices: either to increase revenue to restore the asset turnover, or to increase margin to compensate for the reduction in asset turnover.

An example of this approach is when global food retailers

initiated expansion programmes that required a huge investment in new superstores. For Tesco, the largest UK food retailer, asset turnover halved over a period of three years. However, its RONOA did not suffer as Tesco managed to double its margin over the same period. It did this by expanding the product range with more profitable items.

Percentage of revenue measures

On the left-hand side of the hierarchy shown in Figure 12.1 is a set of measures that express each part of the income statement as a percentage of revenue. This includes gross profit and operating expenses as subtotals, which are then broken down further into individual lines of staff costs, depreciation, administration, marketing, and so on.

The first level of these explores the proportion of revenue that feeds into gross profit and the amount of revenue spent on operating costs (see Table 12.15).

TABLE 12.15 **Gross profit and operating costs as a percentage of revenue**

	Current year	Previous year
$\dfrac{\text{Gross profit}}{\text{Revenue}} \times 100$	$\dfrac{5,490}{13,860} \times 100$	$\dfrac{5,110}{12,540} \times 100$
Gross profit	39.6%	40.7%
$\dfrac{\text{Operating costs}}{\text{Revenue}} \times 100$	$\dfrac{3,750}{13,860} \times 100$	$\dfrac{3,410}{12,540} \times 100$
Operating costs	27.1%	27.2%

Percentage of revenue measures are effective in monitoring trends, particularly when applied to types of costs. For example, the staff cost percentage should stay reasonably constant year on year. If the ratio starts to rise, the business may be paying too high rates or becoming less productive. Both are indicators of unsustainable performance that will lead to profit decline.

These percentage of revenue measures are a form of what is known as vertical analysis (see Chapter 11) and they provide a quick way to evaluate the cost structure of a business. This can also be a starting point for benchmarking, where the proportion spent on costs is compared with competitors within the same sector. For example, two consumer goods companies, Unilever and Mondelēz (formerly Kraft Foods), spend significantly different amounts on advertising and promotion. In the year to December 31st 2012, Unilever spent 13.2% of revenue whereas Mondelēz spent only 5.2% of revenue. This analysis would cause both businesses to explore where the right level of investment should be. Procter & Gamble, although having a different year end, spent 11.2% in the year to June 30th 2012.

For the example business some of the costs are increasing, indicating that it may be becoming less efficient. The increase in employment cost and administration may be signs of a head office that is growing faster than the rest of the business.

The cost reductions in research and selling may be helpful to current levels of operating profit margin and RONOA, but they do not support innovation and customer development, which is the basis for the future growth of the business.

TABLE 12.16 **Costs as a percentage of revenue**

	Current year	Previous year
$\dfrac{\text{Employment cost}}{\text{Revenue}} \times 100$	$\dfrac{2,310}{13,860} \times 100$	$\dfrac{2,060}{12,540} \times 100$
Employment cost	16.7%	16.4%
Using a similar calculation the other cost percentages can be calculated as follows:		
Research	2.9%	3.8%
Selling	7.9%	8.2%
Administration	9.2%	8.7%
Depreciation	10.0%	10.3%

Capital measures

Just as proportion of revenue measures are applied to the income statement to develop the margin concept, so capital measures are applied to the statement of financial position to develop the asset turnover concept. The first two measures are known as fixed asset turnover and working capital turnover (working capital is defined as inventory plus receivables less payables).

Fixed asset turnover monitors what is sometimes known as the "sweat" of assets. The purpose of assets is to work for the company and this ratio, which compares fixed assets with revenue, indicates how well this happens. Declines in fixed asset turnover are caused by either a reduction in volume of business or substantial investment that is taking time to become fully utilised.

A decline caused by volume reductions may lead to asset disposals to resize the business to its new trading level. A decline caused by substantial new investment will require a volume strategy to justify the investment that has been made.

Growth in this ratio may not always indicate success, as capacity constraints may emerge and the appropriate time for asset management, including maintenance and repairs, should not be compromised.

TABLE 12.17 **Fixed asset turnover**

	Current year	Previous year
Revenue	13,860	12,540
Tangible fixed assets	8,520	7,190
Fixed asset turnover	1.63	1.74

Table 12.17 shows that the fixed assets are growing at a faster rate than revenue. The business was earning $1.74 for every $1 of investment which has reduced to $1.63.

The ratio is normally limited to tangible fixed assets, the assets used operationally. If intangible assets are included in the ratio (or evaluated individually), the results may be inconclusive; the majority of these assets usually arise from acquisition strategy rather than operational performance.

Working capital turnover measures how effective a company is in managing the cash tied up in its day-to-day operations (see Figure 12.3).

FIG 12.3 **Working capital cycle**

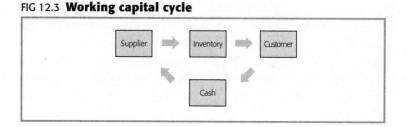

Cash is paid to a supplier who provides inventory. The inventory is converted to finished goods and held in the warehouse until purchased by a customer. The customer pays for the goods which brings cash back into the business. Both suppliers and customers have credit terms, so the key factor is how long cash takes to complete the cycle. Money tied up in this cycle has to be funded and can significantly drain the resources required for investment in assets.

Working capital = inventory + trade receivables − trade payables

For the current year this would be:

$$3,740 = 2,960 + 2,830 - 2,050$$

TABLE 12.18 **Working capital turnover**

	Current year	**Previous year**
Revenue	13,860	12,540
Working capital	3,740	2,860
Working capital turnover	3.71	4.38

East Coast Printers buys paper from its supplier and holds it in inventory. Some time later the supplier will be paid. As customer orders are printed, the inventory is used and invoices for finished orders will be issued. Customers take credit and pay their invoices. In total there is $3.74m tied up in managing this process.

Chapter 14 looks at how to manage this cycle more effectively and even make working capital negative by receiving money from customers in advance of paying suppliers. Mathematically this means the amount of payables is greater than the amount of inventory and receivables combined. The types of businesses that achieve this negative value include airlines, food retailers and insurance companies.

As well as looking at the ratio in total it can be broken down into the individual elements. These are usually referred to as day measures:

- Inventory days – the amount of time inventory is held on site from the moment it arrives to the moment it is despatched. The calculation is:

$$\frac{\text{Inventory}}{\text{Cost of sales}} \times 365$$

- Receivable days – the time taken for customers to pay their invoices. The calculation is:

$$\frac{\text{Receivables}}{\text{Revenue}} \times 365$$

- Payable days – the time taken to pay suppliers' invoices. The calculation is:

$$\frac{\text{Payables}}{\text{Cost of sales}} \times 365$$

In each of these three measures the denominator reflects an annual level of activity in the same terms as the numerator. For example, inventory excludes profit and therefore cost of sales is the best approximation to annual level of inventory consumption.

Table 12.19 shows that both inventory and receivables have increased, which ties up money, but the business has taken advantage by extending its credit from suppliers. Although this may not be sustainable, it has provided a way of retaining cash in the business. However, there may be a risk of losing prompt-payment discounts and even incurring late payment penalties.

TABLE 12.19 **Day measures**

	Current year	**Previous year**
Inventory days	129	94
Receivable days	75	59
Payable days	89	54

Once calculated, all these measures can be included in the hierarchy of ratios (see Figure 12.4) which is a useful way of summarising the operational measures for a business.

If budget data, a third year or even a competitor are added to the chart, the information will highlight weak areas even more clearly.

More operational measures

As well as the hierarchy of ratios, many industries and even businesses have developed their own ratios to help them manage the unique

FIG 12.4 **Hierarchy of ratios example**

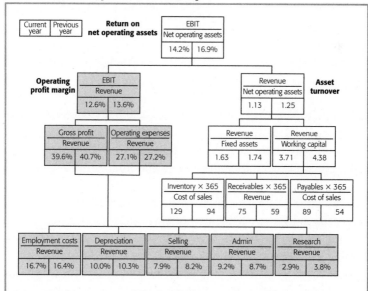

aspects of their operations. Some of these measures are also used by regulators to monitor businesses and provide early warning signals of those that may be in trouble. This is particularly important for the financial services industry to protect investors. Though in the run-up to the 2007–08 financial crisis the measures used neither indicated nor quantified the extent of failure that was exposed. Examples of these measures are as follows.

Employee ratios

In many businesses a set of efficiency indicators can be created by comparing the costs in the income statement on a per employee basis. These are calculated by taking each cost and dividing it by the number of employees in the business, as has been done for the administration cost in Table 12.20.

TABLE 12.20 **Administration cost per employee ($'000)**

	Current year	Previous year
Administration cost	1,270	1,090
Number of employees	46	43
Administration cost per employee	27.61	25.95

These ratios can be calculated using either the number of employees at the end of the year or an average of the numbers at the beginning and end of the year. Table 12.20 shows that the administration cost of running the company has risen from $25,950 per person to $27,610 per person, an increase of 6.4%. Although some of the increase may be caused by inflation and therefore expected, this increase is over the inflation rate and implies the business has become less efficient.

The ratio can be applied to all cost categories and is particularly useful in service industries where many of the costs are employment based.

Some industries, such as car manufacturing, develop this ratio further into man hours per product. This can be useful for continuous improvement programmes in highlighting where productivity might be increased by reducing the man hours spent on products.

Utilisation and revenue per customer ratios

For the group of businesses defined as infrastructure in Chapter 2 (such as hotels, airlines or telecommunications), the main focus is utilisation of their assets and the revenue they earn from each customer. Some of the typical ratios that are useful for this are as follows:

■ Hotels measure occupancy (the proportion of available rooms that are sold) and revenue per available room or REVPAR (with discounting and corporate rates this can be volatile and therefore becomes a focus for management).

■ Airlines measure similar attributes – load factor (the proportion of available seats that are sold) and yield (the revenue per passenger per kilometre, a measure that enables comparison between long-haul and short-haul routes). Over the past decade the load factors of airlines have been rising through the sacrifice of yield. For the low-cost carriers in the market it is discounted pricing that has been critical to customer retention.

■ Telecommunications companies use a measure known as ARPU (average revenue per user) to monitor customer spend. The number of minutes of usage is rising continually and the price per minute has fallen, so it is crucial that the combination of these aspects enhances the overall revenue per customer.

Retail measures

In the retail industry there are similar utilisation measures to those mentioned above. Retailers invest in buildings for which they need to get a high footfall (customers entering), a large basket size (spend per customer) and good use of space, which is calculated as revenue per square foot or metre and profit per square foot or metre. The combination of these aspects focuses management on selling high-volume, high-profit goods.

The profit per square foot measure can be developed further to look at effective use of shelf space rather than floor space. Food retailers also look at profit per cubic foot, which helps them monitor two aspects: the use of space by large items compared with small items; and the number of facings of each product to hold on the shelf.

Expense ratios

In financial services businesses, efficiency in managing the costs of processing and administration matters greatly. There is a range of ratios similar to the left-hand side of the hierarchy which compare costs as a proportion of investors' deposits and earned income.

Efficiency of capturing new business can be measured by expenditure per dollar of new business. Comparing this with past years or competitors shows the effectiveness of marketing and establishing new customer policies and accounts.

In fund management the charges and expenses are expressed as a percentage of the fund value and can influence both product sales and customer retention. Funds that grow well attract interest and new money; those that perform below average or have high charges are unlikely to generate investor loyalty.

Insurance companies monitor their pay-out ratios as a percentage of the premium income. The estimation of claim rates will be the basis of policy pricing and the monitoring of the amount paid out will show how accurate these estimates were.

Investment measures

Several capital expenditure measures help monitor the performance of the investment being made.

Reinvestment ratio

This is the relationship between capital expenditure and depreciation. If the measure is more than 100%, the business is investing more than it depreciates its owned assets and therefore growth in profitability should be taking place to make the investment justifiable. If the ratio is less than 100%, the business may be milking its assets and moving towards an unsustainable state where either the assets will require higher maintenance or significant new investment will be needed.

Investment funding

Where is the money coming from to fund new investment? By comparing the cash flow generated before investment and financing with the amount invested, a business can see whether it is growing through organic development or external support. In the early years of a business there is likely to be heavy reliance on external funding, but in the longer term this should decline and move to less than 50%.

Liquidity measures

In managing a successful business cash is often described as "king"; in other words, the most important resource to focus upon. Through the working capital measures it is possible to monitor the rate at which cash is being collected from customers and paid out to suppliers, and most importantly to determine whether there is sufficient cash available to meet liabilities and payroll costs as they fall due. Liquidity measures will also help evaluate this.

Current ratio

A common test of a company's liquidity is the current ratio, which is calculated as:

$$\frac{\text{Current assets}}{\text{Current liabilities}}$$

The objective is to achieve a value greater than 1. This means that the business has more near cash items (inventory, receivables and cash, all of which should become cash within a matter of months) than short-term liabilities.

There are many flaws in this measure. For example, to achieve a value greater than 1 a business could manage working capital inefficiently: keeping high levels of inventory, slowly collecting receivables and rapidly paying payables. Another flaw is the timing of when the year-end accounts are produced. In a seasonal business the year end may show optimal values which may have been significantly different during the previous 12 months. Similarly, month-end values may not be representative of the position during the month.

Liquidity is really about the ability to generate sufficient cash in the future to meet all liabilities as they fall due. There is no measure that can easily look at the future so this is seen as the best alternative. The availability of borrowing facilities is also a test of a business's ability to meet future liabilities.

Acid test

This is a similar measure to the current ratio, but looks at very near cash items only as the means to pay short-term liabilities. It is calculated as:

$$\frac{\text{Current assets} - \text{inventory}}{\text{Current liabilities}}$$

The objective, as with the current ratio, is to have a value greater than 1. Inventory is excluded as it has to become a receivable before it becomes cash, which may take several months, putting it outside the very near cash category.

The measure has similar flaws to the current ratio as it looks at the ability to meet liabilities as if no future cash would be generated from sales. The key to using both these liquidity ratios is to look at their change from year to year and how they compare with other companies in the same sector.

The balanced business scorecard

The measures described above are sometimes referred to as trailing indicators in that they are known only after the event and will not in themselves predict the future of the business. Although they can be calculated on projections within business plans and budgets to help direct the business to be more efficient, the predictive measures of an organisation's health are in the product and service elements rather than the numbers.

Many would argue that attributes of growing brand awareness, growing customer numbers, levels of repeat business from customers and even employee satisfaction are perhaps better indicators of the future. These measures contribute to a portfolio of measures that are both financial and non-financial and, in combination, help to measure and manage all aspects of a business. This is known as the

FIG 12.5 **Balanced business scorecard**

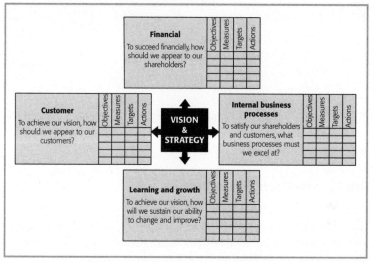

Source: Kaplan, R.S. and Norton, D.P., *The Balanced Scorecard: Translating Strategy into Action*

balanced business scorecard or company dashboard, which is a panel of no more than 20 critical indicators (see Figure 12.5).

Some of the typical measures used under each section in Figure 12.5 for an IT consultancy, for example, are:

- Financial (ROCE)
    - Cash flow
    - Project profitability
    - Profit forecast reliability
    - Sales pipeline
- Customer
    - Market share
    - Customer satisfaction results
    - Proportion of repeat business
- Internal processes
    - Tender success rate
    - Hours of rework
    - Project delivery delays

- Project hours over budget
- Learning and growth
  - % revenue from new services
  - Staff satisfaction survey
  - Staff retention rates
  - Employee suggestions

For more information on this concept see *The Balanced Scorecard: Translating Strategy into Action* by Robert S. Kaplan and David P. Norton.

Measures determine behaviour

In selecting measures to monitor a business and its performance, care is needed to make sure that the resulting behaviour is congruent with the overall business strategy. For example, an insurance company created a response measure for its call centre whereby the staff were told to answer all calls within three rings. Although admirable in intent, this new target led to the call centre staff being "short" with their customers so they could be free to catch the next caller. For those calls that went over three rings, there was no incentive to answer the call at all; such calls had registered as failures and the staff felt that they might as well keep themselves free, ready for the next customer.

Both these behaviours were contradictory to the purpose of introducing the measure at the outset. If staff are measured or rewarded on the achievement of a performance indicator, they will naturally orient their actions for maximum impact on the indicator regardless of the effect on company strategy or customer service. In setting any performance target, it is important to consider the way people may behave in order to achieve it.

13 Stockmarket and investor measures

THE STOCKMARKET is where investors buy and sell shares and make and lose money – in some cases a lot of money. To monitor the performance of stocks there is a range of measures that are regularly quoted in financial media showing absolute and relative performance of shares. This chapter explores a number of these measures.

Why are companies quoted on a stockmarket?

In Chapter 1 the difference was explained between a private company, where shares are typically bought and sold by the owner managers or a small group of investors, and a public company, where shares are bought and sold on the stockmarket. There are many successful private companies such as Cargill, an agricultural commodities and food business, and Mars, a confectionery and pet-food business. Both would be in the top 300 of the *Fortune* 500 biggest global corporations if they were listed on a stock exchange.

The advantage of a quotation on a stockmarket is the ability to gain access to equity investment by issuing tradable shares. Balancing the mix of debt and equity is a fundamental part of managing leverage (gearing) levels to provide optimum levels of WACC (see Chapter 6). Shares have an added advantage of no repayment date and no interest payments. This means that in the growth phase of a business the cash flow can be directed towards the operations and not the investors. The growth in share price provides the investors with their required return.

A stock exchange

Shares in publicly traded companies are bought and sold on a stockmarket. The New York Stock Exchange (NYSE) and the London Stock Exchange are two examples.

The exchanges make buying and selling easy. A stockbroker will act on behalf of its clients and trade on the market. If a client wants to buy some shares, the broker will place a buy order. However, it is not like a supermarket where there are products on shelves waiting to be purchased. At any point in time all the shares are owned by somebody (either an individual or an organisation). For a purchase to take place there must be someone willing to sell. If there are no sellers wanting to part with their shares, the marketmakers will raise the share price to entice a shareholder to sell and complete the trade.

If there are more buyers than sellers in the market, the price of a share will rise and vice versa. Brokers will not take more than a few shares onto their own book so trades have to be matched. Therefore share prices rise and fall as trades take place. Sophisticated investors watch this movement minute by minute when the markets are open to spot opportunities to make money out of even the smallest changes in price.

What drives a share price?

Although there are equal numbers of buyers and sellers at any share price, the views of the shareholders on whether the share price is rising or falling will be at variance with each other. Some of the factors that drive opinion, transactions and ultimately share price are shown in Figure 13.1.

The main factors can be categorised in three groups: track record, external factors and future expectations. The track record, comprising facts and attributes of past performance, is the most tangible of these groups, but it is perhaps the poorest at predicting the future potential of a business.

However, much management credibility is created by the delivery of a strong set of financial results, increased earnings and in particular a strong cash flow. If management has a proven track record and the

FIG 13.1 **Factors affecting share price**

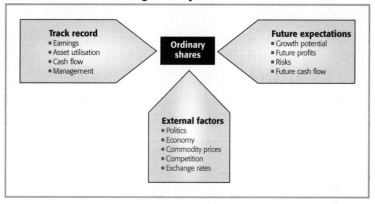

strength to exceed investor expectations, there is justification for trusting them to continue the process in the future.

The uncontrollable influence is the combination of external factors:

- A change of government will create uncertainty in the market.

- Changes in regulation, policy and taxes will alter the market conditions for businesses.

- Rises in interest rates and commodity prices can reduce consumer spending, which in turn can reduce demand across the economy.

- Events in the global economy will affect exchange rates and prices for dealing with foreign suppliers and customers.

Ultimately, the main influence on a share price is the expectation of future returns for the investor. This is a combination of the factors from all three groups, and expectations can be assimilated and then projected into the future to determine whether the current share price offers the potential for gain or loss.

Indicators of future growth potential

The P/E ratio

An important measure used by investors to compare future expectation with the current share price is a price/earnings (P/E) ratio. This is the share price divided by earnings per share and is a factor or multiple.

■ The share price is the current value from the market, and for active shares this will constantly move when the market is open.

■ Earnings is the profit generated by the business that is attributable to the shareholders and is after tax and interest. If the total earnings are divided by the number of shares in issue, a value of earnings per share (EPS) will result. The value is usually small and therefore expressed in dollars and cents.

For example, Coca-Cola had earnings in 2012 of $9,019m and 4,504m shares in issue; dividing one by the other gives an EPS of $2.00. This compares with a share price at the end of 2011 of around $36.25.

The P/E ratio is therefore:

$$\frac{\text{Share price}}{\text{Earnings per share}} \quad \frac{36.25}{2.00} = 18.12$$

Companies with different future expectations for EPS will have different P/E values (see, for example, the three companies in Table 13.1).

TABLE 13.1 **Earnings per share expectations (cents)**

Company	Now	+ 1 year	+ 2 years	+ 3 years	+ 4 years	+ 5 years
Company A	10	10	10	10	10	10
Company B	10	11	13	15	17	20
Company C	10	9	8	7	6	5

Company A has a constant rate of anticipated earnings per share, company B is expected to grow at around 15% a year and company C is expected to decline by around 13% per year.

A company that offers better future returns will be worth more. A crude benchmark for interpretation would be as follows:

- A company with flat performance trades off a P/E ratio around 10. Therefore company A might be in the market trading at $1 (that is, the share price is ten times the current EPS or it will take ten years at the current rate of earnings to pay back the share price). Some utility companies have this profile as their product prices are regulated and their earnings do not grow substantially.

- A company with high growth potential trades off a high P/E ratio. The higher the P/E number, the higher the growth expectations. Therefore company B might trade off a P/E of around 20 and have a share price of $2. High-tech or biotech companies are examples: Apple and Google have had P/E ratios of over 50 at various times in the past few years and typically trade at over 20.

- A company in decline will have a P/E ratio below 10 that indicates earnings expectations are getting worse. Company C might have a P/E of 7 and a share price of $0.70. Companies that are in old technology, out of favour or subject to adverse market conditions trade in this territory. The share price of airlines after a global terrorist event usually falls, making their P/E ratio a single digit. This reflects market uncertainty regarding consumers' confidence and willingness to fly.

The best way to judge the market expectations of a business is to compare the P/E ratio with a market index published in the financial media. If the market or sector index had a P/E of 12, shares with a P/E ratio above the index are likely to outperform and those below to underperform.

To make capital gains on the stockmarket an investor needs to select a share where the growth expectation in the market is less than will be achieved. Therefore, when the company actually achieves a higher than expected growth in EPS, the share price will rise. The greatest potential perhaps lies in very low P/E stocks, where a change of management can turn the business around and return it to growth, making the share price rise rapidly. However, failure to turn around the business can be the end of the company and a loss of investment.

The portfolio of share measures

Many of the portfolio of share measures shown in Figure 13.2 are covered in earlier chapters, and the P/E ratio and earnings per share are described above. Other measures are as follows.

Return on equity

Return on equity is earnings divided by shareholders' funds. It is the rate of return for investors as described in Chapter 6 and is the reward for the risk that the investor takes.

Dividend cover

Dividend cover measures the ability of the company to pay and potentially sustain its dividend. It is calculated by dividing the earnings by the dividend. The result is a measure of how many times the business could have paid the dividend. In mature companies this would typically be between two and three, indicating that the business pays out between one-third and half of its earnings each year. In the long term the ratio should stay constant or rise. Declines in the ratio indicate that the company is raising its dividend faster than it is able to generate the earnings needed to fund the payment.

The inverse of this ratio is known as the dividend payout ratio, the proportion of earnings that are distributed, which might be 30–50% for mature companies.

Dividend yield

Dividend yield measures the rate of cash return on a share if it were bought in the market today. If a company pays a dividend of 8 cents in a year and the current share price is $2.50, the yield is the dividend divided by the share price which, in this example, would be 3.2%. This is a similar measure to an interest rate on a savings account, though it is typically lower as the investor will be looking for not only this cash return but also a capital gain on the value of the share.

Market capitalisation

Market capitalisation is the value of the company and is calculated as the number of shares in issue multiplied by the current share price. If

FIG 13.2 **The portfolio of share measures**

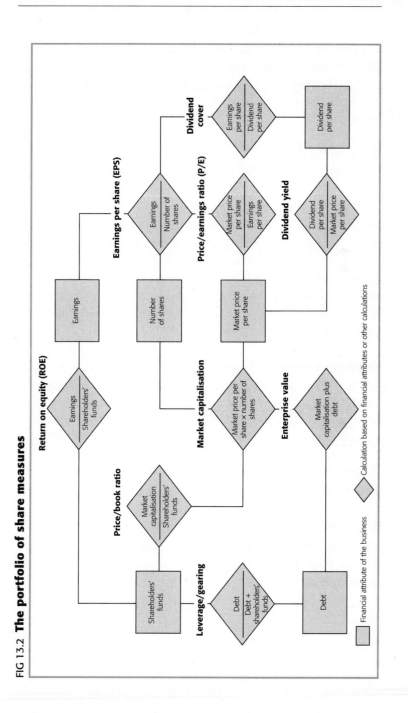

the business were to be acquired, the market capitalisation would be the minimum price that would have to be paid to buy all the shares in issue. To persuade all the current investors to sell, a buyer will have to offer a premium on the current share price, often more than 20%, making a takeover an attractive selling opportunity for an investor.

Price to book ratio

The price to book ratio measures the value of the company as a multiple of the net assets on the statement of financial position. For a branded company this multiple would be sizeable as the value is in the name, which may not be on the statement of financial position. At the end of 2012 Coca-Cola's ratio was 4.9 based on a market capitalisation of $163 billion and shareholders' funds of $33 billion. Compare this with a mining company such as BHP Billiton, where the price to book ratio is 2.8 as the value is in the physical resources in the ground. This ratio is a measure of the intangible value that is within the current share price.

Enterprise value

Much of this chapter looks at a business from the shareholders' perspective, but its profits and cash are earned on behalf of both the debt and the equity holders. If the market value of equity (the market capitalisation) is added to the debt, this provides the value of all sources of finance and is known as the enterprise value (EV). Expressing EBIT as a percentage of EV shows the return made on behalf of all investors.

The financial media

The financial media quote a number of attributes of shares. The *Financial Times* gives the following, and papers such as the *Wall Street Journal* are similar:

Name	Price	Change	52 week high	52 week low	Yield	P/E	Volume
Company A	52.06	+0.12	54.68	40.95	3.4	18.9	356,000

- Price is the closing share price at the end of the previous day's trading.

- Change is the share price movement that took place during the previous day.

- 52 week high and low are the upper and lower extremes of the share price during the previous year, indicating how the share has moved in the year.

- Yield is the dividend yield as explained above.

- P/E is the price/earnings ratio as explained above.

- Volume is the number of shares that were exchanged during the previous day's trade. As all shares are owned at any point in time the number represents the volume bought and sold.

Shareholder value measures

Since the 1980s and 1990s consultancies have developed new measures that have had supporting research to show they have found a better correlation between financial performance and share price for investors than those mentioned in Chapter 12. These are more commonly based on cash flow, removing the distortions that are sometimes created by accounting policies used in traditional profit measures. They also aim to reflect risk more genuinely than simple RONOA measures are able to. However, the more detailed the measure used to identify shareholder value the more difficult it becomes to understand and apply it.

Figure 13.3 illustrates the range of measures that are traditionally used. The measures start at the bottom left with basic revenue and profit growth measures which, although helpful in identifying the operating performance compared with previous years, do not correlate to shareholder value. The third measure shows the cash flow generated. This is the basis for any discounted cash flow analysis and is a better basis for a valuation, but it still ignores the amount of investment required to earn the surpluses. The middle section starts with the measures covered in Chapter 12, which are based on variations of return on investment, the most common measures in an organisation and good indicators of investor return.

FIG 13.3 **Shareholder value measures**

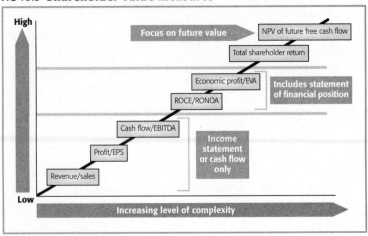

Statement of financial position measures are distorted by three significant factors:

■ Not all assets are on the statement of financial position; they may be rented or leased disguising the true investment required to fund the business.

■ The assets owned are normally held at historic cost less depreciation rather than their current value. This may be insignificant for assets such as equipment, but buildings can be substantially undervalued without a revaluation taking place.

■ The largest asset of goodwill (or brand name) is largely excluded from the statement of financial position, unless it arose from an acquisition.

Economic value added

Economic profit or EVA (economic value added), a measure developed by Stern Stewart & Co, an international management consultancy, looks at the profitability above or below the amount needed to satisfy investors. It is calculated as:

$$EVA = (R - COC) \times \text{Capital invested}$$

R = net operating income after tax/average capital
COC = cost of capital (weighted average cost of capital after tax cost of debt and equity)
Capital = total capital invested

In the Stern Stewart version detailed adjustments are made to arrive at the figures for net operating income after tax and cost of capital, so this measure has been described as "difficult" for operational managers to apply when evaluating the impact of their actions.

Total shareholder return

Total shareholder return (TSR) is a way for a publicly quoted company to express its overall return to shareholders for a year. The return will be a combination of share price growth and cash payments (dividends). Therefore, if an investor held a share at the beginning of the year the TSR would be the annualised growth rate received on that investment.

The calculation is as follows:

$$\frac{\text{Share price at end of year} - \text{share price at the start of year} + \text{dividends}}{\text{Share price at the start of the year}}$$

For example, if a share was $1.00 at the start of the year and $1.08 at the end of the year with $0.03 of dividends paid, the TSR would be:

$$\frac{\$1.08 - \$1.00 + \$0.03}{\$1.00} = 11\%$$

The measure can be applied to longer periods and then converted to an equivalent annual return.

The measure itself should be considered in a relative context rather than as an absolute value. For example, the market as a whole might have gone down by 10% and therefore a company achieving an overall TSR of 1% would be above average. Because of its nature, TSR cannot be calculated at a divisional level or for privately held companies.

Free cash flow

As explained in Chapter 10, the basis for valuing an investment opportunity is through discounted cash flows. This is the same for a business, so the value of the business is derived from discounting the future cash flows that it is expected to generate.

For valuation purposes the cash generated is known as the free cash flow (FCF), which is defined as the cash generated from operations less the interest paid, less the tax paid and less certain capital expenditure (see below). It is therefore the cash generated before dividend payments and any drawing on or repaying of sources of finance.

The calculation is as follows:

EBITDA	(Earnings before interest, tax, depreciation and amortisation.) The majority of income statement items are cash related, apart from depreciation and amortisation, so this is a good approximation for cash generated from operations that will be refined with subsequent adjustments
+ / − changes in working capital	To pick up the effect of cash tied up in or released from inventory, receivables and payables, the movement in each balance is included. For example, if receivables at the end of last year were $1.3m and this year they are $1.5m, an additional $200,000 has been tied up in working capital and should be deducted from the calculation
− interest paid	The cost of the debt that is paid
− tax paid	The amount of tax paid on profits which may not match the amount on the income statement as tax rules may allow tax payments to be deferred to later accounting periods

− capital expenditure	The money invested in new fixed assets. This number is normally split between two types:

- stay in business (SIB) capital – the money spent on the replacement and renewal of assets that are already in use in the business;

- expansionary capital – the money spent on incremental assets to expand operations (resulting in the creation of new revenue streams or saving of operating costs).

For the calculation of FCF it is only the SIB expenditure that is deducted; in other words, the FCF can be described as the cash flow effect of running the current business activities

= FCF	The cash generated from operations less the interest paid, less the tax paid and less SIB capital expenditure

Cash flow can be expressed as a per share measure much like earnings per share. The FCF for the whole business is divided by the number of shares in issue.

To value a business the FCF can be projected and discounted. Some organisations use an unleveraged FCF for this purpose, which means that the interest paid is removed from the calculation (as inevitable changes in leverage that would take place on a purchase of a business could potentially undervalue the business). The result is an enterprise value for the business from which debt can be deducted to value the equity.

Company valuations

As mentioned in the previous section, the basis for valuation is the discounted future cash flows. However, there are other measures and multiples that help validate the result. A valuation that is similar on all measures supports its acceptance.

The techniques for valuing a business are summarised in Figure 13.4. The base of the chart is split into the measures that are either

FIG 13.4 **Ways to value a company**

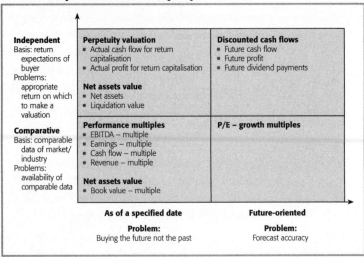

future-oriented or based on the current financial results (as of a specified date). The left-hand side of the chart is split into comparative (relative) and independent (stand-alone) measures.

Each of the quadrants can be explained as follows:

■ **Future-oriented comparative measures** – typically P/E based assumptions, taking similar businesses or a sector average P/E and applying it to the current earnings.

■ **Specific-date comparative measures** – a set of measures based on multiples of attributes: EBITDA, FCF, revenue and assets. In the dotcom boom, where start-up companies had no cash flow, assets or profit, the only measures available to value the companies were revenue multiples or even customer number multiples. The dotcom crash perhaps shows that valuations which are not made on cash flow are based on highly risky expectations.

■ **Future-oriented independent measures** – the discounted cash flow valuations which form the basis of most analysts' and merger and acquisition valuation models. Projections are made of future cash flows on which NPV (net present value; see Chapter 10) calculations are made.

■ **Specific-date independent measures** – a set of measures based on perpetuity calculations, which for dividend valuations are determined by Gordon's growth model as explained below.

Using this model a share price can be calculated using the future expected series of dividends, the growth rate in the dividends and the expected return required by an investor.

For example, if investors require a 10% return on their money and a company pays a dividend of $0.10 a year with no growth, investors would value a share in that company at $1. If the company expects its dividends to grow by 3% a year in perpetuity, the share will be worth more. The formula is as follows:

$$\text{Share price} = \frac{\text{Value of the next dividend}}{\text{Investors required return} - \text{dividend growth rate}}$$

$$\text{Therefore the share price} = \frac{\$0.10}{10\% - 3\%} = \$1.43$$

Because it uses a simple perpetuity growth rate, Gordon's growth model is generally applied only to mature companies with low dividend growth. The result is only a broad indicator of value rather than the basis of a transaction.

Under specific-date independent measures a break-up scenario or liquidation value can also be calculated. These are more relevant for asset-based businesses such as property companies than trading companies.

In bidding to take over a company it is crucial to decide how value can be added and why one acquirer can add more value than another. The highest bid is likely to come from the bidder who relies on one or more of the following:

■ higher expectations of value;
■ greater identifiable synergies;

■ lower acceptable returns.

Therefore the bid price is partly dependent on synergy gains, which are derived from several sources:

■ Economies of scale – where corporate functions provide services to the whole organisation, such as treasury, investor relations, human resources and IT, and can be used without necessarily incurring incremental cost.

■ Supply chain efficiencies – where the output of one part of the group is the input to the next; for example, tour operators owning their own airlines.

■ The buying power of the company as a whole – which enables input costs to be reduced for all parts of the company.

In an analysis it is important to state what assumptions on synergy have been made in deriving the valuation. Many organisations admit that synergies are often valued but rarely achieved, particularly when headcount savings form a significant part of the calculation.

Brokers and broker reports

The role of brokers is to buy and sell shares on behalf of their clients. In providing this service they also offer research reports to help guide clients with regard to the potential of various stocks. Their recommendations identify target prices that they expect a stock to reach and advise on whether an investor should buy, hold or sell the stock. An example of a rating system used by JPMorgan Chase is as follows:

■ Overweight – over the next 6–12 months, we expect this stock will outperform the average total return of the stocks in the analyst's coverage universe.

■ Neutral – over the next 6–12 months, we expect this stock will perform in line with the average total return of the stocks in the analyst's coverage universe.

■ Underweight – over the next 6–12 months, we expect this stock will underperform the average total return of the stocks in the analyst's coverage universe.

The analyst's coverage universe is the sector and/or country shown for each stock.

To compile their analysis, brokers will attend meetings with the company, interpret economic and market trends, and compare operations with sector competitors. This information will be used to develop a projection of the company's performance for up to ten years with simple perpetuity trends for the years beyond.

TABLE 13.2 **Principal measures found in a broker's report**

Metric	Explanation	Meaning
EPS	Earnings per share	Described above
CFPS	Cash flow per share	Described above
DPS	Dividend per share	The dividend paid out per share in one year
Payout ratio	Dividend payout ratio	The proportion of earnings that is paid as a dividend. For example, if EPS was $2 and the dividend was $0.80, the payout ratio would be 40%
ROCE	Return on capital employed	Explained in Chapter 12
ROE	Return on equity	Explained in Chapter 6
ROA	Return on assets	See return on total assets in Chapter 12
P/E	Price/earnings ratio	Described above
P/CF	Price/cash flow per share	This is a similar measure to P/E but it compares the current share price with the cash flow per share. In theory this is a more relevant ratio than P/E as investment decisions should be based on cash, not accounting profit

Metric	Explanation	Meaning
EV/EBITDA	Enterprise value/earnings before interest, tax, depreciation and amortisation	This measures the relationship between the cash flow generated this year (EBITDA) and the market value of the investors' capital (both debt and equity)
Dividend yield	Dividend yield on current share price	Described above
Net leverage (gearing)	Leverage (gearing) with cash balances deducted from loans	Explained in Chapter 6
BVPS	Book value per share	This is based on similar principles to the price to book ratio described on page 268. The calculation is to divide the shareholders' funds by the number of shares. This will typically be less than the share price as it will exclude the value of goodwill present in the business
EBIT margin	Earnings before interest and tax margin	See operating profit margin in Chapter 12

A forecast income statement, cash flow and statement of financial position will be created. A WACC (see Chapter 6) will be estimated, and by applying discounted cash flow principles (see Chapter 10) to the forecast cash flow a company valuation can be calculated. This value will in turn provide a target share price to form the basis of the recommendation.

Table 13.2 summarises principal measures used in brokers' reports. They provide comparative indicators over a ten-year period and benchmarks against other companies in the sector. The focus of the analysis is on profitability and cash flow generation.

Share options

The principal business of stock exchanges is trade in physical shares, but they also trade in share options in the major stocks. An option gives the holder the right to buy or sell a share at a predetermined price at some point in the future – for example, the right to buy shares in three months' time at a price set today.

An option which gives the buyer the right to buy a share is a "call" option. An option which gives the buyer the right to sell a share is a "put" option. The specific share on which an option is placed is called the underlying asset. The price at which the underlying asset is to be bought or sold is called the strike price or exercise price.

The buyer of an option is not obliged to either buy or sell the underlying asset; it is only a right that can be exercised. The originator of an option, the option writer, must be able to carry out its side of the transaction, should the option holder exercise its right.

Most options traded on exchanges are not settled by physical delivery (actually transferring the underlying asset) but by a payment of the value of the option at expiry. The value is the difference between the option price and the current market value. This value is either:

- out-of-the-money (worth zero), in which case the asset can be purchased for less than the option price – for example, an option conferring the right to buy shares at $5 when they are trading at only $4.50; or

- in-the-money, in which case the option price is lower than the market price – for example, an option to buy shares at $5 though the market price is now $7.

Traded options bought on exchanges are a means of having exposure to share performance without having to invest the capital required to buy the stock. The risk is much greater with options as they expire on a fixed date and may end up being worthless.

Some companies issue share options to senior staff as part of incentive and retention packages. For example, senior managers may be offered a right to buy shares in their company in five years' time at today's share price. This gives them an incentive to work hard, create shareholder value and share in the reward. If the share price rises over the five years, on expiry of the option the company will issue additional shares at the predetermined price. This will of course dilute the ownership percentages and the value of holdings for existing investors, but in practice the effect is minimal and is more than compensated for by the focus management has on driving value creation.

The effect of these staff options will potentially lower the earnings per share (see page 264). The normal calculation is to divide the earnings by the number of shares in issue, but there is another calculation that brings the effect of all the staff share options being exercised and turning into additional shares. This is known as the fully diluted earnings per share, which will always be a lower number than the undiluted EPS as the denominator is greater.

14 Working capital management

WORKING CAPITAL WAS DEFINED in Chapter 4 as the money tied up in inventory and receivables less payables. For most product-based businesses, the amount of money tied up in working capital can be substantial. For example, in 2012 Pirelli had over €1.8 billion of inventory and receivables and total debt of a similar amount, on which it was paying €172m interest a year. If it could reduce its inventory and receivables, it could repay some of its debt and related interest costs. This chapter looks at ways of managing working capital at an optimum level, using techniques for reducing the amount of inventory that is held, speeding up the collection of receivables and deferring the settlement of payables.

The working capital cycle is shown in Figure 14.1. There is often debate about whether cash should be included or excluded as part of working capital. Because cash is not "working" for the business, it is normal to exclude it from the calculation and limit the definition to just the trading items of inventory, receivables and payables.

The common measures used to monitor the levels of these

FIG 14.1 **Working capital cycle**

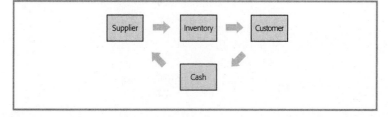

FIG 14.2 **Working capital management**

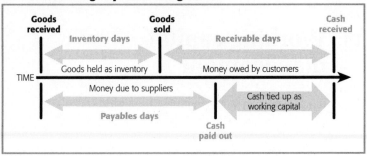

assets and liabilities are illustrated in Chapter 12. These are the day measures: inventory is measured by the number of days it is held for resale; receivables by the number of days it takes to collect cash; and payables by the number of days a business waits before settling its accounts with suppliers. The aim of effective working capital management is to minimise the number of days taken for cash to complete the cycle (see Figure 14.2).

The number of days for cash to complete the cycle is:

Inventory days + Receivables days − Payables days

It is possible to create "negative" working capital where inventory levels are low, sales are in cash (thus creating no receivables) and credit is taken from suppliers. This structure is found in food retailers and generates cash for the business, which can be used to fund property and equipment.

For a company involved in the automotive sector, the working capital cycle might be:

	Days
Inventory days	109
+ Receivables days	77
− Payables days	60
Working capital cycle	126

Compare this with a supermarket, where the working capital cycle might be:

	Days
Inventory days	15
+ Receivables days	0
− Payables days	28
Working capital cycle	−13

The optimisation of this cycle can be measured by the working capital turnover (as explained in Chapter 12). This is calculated by dividing revenue by working capital to give a value which is a multiple. Therefore as working capital becomes leaner the multiple will increase. However, this will not always be true, as shown in Figure 14.3.

Starting on the right-hand side of Figure 14.3, as a business lowers the amount of working capital (on the horizontal axis) the working capital turnover will increase, illustrating the efficiency that has been gained. If the business manages to reduce working capital still further until it becomes negative, the additional improvements will be delivered by a decrease in the ratio, showing that more cash has been released.

FIG 14.3 **Working capital turnover**

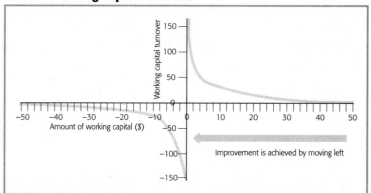

The techniques to manage these three items are explained below. The working capital cycle starts with the purchase of inventory.

Reducing inventory

Inventory is an inevitable consequence of trading in products. It can be in the form of raw materials, work in progress (known as WIP – products in the process of being manufactured) and finished goods ready for sale. There can also be spare-parts operations for businesses such as car manufacturers.

A business needs to hold inventory for the following reasons:

- as a buffer to manage uncertainty in supply such as lead times, quality and order fulfilment;
- to purchase quantities that are economic (see below);
- to ensure continuous production runs with a complete set of components;
- to stabilise manufacturing by using batch production;
- to cope with unpredictable demand and the desire not to pass up a sales opportunity;
- to provide customer choice.

The aim is to reduce inventory because it not only ties up cash in the business but also exposes the business to other financial costs, such as:

- storage – the cost of warehouse space, warehouse staff and any particular storage conditions (such as chilled or secure storage);
- management – the cost of management time in counting, finding, moving and inspecting;
- obsolescence – the risk that the product will become unsaleable if held for too long or because product enhancements are required;
- damage – the inventory has the potential to be come unsaleable;
- theft – the removal of inventory.

Inventory can be likened to a reservoir holding water. The "supply"

FIG 14.4 **Types of inventory**

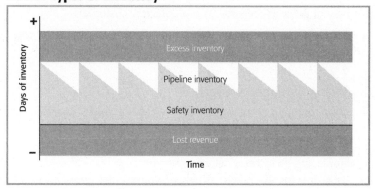

of rain is unpredictable and therefore replenishment is unreliable. A large reservoir enables demand to be consistently met (apart from at times of extreme drought). If supply were more reliable, the amount of water, or inventory that has to be held, could be reduced. Therefore to optimise inventory is to increase certainty in both supply and demand.

The profile of inventory is summarised in Figure 14.4. Time is shown on the horizontal axis and the level of inventory on the vertical axis. Four separate areas are identified:

- **Pipeline inventory** – the saw-tooth pattern in the middle of the chart. The points where it peaks represent inventory arriving followed by sales, causing inventory to slowly fall over the subsequent days or weeks. When inventory levels are low a reorder takes place and the amount of inventory climbs back to a peak.

- **Safety inventory.** This is buffer inventory to ensure sales can continue with the uncertainties in demand and supply. The amount of uncertainty dictates the amount of safety inventory that needs to be held.

- **Lost revenue.** When inventory runs out this area represents the sales that could have been captured. Although specific unfulfilled orders can be identified and measured, the impact on long-term customer behaviour is more important as dissatisfaction can lead to customer accounts being closed.

Managing and inquiring about lapsing accounts is an effective way of gathering feedback from defecting customers.

■ **Excess inventory.** The needless holding of inventory that wastes resources in storage and may become obsolete.

Reducing pipeline inventory

To reduce pipeline inventory a business needs to make more frequent and smaller orders. Although this will reduce inventory levels it may push up supply costs, and the business may lose out on volume discounts and incur extra delivery charges.

To deal with the potential loss of volume discounts on orders, a call-off contract can be established, whereby an annual purchase volume is agreed with appropriate discounts and when inventory is required in the business it is called off for delivery. The benefit of this approach is achieving the prices of bulk buying combined with the convenience of small deliveries and low inventory levels. This type of deal is appropriate only for products or services where an annual level of demand can be predicted with certainty. There are also advantages for the supplier, which will have a confirmed order and will be able to produce the inventory at slack times.

There is a well-established method for calculating an economic order quantity (EOQ) using the following formula:

$$\sqrt{\frac{2RS}{CI}}$$

Where:
R = Annual usage of an item
S = Ordering cost (in total not per unit)
C = Unit cost
I = Holding cost per unit for one year

For example:

Annual demand	3,000 units
Average order cost	€20
Item cost	€12
Average holding cost	25%

Applying this through the formula would suggest the economic order quantity is:

$$\sqrt{\frac{2 \times 3,000 \times 20}{12 \times 25\%}} = 200 \text{ units}$$

A graph of the relationship between holding cost and order cost is shown in Figure 14.5. Where the total cost line is at a minimum identifies the optimum order quantity, which is 200.

This formula is used to set a reorder quantity (ROQ), but in some inventory systems a reorder level (ROL) is also required. This is the amount of remaining inventory at which an order will be placed. There is a balance between running the inventory too low with the risk of missing a sale, and being overcautious and ordering too early. This is covered in the next section.

In principle, the strategy on EOQ will suggest that:

- high-value items should be ordered often and low inventory levels should be maintained;
- low-value items should be ordered infrequently and higher inventory levels should be maintained.

FIG 14.5 **Relationship between holding cost and order cost**

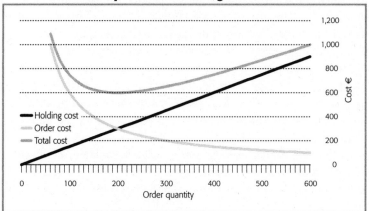

Reducing safety inventory

This is a combination of improved demand forecasting and supplier reliability. When these are worked through an inventory modelling tool, supplier reliability is normally shown to have the greatest impact on safety inventory, as explained below.

Demand forecasting

Demand forecasting is the process of predicting future average sales on the basis of historic data samples and market intelligence. The volatility of demand from an average level is supplied from the safety inventory.

Any forecast is likely to be wrong, so the focus should be on understanding the range of potential forecast errors and the level of safety inventory that will cater for peak demand. An important additional calculation is forecast bias. This is the cumulative sum of under- or over-forecasting over a period of time. If, for example, the staff continually over-predict sales there will be a negative forecast bias, which will result in excess inventory and vice-versa.

A good process for demand forecasting involves collecting information as far down the supply chain as possible. For example, orders or bookings are better than sales when planning inventories and production. When forecasting the average demand it must be adapted for products with seasonal patterns – for example, garden products in summer and festive products for Christmas. The customer demand needs to be anticipated and a final date for reordering determined. Historic patterns of sales volumes can be a valuable source of reference for identifying appropriate inventory and ordering dates.

In the retail sector, the weather can play a large part in consumers' desire to go shopping and what they will buy. Care needs to be taken to manage inventory and potentially use sale or return as a way to reduce the risk of being left with inventory after the period of demand.

There are numerous forecasting packages available, all of which use combinations of mathematical models to simulate and predict future demand. The most common basic forecasting techniques are as follows:

- Simple average. The average of a selected range of past figures becomes the forecast for future periods. The more past data that are selected, the more the fluctuations are dampened.

- Moving average. The average of a specified number of past sales figures becomes the forecast on a rolling basis (see Table 14.1).

- Exponential smoothing. A weighting factor called alpha (a value between 0 and 1) is used to place a higher exponential bias on recent data and a lower exponential bias on older data. An alpha near 1 decays past data quickly (or weights current data more highly) and an alpha near 0 decays data more slowly (putting more emphasis on past data).

- Adaptive smoothing. This is where the weighting factor alpha is automatically selected based on the previous period's forecast error.

TABLE 14.1 **A four-period moving average forecast**

Period	Actual demand	Four-period total	Moving average forecast
1	68		
2	65		
3	58		
4	61	252	63
5	50	234	59
6	48	217	54

Supplier reliability

The factors in supplier reliability cover both response time and quality. The more often a supplier is unreliable, the greater is the tendency for its customers to hold more safety inventory to compensate for supplier incompetence. By changing suppliers or improving existing supplier reliability, a business can reduce its safety inventory levels in the knowledge that the supplier can support the business efficiently. The main considerations are as follows:

■ **Response time** – the lead time from a supplier receiving an order and being able to deliver it. Sourcing supplies from another continent to drive down cost may be advantageous at one level, but it is likely to extend lead time (for transport) and require higher inventory levels to cover for uncertainty and potential delay. The risk of delays in supply can be passed back to the supplier in the form of guarantees and penalties, but the supplier providing the guarantee is likely to pass on the cost in its pricing, as it will with any fulfilment obligation imposed on it. The way to reduce response time and unit cost is to work with the supplier on how efficiencies can be jointly achieved.

■ **Quality**
  - supplier error (failures in fulfilling an order to specification);
  - short or delayed delivery (the inability to supply on time and in full, which is critical in supplier performance – failure on this measure can be one of the biggest contributors to holding safety inventory);
  - product quality (supplies that are not fit for purpose, damaged, fail in service or are not to specification).

Lean versus agile

In structuring a supply chain for sourcing it is important to balance each supplier's ability to manage demand response times with reliability and split requirements between supplies that need to be agile and those that can be lean:

■ **Agile** – the primary goal is revenue and growth. These are supplies where there is high volatility in demand and a quick response time to replenish is crucial. An example is fashionable clothing, where demand is unpredictable. Retailers need to be able to replenish inventory quickly should the product be popular, but they do not want to hold inventory in case demand is low. Agile typically means that products need to be manufactured near to the point of sale and therefore a short transport time is important.

■ **Lean** – the primary goal is cost reduction. These are supplies where demand is predictable and low-cost sourcing can be the focus. An example is basic clothing such as underwear, where retailers can plan volumes with reasonable accuracy and inventory does not become obsolete. As volumes are predictable, slow and lengthy transport is not a problem.

Managing the portfolio

As a manufacturing business grows it can develop an increasingly complex portfolio of products, variants, components, spares and sub-assemblies. The number of separate product items or stock-keeping units (SKU) determines the range of inventory held. A variety of methods can be used to reduce the value of this increasing investment in inventory.

Simplification and standardisation

The first stage in reducing the volume of separate inventory items is to simplify the range of products and components that are held. Some of the ways to achieve this are:

■ reducing the number of variants, such as sizes, colours, flavours or formats of products;

■ standardising components where products share common parts – many of the car manufacturers use this approach; for example, Ford and Volkswagen Group use common parts across their range of brands;

■ single sourcing to reduce safety inventory and make more frequent supplier deliveries economical.

Vendor-managed inventory

Vendor-managed inventory (VMI) is a process where a supplier will retain ownership of inventory and manage its provision within a customer's site. An example is greetings cards in supermarkets. There are numerous types of cards, slow rates of stock turn and complexity in co-ordinating the replenishment of shelves. Many supermarkets have entered into VMI arrangements with their suppliers: the supplier is responsible for shelf filling and the supermarket does not buy the product until a customer purchases it. The benefit of this approach for the supermarket is that there is neither investment in inventory nor disposal of unpopular or seasonal styles that remain unsold.

The same approach can be applied in manufacturing where contracts with suppliers can be structured for the provision of components straight into line-side storage areas. The management of lead times and safety inventory remains with the supplier. Penalties can be built in whereby a supplier is "fined" when a component has run out and continuous manufacturing is prevented.

Sale or return

Where there is uncertainty about the use or sale of a product the risk can be left with the supplier, with inventory being taken into a business on a sale-or-return basis. If the product is used it is paid for, and if it is not used it is simply sent back to the supplier. This involves no risk or inventory for the customer and is an efficient way to try out new product ideas and suppliers. However, because unit costs may be higher under such an arrangement, once volume levels are established it may make sense to revert to an outright purchase model.

Supply models

A range of supply models is used to decouple supply and demand. A supply model determines the point at which components are assembled into a finished product, committing a manufacturer to a particular variant of its product portfolio. For example, a car manufacturer that builds cars in advance of receiving a customer order needs to pre-select attributes such as paint colour and interior fabric. If the combination proves unpopular, the variant will remain in inventory a long time. However, if the car is painted and trimmed after an order is placed, there will be no need for inventory to be held and far more colour options can be offered. The disadvantage of this approach is the time delay between an order being placed and the finished product being delivered. Five types of supply model are listed in Table 14.2.

TABLE 14.2 **Supply models**

Style	Example	Inventory issues
Fulfil and sell from inventory	Retailer with lots of outlets	Limited range. Demand in each location may not even require high levels of safety inventory to be held in each outlet
Fulfil and deliver from inventory	Amazon with centralised distribution points	Delay in distribution and fulfilment of customer need. Demand is more predictable requiring lower levels of safety inventory. Greater range can be offered
Assemble to order	Dell with products built from sub-assemblies	Delay for production, though products can be highly tailored to customer requirements enabling a wide range of options and choices to be offered
Make to order	Restaurant where meals are made to order from pre-purchased raw ingredients	Personalised product provision enabling wide choice and minimal waste from pre-empting customer selection
Source and make to order	Shipbuilder where components and raw materials are purchased after an order is received	Long time to design and source before production can be commenced. Highly individualised products without any obsolescent inventory

Much of the advantage of "fulfil and deliver from inventory" can be gained by those that "fulfil and sell from inventory" by using central warehouses that frequently deliver to the outlets. This enables each outlet to maintain low levels of safety inventory.

The operational advantages and disadvantages of each model are illustrated in Figure 14.6. This shows that there is no ideal position; depending on the nature of the business and customer requirements, the optimum decoupling point can be identified.

Distributors

For businesses that have a large portfolio of products and a wide and diverse customer base, a route to market is to use distributors to manage the inventory and the high-volume, low-value transactions. An example is Unilever. The company distributes directly to major retailers, but small owner-manager shops have to source Unilever

FIG 14.6 **Operational advantages and disadvantages**

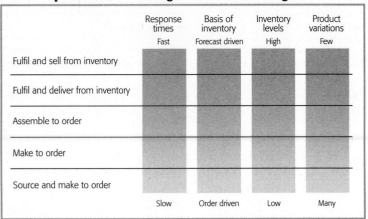

	Response times	Basis of inventory	Inventory levels	Product variations
	Fast	Forecast driven	High	Few
Fulfil and sell from inventory				
Fulfil and deliver from inventory				
Assemble to order				
Make to order				
Source and make to order				
	Slow	Order driven	Low	Many

products through a wholesaler. This means that Unilever delivers whole pallets of products to a few large customers. The distributors and wholesalers break the pallets down into individual cartons and products to sell in smaller units.

For Unilever, there are substantial cost savings in handing over the high-volume, low-value transactions. This is the principle of Pareto analysis or the 80/20 rule, which suggests that 80% of revenue is derived from 20% of customers and vice versa. The percentages may not be precise, but a substantial part of any organisation's infrastructure is set up to service a large group of small-value customers from which little profit is derived.

The advantage to the distributors is that they can consolidate the portfolio from a number of manufacturers (Procter & Gamble, Nestlé, Danone, Heinz, Coca-Cola, and so on) and derive higher value sales per customer than would be achieved from any single manufacturer.

Reducing receivables

In the business-to-business market customers expect to purchase on credit; inevitably, this will delay the receipt of cash from one to three or more months from the point of sale. In the consumer market cash sales are more common. Credit-card settlement, although similar to cash in speed of payment, carries a cost as credit-card companies charge a fee for handling the transaction which is equivalent to an interest payment for credit plus administration.

The credit terms that a business offers can be an intrinsic part of the overall customer proposition; for example, furniture companies that offer interest-free credit for a year or car companies that provide extended credit over three years. These terms aid sales but have a cost, which needs to be recognised, and a cash flow effect, which the business will need to fund. Accelerating cash collection may not always be optimal for the overall business model and therefore only actions that are consistent with the model should be considered.

All settlement involves the risk of bad debt from non-payment through companies becoming insolvent, credit-card fraud or even forged bank notes. Care taken in validating the counterparty and the means of settlement can reduce such losses but will never eliminate them entirely.

Credit checks

Before advancing credit to customers it is important to check that they are bona fide and able to pay. Typically, this would be through a credit check and perhaps a bank reference. These procedures do not guarantee payment, but they will usually prevent dealings with high-risk customers.

A credit check completed by one of the credit agencies will be an analysis of the customer's accounts and will be similar to the ratio analysis explained in Chapter 12. The areas of focus will include:

- evidence of a sustainable and profitable business;
- leverage of under 50%;
- track record of payment history;
- tangible net worth – the surplus uncharged assets available to creditors;
- the relative performance of the business compared to others in its industry sector;
- details of court judgments against the business;

- details of existing mortgages and charges taken by lenders over assets;
- details of directors and their other directorships.

From this information the agency will form its view on financial strength, risk and maximum credit limit.

Using a credit reference a business can create its own credit limit. The amount will typically start low and increase with good payment experience.

Once a credit limit is in place it is important to have procedures to prevent a customer from exceeding the limit. This is achieved by careful monitoring of the account and either suspending additional sales until the account has been reduced with a cash payment or by increasing the limit in line with good credit history.

Account management

When a large organisation receives an invoice there is usually a well-defined procedure for validation and payment. Smaller organisations will have similar systems, but they may not be as sophisticated. Failure to comply with these systems will trigger a rejection of the invoice and a delay in payment while the invoice is returned and corrected. Understanding a customer's invoice processing system is a simple way to ensure that there are as few barriers as possible to prompt payment. For example:

- **Purchase order numbers.** Many systems require a purchase order to be raised before any goods or services are accepted. The invoice needs to state the purchase order number to be approved for payment. The basis of the purchase order will be either a contract or a specific quote that has been provided.
- **Correct information.** Although this may be obvious, it is a common cause of invoice rejection. Errors include incorrect quantity (particularly if there was a short delivery), price (not matching what was agreed), discount (terms not agreeing to contract).
- **Incorrect address.** Centralisation of organisations has meant that transactional accounting may be based at a different site or

even in a different country from where the product or service was delivered.

An important response to having an invoice rejected is to make sure that the relevant staff avoid making the same mistake again. Their role should be as much about correcting the error as about putting processes in place to avoid it being repeated.

Aged debt report

Most accounting systems will be able to produce an aged debt report which lists all the unpaid invoices by the date they should have been paid. Payment of overdue invoices should be rigorously chased and some rules should be set, perhaps as follows: once an invoice is over 60 days old (overdue for payment), further sales should be suspended until the arrears are cleared; enforcement notices should commence after 90 days and legal proceedings to recover the cash after 120 days. A disciplined approach that is understood by customers helps to focus attention on the issue and encourage payment ahead of others that are less forceful. Getting cash in on time is one of the most important controls for any business.

Many accounting systems will report the status of customers' accounts at the end of the month, which may not be representative of the payment system they adopt. For example, many businesses pay their suppliers on the last trading day of the month which means the cash is received in the first few days of the next month. Therefore a customer account may look over the limit at the end of the month but be regularised a few days later. To manage the effect of this common practice, enforcement action should only be taken once cash sent in the previous month has been received (potentially the third working day of the month).

This process may not please customers, but it should be balanced against the risk of a bad debt. There are of course good and bad customers. The bad customers are those that demand considerable attention and do not pay their invoices. A business may be more successful by choosing not to deal with them and focusing on the good customers that are easy to serve and pay their invoices on time.

Changing the business model

It may be possible to avoid having, or to reduce the volume of, receivables by changing the business model, as mobile phone companies have done with "pay-as-you-go" services. Their original model was to have account customers who paid invoices once a month in arrears. For low-use customers the cost of issuing, collecting and even chasing small amounts was more expensive than the amounts involved. They therefore introduced the prepay service where the mobile phone company receives the cash in advance of the usage and the low-use customers spend their advance as they use the service. There is no bad debt risk and there is the benefit of receiving cash in advance. Some prepaid cards also have a time limit so that a proportion of cards will have a value that expires without any service being provided.

Changing the model can be a way to achieve an accelerated profile of cash receipts and a reduction in risk to the business.

Prompt-payment discount

A way to accelerate the receipt of cash is to provide an incentive, usually a discount that is well worth the customer accepting: 1–2% discounts on the invoice amount are quite common for payment within 30 days. However, this process has to be carefully managed as some customers will not only take the discount but also continue to pay late. Businesses that offer the discount may be reluctant to chase the missing part, particularly from important customers.

The percentage may seem high in relation to the cost of capital (see Chapter 6), but a business will save the cost of both administration time and despatching reminders if the profile of receivables is made more efficient by the incentive. In the UK utility companies offer a discount for payment by direct debit within ten days of invoice. The objective is to collect the huge number of small amounts as quickly and as efficiently as possible. The chasing process for the small amounts could well cost more than the invoice value, especially if reminders have to be sent out.

Converting receivables into cash immediately

For a new or small business, where cash flow may be tight and administrative resources scarce, it is possible to convert receivables into cash immediately. This is achieved by letting another business take responsibility for collection. Two common methods are as follows:

- **Factoring** – when book receivables are sold to a bank or other financial institution. The bank, often using client stationery to disguise its role, manages the collection process. It takes responsibility for issuing statements and chasing slow payers. There is a cost for this as the bank will charge an administration fee and interest on money advanced ahead of collection from customers. There is also the question of bad debts and who should bear the cost. Factoring is therefore structured either with or without recourse. With recourse means the bad debts are passed back to the business and the bank has a low risk (that is, the ability of the business to refund the money advanced). Without recourse means the bank has to absorb any bad debts and therefore it will want to check the credit history of the customers and charge a fee to cover itself for potential default.

- **Securitisation** – when the book receivables are sold to a shell (or new) company and investors, seeking a short-term investment, can make an appropriate return for the risk in collection. This type of transaction is appropriate only for large value amounts and was used by mobile phone companies in their early years as a way to accelerate cash receipts while they built their networks. It is also a way for small mortgage companies to operate – their size prevents them taking on too much debt so they build a mortgage book and periodically sell it off to fund the next book. This contributed to the collapse of some small mortgage companies in the 2007–08 financial crisis, mainly because the debt was sold without recourse. As mortgage payers defaulted the losses mounted, revealing huge exposures that were not apparent from the mortgage companies' financial statements.

In both types of transaction the counterparties are seeking to make a profit, so the decision on whether to use this approach is a result of careful cash flow planning, knowing the expected leverage position and anticipated WACC percentage (see Chapter 6) to determine the most cost-effective way of operating.

Making invoices and statements fun

Consumers usually expect a plain, buff-coloured window envelope to contain an invoice or statement. This does not entice them to open it or, indeed, pay the invoice. Organisations have an opportunity to motivate consumers to open the envelope and pay promptly by offering incentives, such as competition tickets or discount coupons. One mobile phone company included footballer collector cards, encouraging children to make their parents open the invoice.

Guaranteeing payment

When businesses trade across country borders the ability to collect cash becomes more difficult. There are potentially two legal systems operating and pursuing the customer can be expensive. Therefore a letter of credit (LOC) is used to provide a payment contract for goods or services. The LOC is an irrevocable payment undertaking drawn up by the customer's bank that binds the bank to pay a fixed sum of money to another party on fulfilment of certain criteria (the delivery of goods). The credit risk is therefore with the customer's bank and not the customer itself.

With international trade there is also the potential for government support, as governments are always keen to promote exports. Some will operate credit guarantee schemes which act much like insurance. For a small payment the debt can be guaranteed and on various conditions the government agency will pay the debt and assume responsibility for its collection.

Direct debit settlement

For consumers making frequent payments, typically for services or utilities, a way to take control of their settlement is to ask them to pay by direct debit. This is the process where the supplier is authorised to initiate withdrawals from consumers' bank accounts. There are strict controls on this; in the UK it enables funds to be withdrawn 14 days after advice of the amount to be taken. Although consumers need to have cash in their bank account for this to work, it is a highly efficient way to automate settlement and reduce administration costs.

Vendor finance programme

The credit terms offered to customers can be a significant part of the overall value proposition. This is particularly important for selling high-price consumer goods. The offer of extended credit with low-interest or even interest-free finance is common. The manufacturers or retailers offering these deals may not want to carry the cost of funding this credit and will therefore set up an arrangement with a bank, which takes on the debt and collects it in the same way as it would any normal loan. The incentive for the bank is that it will pay the retailer less than the amount it collects. For example, if a piece of furniture is on sale for $1,000 with interest-free credit, the bank will give the retailer, say, $900 and take the difference of $100 to cover the cost of interest until cash is received from the customer. These finance packages can be branded so the customer does not know the financial institution behind the transaction.

Funding construction projects

Many businesses invoice customers on completion of services or delivery of products. For businesses involved in construction projects, where there will be significant investments in raw materials and work in progress, a substantial amount of working capital can be committed. To offset this investment it is important to have a schedule of "payments on account" which match the investment or even provide a cash-positive position. To satisfy customers that they are paying for genuine work that has been completed, it is normal to have the work in progress "certified" by an independent expert. The advance payments need not be limited to just the costs incurred to date; they can also include a proportion of the profit that will arise on the whole transaction. The recognition of this profit is explained in Chapter 16.

Deferring settlement of payables

An important part of optimising working capital is to defer the settlement of payables. This might be the easiest of the three areas to control (as a business has the ability to dictate when payables are settled), but there are implications regarding the relationship this creates with suppliers and the overall image of the business. An abuse of credit terms will jeopardise the willingness of suppliers to continue supplying or motivate them to offer sub-optimal prices in an attempt to cover the cost of the credit provided.

The actions of a business that is trying to defer payment are in direct contradiction to a supplier that is trying to apply the principles of reducing its receivables. A contractual agreement is needed that is accepted by both parties and complied with for all payments. Without such agreement relationships are likely to become strained as each party pushes its preferred position. The attitude of suppliers at times of urgent need will be crucial, particularly if products are required at short notice or to a certain specification.

When to set terms

In setting up supply agreements, the easiest time to agree payment terms is when a supplier has the opportunity to win a new contract. The supplier will be hungry for the business and may be soft on terms as it concludes the supply agreement. Once the supplier is in place and the business's dependency on it grows, its position is stronger and terms will be more difficult to renegotiate.

One of the most common terms for settlement is to pay at the end of the month following the month of invoice. Therefore any products or services purchased in, say, March will be paid for at the end of April. Once terms have been agreed they should be complied with.

However, if a business is on the typical terms mentioned above, the most advantageous time to purchase products or services is at the beginning of a month as payment will not be required for 60 days, compared with purchases at the end of the month that will need to be paid for after only 30 days.

Supplier discounts for volume

Suppliers are keen to see their order books grow and consequently offer volume-based discounts that are justifiable through the economies of scale that result from large orders. Several types of discount are offered:

- **Order size** – placing large orders that are fulfilled with long and efficient production runs. The larger the size of order the higher the discount offered.

- **Delivery discount** – having one bulk delivery rather than several small deliveries enables efficiencies in logistics that can be encouraged with discounts.

- **Overrides** – annual discounts based on total purchasing during a year. Suppliers will often set these at levels above the previous year's volume to encourage growth. The temptation is to place a large order at the end of the year to hit the override discount. This will create high inventory and is likely to prevent the following year from reaching the volume where the next override discount takes effect.

In managing payables it is important to secure a low unit cost in sourcing. Bulk purchasing creates inventory and accelerates payables, but it may be more cost effective overall.

Prompt-payment discounts are also offered by some suppliers (see reducing receivables above). The cost of funding the accelerated payment needs to be balanced against the value of the discount achieved. If the WACC of the business is 12% (see Chapter 6), the prompt-payment discount needs to be more than 1% per month to be worth accepting.

To optimise the cost and cash flow benefit from suppliers it is important to set appropriate performance measurement for purchasing departments. If a department is measured on cost reduction, its staff will be tempted to give away payment efficiencies to secure higher discounts. The measures need to encourage a balanced response that minimises the total supply cost to the business.

Changing the business model

A way to avoid holding inventory and defer payables is to delay the purchase of products from a supplier until they are actually required in the business. For example, in a manufacturing business where there is a regular supply contract in place, it is likely that both the business and supplier will hold a buffer of inventory. The business will hold inventory to meet volatility in demand or delays in supply. The supplier will hold inventory to meet volatility in demand and to fulfil orders at short notice. By the two parties combining their inventory in one location, both reduce inventory and only hold one buffer to meet all demands. This involves the business providing the supplier with space to store the inventory and the purchase of inventory takes place as it is used in the business. There are several ways of doing this (see reducing inventory above).

The system can be further enhanced to include automated billing. This is possible because as products are made the number of components in each finished item is known. Therefore computer systems can identify the number of items that have been purchased from the supplier and using a price list an automated invoice can be generated. The invoice can be settled on agreed terms.

This whole process becomes highly efficient in terms of combining a reduction in inventory, a delay in payment and a reduction in administration (including fewer inventory counts, automated invoicing, a lack of invoice errors and automated settlement).

15 Published reports and accounts

TO HELP BOTH potential and existing investors understand how a business is performing the directors have a legal responsibility to publish a set of reports and accounts at least annually (for businesses listed on a stock exchange these can also be half yearly and quarterly – known as interims). To make sure the accounts provide a valid basis for making judgments about the business they have to be independently verified by auditors.

In most countries, once the set of reports and accounts is published it can be seen by anyone with an interest in the business (in some countries there is no requirement to make the accounts of private companies available). This includes not only the investors but also those interested in understanding the viability of the business such as customers (checking the business will be around to maintain their product), employees (to interpret their job security and pension protection), suppliers (to check that the business has sufficient resources to pay invoices as they fall due) and those interested in investing in or even acquiring the business. Although this publicly available document exists for all to see, it must be remembered that it only reports history (how well the business did last year) and gives little or no indication of what the future holds. The deterioration of many businesses has not been foreseeable from their published reports and accounts.

The reports and accounts must be prepared in accordance with legal and regulatory standards to make sure that they are comprehensive. The rules are not only detailed and extensive but also vary from country to country. This chapter explores the composition of the reports and accounts and how to read them. Chapter 16 provides an overview of some of the technical areas that are commonly encountered. This book is not intended to be a detailed reference resource for preparing published accounts, for which the regulatory authorities issue more appropriate publications.

The regulatory framework

There is a hierarchy of regulatory bodies that define the rules for preparing a set of reports and accounts (see Table 15.1). The rules are constantly evolving, now largely because of a desire for greater global harmonisation. The general ethos behind the new rules is to move the focus more towards the statement of financial position, increasing disclosure of the fair value of assets and liabilities. Some corporate failures such as Enron have gone undetected because of mis-statements in the statement of financial position.

TABLE 15.1 **Regulatory bodies**

National law	The legal framework has the highest authority; in Europe, EU directives rank above national law
International Accounting Standards Board (IASB)	This was created to produce International Financial Reporting Standards (IFRS) to harmonise reporting around the world
National accounting standards	These are being aligned as IFRS take precedence
Listing rules	National stock exchanges have additional reporting requirements for companies that are listed and increasingly require IFRS compliance

The evolution of published accounts

Published accounts used to be exactly what the title described, simply a set of accounts comprising a profit and loss account (the former name for an income statement), balance sheet (the former name for statement of financial position), accompanying notes and an audit report. In the 1970s this document, which had to be sent to all investors, seemed a communication opportunity too good to miss and marketing departments sought to embellish it with corporate success stories. As glossy colour printing became cheaper, the document took on a new format, with the first section full of reports, photos, charts and details typically found in a corporate brochure and the second section, containing the accounts, often printed in a smaller font on matt paper.

In the 1980s the regulations and disclosure requirements grew and the accounts become more comprehensive, making the booklet a more substantial document. In the 1990s companies started to split the two parts into two separate booklets: the annual report and the annual accounts. Now much of the annual report part is the essence of a company's website, leaving the accounts as a comprehensive set of business reports and financial information – almost back where they started, but far more detailed and prescriptive in their format. However, format and structure of the accounts still give the impression that they are designed to deter rather than absorb a reader.

Typical contents of a set of reports and accounts

Although each company produces its own personalised set of reports and accounts, the typical set is shown in Figure 15.1.

The heart of the document comprises the five financial statements. Around these is the supporting financial information comprising the accounting policies, the detailed notes and disclosures and the audit report. In a set of reports and accounts these are usually presented after the financial statements.

The annual reports, which are represented by the outside layer, make up the first half of the document and consist of executive business reviews and committee reports.

To understand the components within the reports and accounts it may be helpful to look at examples as you read the remainder of this chapter. The reports and accounts can be downloaded from the websites of any large and many small companies. Select a company that you are interested in and go to the "investor relations" part of its website. There is usually a section for reports, and the annual reports and accounts can be found either in one document or in two: annual reports and annual accounts.

American companies or companies that have their shares traded in the United States must produce their accounts in the format for

FIG 15.1 **Layers of reports and accounts**

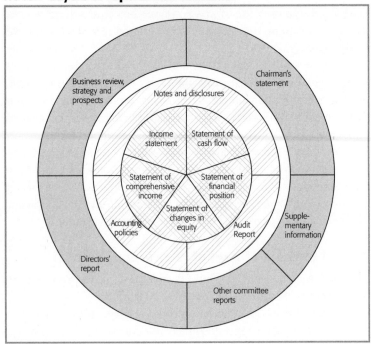

filing with the Securities and Exchange Commission. For American companies that are publicly traded and private companies that are over a certain size, this is known as a 10K report and must be filed within 60 days of the year end. Foreign companies that are publicly traded in the United States must file a 20F report within six months of the year end.

The financial statements have five parts:

- Income statement
- Statement of comprehensive income
- Statement of changes in equity
- Statement of financial position
- Statement of cash flows

To enable business performance to be interpreted from these statements the current results are shown beside those for the previous year. Thus improvements and deteriorations can be easily identified. Where there have been changes in the business or in accounting policy or material errors, the previous year's numbers are adjusted to make comparisons possible on a like-for-like basis. (Changes in the basis of accounting measurement do not require previous year restatement, such as changing the depreciation period for an asset from five years to four years.)

The income statement, statement of financial position and statement of cash flows are explained in Chapter 4. The two other statements are needed to reconcile the changes that have taken place in shareholders' equity during the year. This includes items that are taken directly to reserves rather than passing through the income statement.

Statement of comprehensive income

This extends the income statement to cover the non-trading activities that are taken direct to reserves such as revaluations in property, pension funds and assets held in foreign currencies. The typical layout is as follows:

Profit for the year (profit after interest and tax, but before any distributions)

$+/-$ Asset revaluations

$+/-$ Pension fund deficit revaluations based on actuarial valuation of defined contribution pension schemes

$+/-$ Foreign exchange revaluations (see Chapter 16)

$+/-$ Other comprehensive income such as gains and losses on hedging instruments

Total comprehensive income

Statement of changes in equity

This reconciles the changes that have taken place in shareholders' equity during the year. Shareholder's equity includes share capital, retained profit and other reserves. The typical layout is as follows:

Opening balance on each item within equity (this means it is a normally a multi-column report showing the opening balance of shares, share premium, retained profit and other reserves)

$+/-$ Total comprehensive income
$-$ Payment of equity dividends
$+$ Share issues
$-$ Share buy-backs
Closing balance on each item of equity

Following these statements are notes that provide the supporting schedules and disclosures, giving details of each of the significant items on the financial statements.

Supporting financial information

The accounting policies and detailed notes provide information about the financial statements. The audit report gives an independent opinion on whether the reported financial information provides a true and fair view of the company, not a guarantee that all the figures are correct. It is therefore important to read the audit report when analysing company performance to make sure that it is not qualified (see the section on the audit report below).

Accounting policies

As has been seen in many of the chapters in this book, finance is as much a matter of judgment as it is fact. For example, the expected useful life of an asset for depreciation purposes is a judgment (as explained in Chapter 5). The accounting policies note is a description of all the significant accounting bases (or judgments) that have been selected as being the most appropriate way to record the activities of the business; for example, the depreciation period and method that are used for each type of asset. The accounts of Cathay Pacific state that the accounting policy for depreciation of flight equipment (aircraft) is to use the straight-line basis over a period of 20 years. Other policies cover revenue recognition, basis of valuing inventory and so on.

The accounting policies a company applies in its accounts are the choice of the directors, but they will have been reviewed by the company's auditors to make sure they are appropriate and have been consistently applied.

When comparing the financial performance of one business with a competitor, it is useful to know whether they have consistent accounting policies as this will help explain any differences. For example, an airline that depreciates its aircraft over 25 years will have a lower depreciation charge than one which depreciates its aircraft over 20 years.

Notes and disclosures

The notes to the accounts combine detailed explanations of the figures in the financial statements with additional disclosures to help readers appraise the financial condition of the business. For major international companies the number of notes will typically exceed 40 and run over as many pages. Each line of the financial statements identifies the note number to which it is linked, so this information can be read in conjunction with the relevant financial statement.

Such information is hugely valuable to competitor businesses as they can interpret items such as margins, customer terms and investment activity. Therefore businesses are keen to disclose the minimum information that meets the legal requirement. Consequently, the structure usually blandly follows the law rather than being embellished with interesting supplementary details.

The amount of information that is shown in a set of accounts depends on the nature and scale of business activities. The overview of common notes in Table 15.2 is typical of a substantial business. Many of the details would not be relevant for a small business. The first note typically concerns the accounting polices so the numerical analysis normally starts at note 2.

TABLE 15.2 **Notes to the accounts**

Note	Explanation
Supporting information providing further analysis of each line in the financial statements (primarily the income statement and statement of financial position)	Explanation of the component parts that make up the summarised number that appears on the face of the financial statements. For example, inventory on the statement of financial position will be separated in the notes into the amount of raw materials, work in progress and finished goods. Costs on the income statement will be separated into materials, staff costs, depreciation, transport, and so on
Segmental information	Small businesses may have one principal activity taking place in one country, but a multinational will have many activities in many countries. For readers to understand the performance of these large organisations the financial statements need to be split into geographical region as well as business activity. Summarised income statements and statements of financial position will be shown for each part
Auditors' remuneration	The amount paid to an accounting firm for audit work and other services has to be disclosed in a UK set of accounts (though not in the notes to accounts in many other countries). The information is of interest in interpreting their independence. Sizeable fees mean the company is a valuable client
Acquisitions and disposals	Details of the companies that have been bought and sold in the year. This includes the value of each transaction and amount of goodwill paid for on purchases (see Chapter 16)
Earnings per share	The income after tax divided by the number of shares in issue (see Chapter 13 for details about how this measure is calculated)
Deferred tax	Tax is normally paid on the income earned in the financial year; however, tax rules can mean that it is deferred or accelerated to a different financial year. Therefore a company can have a deferred tax liability (tax that will be payable in a future financial year which relates to activities in the current or previous year) or a deferred tax asset (tax payable in a past year which relates to activities that will happen in a future year). With deferred tax it is a question of recognising the timing difference between when an income is earned and when the tax on that income is paid

Note	Explanation
Financial instruments	To protect a company from the volatility of external factors such as foreign-exchange rates and interest rates it can use financial instruments that fix or hedge against future movements in rates (see Chapter 16). The extent of these instruments has to be explained so that readers will understand the exposure of the business to global events which may cause sudden movements in rates
Share options granted to executives and employees	As part of an executive incentive plan, management may be granted share options. These allow them to buy shares at a future date based on a predetermined price. The benefit to the investors is that it encourages their actions to be congruent with shareholder value creation as they personally gain from increases in the share price (see Chapter 13)
Pension/retirement benefit fund report	Organisations that offer their staff a defined benefit pension scheme have to report the position of the assets and liabilities in the scheme. The two main types of scheme were explained in Chapter 5. In recent years many companies have found that their defined benefits schemes (where the payments on retirement are linked to final salary and years of service) have a shortfall in assets to meet their future obligations. The note has to explain the assumptions used to derive the present value of future obligations (using discounted cash flow techniques as explained in Chapter 10) and the current value of scheme assets. Although the assets are held separately from the business and not shown on the statement of financial position, any deficit or surplus in the pension fund is shown. The note needs to describe how the company plans to close any gap and thereby fulfil its obligation to its staff. The risk for employees is that the company does not have sufficient resources to close the gap and the pension scheme will not be able to meet the contracted expectations
Contingent liabilities (guarantees and indemnities and lawsuits)	A contingent liability is a condition that exists at the statement of financial position date but the outcome will be known only by the occurrence of one or more uncertain future events; for example, a guarantee offered (that may or may not need to be called upon), or a lawsuit (where a company has substantial litigation that may result in a cost or benefit). A good illustration of this is to be found in the financial statements of Dow Chemicals, which have several pages of contingent liabilities in the form of lawsuits for damages caused by asbestosis, silicon breast implants and pesticides, and environmental damage

Note	Explanation
Commitments (future obligations, typically leases)	As the financial statements are based on reporting history, this note is used to identify the future obligations that the company has entered into; for example, the placing of a substantial purchase order (such as airlines buying future aircraft) or lease agreements that contractually require the company to make future payments for use of the property
Related party transactions	Material transactions entered into with related parties are clearly of significance to the readers of financial statements because they may not have taken place on an "arm's length" basis. Therefore details help readers understand the nature of these transactions. Related parties include companies where there are direct investments or common investor ownership and control
Principal investments	Large organisations are likely to have evolved by buying businesses and this section lists the primary companies that form the group results (see Chapter 16 for details of a group structure)
Post-statement of financial position events	These are substantial events that have happened since the end of the financial year; for example, events that change the judgments made, such as revised inventory valuation or settlement of litigation. Information on an acquisition or disposal will also be disclosed

Audit report

Independent auditors are appointed by the shareholders to report on whether the financial statements prepared by the directors provide a true and fair view of the financial position of the company.

The audit covers only the financial statements (which include the accounting polices and notes); the executive business reports and committee reports are excluded. However, auditors are unlikely to sign their report if there are statements in the first half of the document that are either inconsistent or discordant with the numbers presented in the second half.

A "clean" or "unqualified" audit report is one that says the financial statements provide a true and fair view and are free from material error. There are four types of "qualified" reports:

- "subject to";
- "except for";
- disclaimer (unable to form an opinion);
- adverse (the accounts do not provide a true or fair view).

A company that has a qualified report will find it difficult to maintain loan finance and take credit from suppliers. Where possible, directors and management will take steps to rework their accounts and resolve issues so a clean opinion can be formed.

Annual reports

The structure of the annual reports can vary considerably from company to company, but some of the typical contents are listed in Table 15.3. This section may be prepared by a public relations department and therefore it is often criticised for being "good news" reporting, sharing all the strengths in the business and usually thin on any difficulties experienced. Readers of a set of reports and accounts should not base their judgment on this part alone as they are likely to come away with a rosy and warm view.

TABLE 15.3 **Contents of the annual reports**

Key results	An overview of the business and a list of around five key measures typically showing revenue, income, EPS, cash flow and ROI. Management can select the measures they want to show or omit this part altogether, and often those selected are ones that, when plotted, provide nicely climbing graphs
Chairman's statement/ message from chairman	A short summary of the main events in the year and significant developments that will happen in the next year. It always ends with thanks to those that made it possible, in particular the staff
CEO review or management discussion	This is a more detailed analysis of the company's performance by business area or region. The expectations or strategy for the future are often general or based on information already in the public domain. The competitive implications of revealing anything more informative mean it is always light on detail. It is rare that companies will commit to specific numbers in terms of performance and growth projections, as they are creating a target that can only generate criticism when it is not achieved

Directors' report	A summary of important details about the company ranging from a statement of the principal business activity through to amounts paid in charitable and political donations
Financial review	An overview of financial performance, significant events during the year, measures and changes to accounting policies or reporting. More recently, an overview of risk factors in the business model has also been included.
The board and remuneration	The directors have to disclose information about themselves (profile and background) and also their pay, pension and share options, so that investors can form a view on their expertise and the level of their remuneration
Corporate governance	A report to show the company's commitment to operating at the highest level of business principles and ethical standards. It will describe the code of practice, methods for ensuring compliance and review systems. For US listed companies this will also include compliance with Sarbanes-Oxley (see Chapter 3)
Audit committee	A monitoring committee made up of non-executive or external directors with three purposes: ■ to review the financial statements to ensure they fairly reflect the business; ■ to review the company's system of internal controls; ■ to oversee the external audit process. The report describes the terms of reference and the work completed on behalf of the shareholders to ensure sound financial governance
Nominations committee	A committee made up of non-executive or external directors with two purposes: ■ to hire (and if necessary fire) board members; ■ to monitor the performance of board members. The report notes the details of board changes that the committee has overseen during the year
Remuneration committee	A committee made up of non-executive or external directors which sets the remuneration package (including pay, pension and share options) for the board and senior management. The group, acting in the best interest of the company, has to balance the need for hiring the most suitable talent with the cost of attracting and retaining that talent
Corporate responsibility	The organisation's statement of responsibility and a summary of initiatives taken towards improving safety, health and environmental performance. The latter often involves describing programmes for using more sustainable resources and reducing the organisation's carbon footprint

5–10 year record	A set of headline numbers, operating statistics and measures to show the growth and evolution of the business. Walmart, an American retailer, shows 11 years of data. The better looking the trends the longer the period that is shown. Companies with chequered histories often limit or exclude this information
Glossary	Businesses in specialist sectors such as insurance or airlines use industry-related terminology and measures. To help readers they provide a short glossary of the terms that have been used in the reports and accounts
Investor relations	A summary of investor matters consisting of the financial calendar (for dividend payments) and share prices at quarter dates

The reports and accounts constitute a substantial document which provides a wealth of corporate information as well as insights and benchmarks for interested parties.

16 Accounting complexities

MOST DAY-TO-DAY BUSINESS TRANSACTIONS involve buying in resources (people, materials or equipment), combining them and selling them in the form of goods and services. There are also more complex transactions such as buying companies, managing long-term projects and international trading, which has foreign-exchange implications. This chapter explores the principles in accounting for these more complex matters.

Buying companies

Growth in a business can be achieved either organically (expanding existing operations) or through acquisition (buying other existing businesses). The acquisition route is a quicker way to build scale, but it requires careful planning to make sure that the value of what has been acquired is retained, for example employees or loyal customers. Acquiring another business can be achieved by:

- purchasing the assets, such as buildings and equipment; or
- buying a majority of the shares in the business.

The second method, where one business (the bidder) buys another business (the target), is more common. As shareholders are the owners of a business, the purchase of shares by the bidder is equivalent to buying control of the target. The amount of control is normally determined by the owned proportion of the available shares. Hence bidders that buy 1% of the shares will have little or no influence over the way and direction in which the target company is run; whereas an entity that buys over 50% will normally have complete control as no other investor or group of investors can outvote them. However, in some companies there are different categories of shares with different voting powers: for example, at Ford, an American automotive company, the 50 or so members of the Ford family have 40% control of the company through B shares, even though they own less than 4% of the shares. Google and Facebook have similar structures to maintain their founders' control. In this chapter it is assumed that the share ownership proportion determines the level of control.

Once a target has been acquired, the owner (often known as a holding or parent company) has to produce financial statements to show not only how its own business has performed, but also what has happened to the investment it made in the target. Unfortunately, this cannot be done simply by supplying the financial statements of the target; instead a "consolidated" set of accounts has to be produced that adds together all the investments as if they were one business. The process of adding businesses together is not straightforward and is based on two factors:

■ the level of control exercised (which defines how much of each business should be included);

■ how any premium paid on acquiring the target (known as goodwill) should be presented.

FIG 16.1 **Group structures and their treatment in consolidation**

Holding company	Investment	Income statement	Statement of financial position
Investment	Under 20% control	Dividends	Cost
Associate	At least 20% but less than 50% control	Share of profits and losses	Share of net assets
Joint venture	50% control	Share of profits and losses	Share of net assets
Subsidiary	At least 50% control	Include 100% and show minority interest	Include 100% and show minority interest

Levels of investor control

Depending on the proportion of shares acquired, the level of investor control determines how a business will be included in the consolidated accounts. There are four main levels of control over another business as defined in the International Financial Reporting Standards (IFRS):

■ A holding of under 20% is known as an investment.

■ A holding of 20% or more but less than 50% can exercise significant influence and is known as an associate.

■ Where the holding is exactly 50% with another party this is a joint venture – at this level neither party has overall control.

■ Where the holding company has more than 50% control this is a subsidiary.

The differences in the way these are treated in the income statement and statement of financial position are illustrated in Figure 16.1 and explained in more detail in Table 16.1.

TABLE 16.1 **Details of group structures and their treatment in consolidation**

	Income statement	Statement of financial position
Investments	Dividends from investments are shown as finance income, which appears on the income statement after the line of operating income	Held as a fixed asset investment at original cost or a lower written-down amount based on a permanent diminution of value (not a temporary loss)

	Income statement	**Statement of financial position**
Associates and joint ventures	The holding company's share of net profits after tax, shown as a separate item after finance income. For example, if an associate had earnings of $100,000 and the shareholding was 30%, $30,000 would be shown on the income statement	On acquisition the fair value of the net assets of the associate or joint venture is shown at cost on the statement of financial position as a fixed asset investment known as equity accounting and for joint ventures as gross equity accounting because of the additional disclosures required. In subsequent years this is adjusted for the holding company's share of earnings which is recognised on the income statement less any dividends received by the holding company. Therefore, if the cost was held at $120,000, the value would be increased by the earnings of $30,000 to show a value of $150,000
Subsidiary	As the holding company controls the subsidiary, all its revenue and costs are added to those of the holding company on each line of the income statement. Although the subsidiary may be controlled by the holding company, not all of the subsidiary may be owned by it. For example, in a 75% owned subsidiary all the revenue and costs will be added to those of the holding company, but at the foot of the income statement the proportion of the subsidiary that is not owned by the holding company is removed as a minority interest. This leaves only the earnings that are attributable to the shareholders of the holding company	As with the income statement, all the assets and liabilities of the subsidiary are added to those of the holding company. In the equity section the shares will be only those of the holding company. The reserves will be those of the holding company plus the holding company's share of the subsidiary company's earnings since it was acquired. There will also be a minority interest, which represents the minority's share of the net assets of the subsidiary. Goodwill from the acquisition will also arise (see below)

Table 16.2 summarises part of the income statement to show how the income presentation of all these levels of shareholding would appear.

TABLE 16.2 **Income presentation of levels of shareholding**

	$'000
Operating income (revenue less trading costs of holding company plus 100% of subsidiaries)	100,000
Finance cost (interest on debt)	(23,000)
Finance income (dividends from investments)	5,000
Share of profit after tax from joint ventures and associates	9,000
Taxation	(28,000)
Net income/earnings	63,000
Attributable to minority interest	7,000
Attributable to shareholders	56,000

Benefits of different investment levels

A business might choose a particular investment level for two reasons:

- **Risk sharing.** Where a venture involves substantial initial investment with uncertainty of reward, it may be advantageous to bring two or more parties together to share the risk. For example, oil companies will share projects where there are considerable exploration uncertainties and mutual benefits from pooling experience and sharing risk.
- **Protecting profitable activities from start-up losses.** On the income statement the financial results of a holding of 50% or less in a business is a single-line entry shown below the line of operating income. Therefore headline income numbers can be protected from showing any losses that arise in an associate or joint venture. By setting up share option agreements, a holding company can increase the proportion of its investment once a venture has become profitable and is worth including with other results as a subsidiary.

Accounting for an acquisition

When acquiring a controlling interest in a business the purchase price will be based on the value of the business as an earning machine, rather than the market price of the assets on its statement of financial position (see Chapter 13 for business valuation principles). However, a share of the statement of financial position is what is actually acquired, with the remainder of the purchase price being an expectation of potential rather than substance. The expectation part is known as goodwill, which is defined as the cost of acquisition less the fair value of net assets acquired.

For example, if a business is acquired for $3 per share and the fair value of the net assets is $1.20 per share, the goodwill will be $1.80 per share. Goodwill represents the value of assets that are not on the statement of financial position, such as the employees, knowledge, brand, customer base and supplier base, which provide the trading momentum to the business and thus its earning potential.

Goodwill arises when producing a consolidated set of accounts because the purchase price paid by a holding company for shares in a subsidiary is replaced by the individual assets and liabilities acquired as if the companies were one business. The goodwill is treated as an intangible fixed asset on the statement of financial position. As time passes the value of the goodwill paid on acquisition may not be maintained as competition may reduce the customer base, or new technology may cause the attractiveness of the products and the value of knowledge to fade. A set of accounting rules has evolved to account for the effect of fade. Initially, goodwill was written off to reserves. Accounting standards were amended to require it to be amortised over a period of time, such as 20 years. This was based on the assumption that after 20 years there was unlikely to be any of the original goodwill still driving earnings. This view has changed and in IFRS instead of amortising goodwill, the board of directors have to complete an annual impairment review of goodwill (and other assets) to make sure they can justify the value at which they are held and identify whether any write-down is required. An example is Hewlett-Packard, which in its 2012 accounts wrote down by $8.8 billion the carrying value of goodwill paid when it acquired Autonomy, a British software business.

Fair value adjustment

In the definition of goodwill the purchase price is compared with the fair value of the net assets. The fair value is not necessarily the book value of the assets and liabilities acquired. These can be adjusted to a value at which they could be sold in a commercial transaction. Some examples of fair value adjustments are as follows:

■ Tangible fixed assets should be based on their market value or depreciated replacement cost (provided they do not exceed their recoverable amount).

■ Receivables should reflect the amount expected to be received allowing for bad debt expectation.

Income recognition

The principle of income recognition for group companies is clear for a whole year of ownership, but in the year of an investment purchase only the income after the date of acquisition can be shown on the income statement. Any income prior to acquisition becomes a component of the value acquired and is used in the calculation of goodwill.

Accounting for long-term projects

Long-term projects are those that take several years to complete, such as a big IT or construction project. In Chapter 5 the point at which revenue should be recognised was defined as "when goods or services are delivered". If this principle were to be applied to these long-term projects, the contract provider would have a volatile income statement; some years, when projects finished, would be highly profitable, but in others the profits would be lean, and there might even be losses.

To make the income statements of these businesses more representative of their activities, there needs to be a way of recognising profit for these types of transactions which reflects both the nature of the transaction and the need to recognise revenue on delivery. The procedure is to break the project down into a series of smaller stages and recognise revenue as each of these smaller stages is completed.

BAE Systems, a defence, security and aerospace company, has the following accounting policy for long-term contracts: "Sales are recognised when the group has obtained the right to consideration in exchange for its performance. This is usually when title passes or a separately identifiable phase (milestone) of a contract or development has been completed. No profit is recognised on contracts until the outcome of the contract can be reliably estimated. Profit is calculated by reference to reliable estimates of contract revenue and forecast costs after making suitable allowances for technical and other risks related to performance milestones yet to be achieved. When it is probable that total contract costs will exceed total contract revenue, the expected loss is recognised immediately as an expense."

The principle for calculating the amount of profit to recognise is to spread it evenly over the life of the project in proportion to the value of work completed. There is also a principle that requires all potential losses to be recognised in total as soon as they are encountered and not to be spread. The formula for calculating the profit to recognise is:

$$\text{Expected total profit} \times \frac{\text{Costs incurred to date}}{\text{Expected total costs}} = \text{Profit to recognise to date}$$

$$\text{Expected total profit} = \text{Expected total revenue} - \text{Expected total costs}$$

$$\text{Expected total costs} = \text{Costs incurred to date} + \text{Expected costs to complete}$$

The danger with this approach is that optimism in the early stages of a project can release profits that may turn out to be unrealised if there are cost overruns in the later stages. Businesses that undertake long-term projects need to be cautious: they should not only release profit slowly in the early stages but also delay releasing any profit until they can foresee the overall outcome with some certainty.

Transactions in foreign currencies

The effects of exchange rates on transactions in foreign currencies can be favourable or unfavourable. They arise in three ways:

■ At a transactional level, where a business buys and sells products or services in one currency yet operates in another – for example, a retailer that imports products from another country.

■ At an investment level, where a business has assets or liabilities based abroad and denominated in a different currency from the one with which it accounts for its business – for example, a branch of a business that is based abroad.

■ At a multinational level, where an organisation has operations and businesses around the world with transactions, assets and liabilities in a variety of currencies yet has to report its results to its shareholders in a single currency.

The management and accounting treatment of these transactions and hedging techniques that can be used to protect a business from losses caused by adverse currency movements are explained below.

Transactions

When transacting with a business in another country, the potential for foreign-exchange gains and losses arises as a result of differences between the exchange rate on the date the transaction was recorded and the exchange rate on the date the cash is received or paid. For example:

■ A UK business sells $1,600 of goods to an American customer when the exchange rate is $1.6 to £1.

■ The sale is recorded when the goods are delivered as $1,600 ÷ 1.6 = £1,000 in the UK company's income statement.

■ There is a period of 30 days before the customer has to settle the account, during which time the pound weakens to $1.5 to £1.

■ The amount actually received is therefore $1,600 ÷ 1.5 = £1,067.

■ The difference between the £1,000 originally recorded and the £1,067 actually received represents a foreign-exchange gain and is taken to the income statement as part of the operating income for the year.

Foreign-exchange gains and losses can arise on transactions such as importing raw materials, buying services and exporting goods. Standard accounting policies require that transactions during an accounting period should be translated at the rate of exchange at the date of transaction.

Asset and liabilities

Monetary items, such as receivables, payables or loan balances outstanding in the statement of financial position at the end of the financial year, should be converted at the closing exchange rate for the period or at the rate the transaction is contracted to settle (including any hedging contracts used to minimise exposure). Once again, the difference between the transaction rate when the cash is received and the rate used to convert the closing balance will result in a foreign-exchange gain or loss.

Gains or losses from year-end translations are normally included under "other operating income or charges" on the income statement. Gains or losses arising from financing arrangements are disclosed separately, usually as part of "finance costs".

Hedging techniques

For overseas investments, hedging techniques for funding them can be used to mitigate some of the foreign-exchange risk. A common hedging technique is to borrow money in the same currency as the investment and try to match the amount of borrowing to the value of the net investment. Thus as exchange rates move the exchange gains made on the net investment are matched by an equal exchange loss on the borrowing, and vice versa.

For example, a UK company makes an investment of £500,000 in the United States, borrowing in dollars when the rate was $2 to £1. This gives an initial investment and borrowing of $1m (see Table 16.3).

TABLE 16.3 **Initial investment overseas**

	£	Exchange rate	$
Net investment	500,000	2:1	1,000,000
Borrowing	500,000	2:1	1,000,000

TABLE 16.4 **Effect after a change in the exchange rate**

	$	Exchange rate	£
Net investment	1,000,000	1.8:1	555,556
Borrowing	1,000,000	1.8:1	555,556

One year later the exchange rate has moved to $1.8 to £1. The US investment has changed its UK value from £500,000 to £555,556 (see Table 16.4). There are no foreign-exchange gains or losses as the gain on the investment is exactly matched by the loss on the borrowing.

With overseas investment some governments impose tight operating constraints by, for example:

■ not allowing profits to be remitted to other countries so any surpluses have to be reinvested back in the business;

■ encouraging further inward investment of profits by levying withholding tax, typically between 10% and 15%, on any remittance out of the country.

Businesses should explore the funding environment thoroughly before identifying funding sources. Even with careful planning, it is impossible to predict the future actions of governments on investment in their country.

Another technique for protecting a business from foreign-exchange movement is to buy or sell currency forward. This is done by contracting through a bank to buy or sell currency at a future date based on an exchange rate determined today. For example, if the $:€ rate is currently 1.3:1 and an American company knows it has to make a sizeable euro payment in three months' time, it can buy the currency forward. Thus whatever happens to the exchange rate over the next three months the company has locked in its euro rate and there will be no gains or losses on settlement.

Multinationals

For groups of companies that are consolidated for financial reporting the holding company needs to select a reporting currency into which all the businesses will be converted. Typically, this will be the currency of the country where the shares are listed. An exception is BP, a British oil company, which reports its results in dollars because oil is priced in dollars and this currency reflects its business operations more appropriately.

The income statement for each company in the group will be converted at the average exchange rate for the year of trade. All items on each statement of financial position will be revalued at the year-end closing rate of exchange. The total of all foreign-exchange gains and losses that arise on consolidation (which is the difference between converting the statement of financial position at the old closing rate last year and the new closing rate this year together with the difference between converting the income statement at the average rate and the closing rate) is shown as a movement in the statement of recognised income and expenses rather than in the income statement.

An extract from Unilever's *Foreign Exchange Accounting Policies Note* explains a common approach used by multinationals: "In preparing the consolidated financial statements, the balances in individual group companies are translated from their functional currency into euros. The income statement, cash flow statement and all other movements in assets and liabilities are translated at average rates of exchange as a proxy for the transaction rate, or at the transaction rate if more appropriate. Assets and liabilities are translated a year-end exchange rates."

Glossary of financial terms

Cross references are in **bold**.

Accounting period	The length of time between two reporting dates, typically a year.
Accounting policies	The accounting principles chosen by the board of directors and shown in the annual reports and accounts.
Accounts payable	A US term for amounts payable to suppliers, usually due within one year.
Accounts receivable	A US term for amounts receivable from customers, usually due within one year.
Accrual	A type of payable where the products or services have been received in one accounting period, but the invoicing and payment take place in a subsequent accounting period.
Activity-based costing (ABC)	The allocation of indirect costs to products or services in proportion to the activities that drove the cost to be incurred.
Amortisation	The writing off of an **intangible asset** over a period.

Annual reports and accounts	A review of a business comprising chairman's statement, report of directors, review of operations, together with financial statements, notes and disclosures. These are produced for the shareholders, although they are used by many other stakeholders.
Apportionment	The spreading of overheads across various cost centres as part of calculating the cost of a product or service.
Asset	Something owned or controlled that has a future economic benefit.
Audit report	A report by an auditor on whether the financial statements provide "a true and fair view" of the business.
Balance sheet	Now known as the **statement of financial position.**
Bonus issue	Shares issued to existing shareholders in proportion to their existing shareholding at no charge.
Book-keeping	The recording and summarising of business transactions.
Break-even point	The volume of activity at which the total **revenue** of a product, service or business equals the total costs, and neither a profit nor a loss is made.
Budget	A financial plan comprising an estimation of the **revenue** and costs for a future period of time.
Budgetary control	The comparison of a budget with actual results, using variance analysis.
Business case	The evaluation of an investment opportunity.
Business plan	The blueprint for achievement in a business over a 3–5 year horizon.

Capital expenditure (capex)	The purchase of **fixed assets**, typically involving justification with a **business case**.
Cash flow statement	A statement showing the funds generated by the operations and funds from other sources. It also indicates how funds have been applied and whether there is a net surplus or deficiency.
Common stock	See **ordinary share**.
Company	A legal entity that is separate from its owners.
Consolidation	The adding together of the financial statements of a group of companies as if it were one company.
Contribution	The surplus after deducting **variable costs** from **revenue**.
Contribution analysis	A method of preparing analyses based on identifying **variable costs** and **fixed costs,** which can be used to evaluate the most profitable areas of a business and how best to use scarce resources.
Cost centre	A department or function to which costs can be allocated for control purposes.
Cost of capital	The required return for investors used in the evaluation of capital projects. Also known as the **weighted average cost of capital (WACC).**
Cost of sales	The **direct costs** involved in providing goods or services (also known as cost of goods).
Creditors	Amounts owing to suppliers and usually payable within one year.
Current assets	The short-term operating assets, including **inventory**, **receivables**, short-term investments, bank and cash balances.

Current liabilities	The liabilities arising as a consequence of trade, including payables and bank overdrafts.
Current ratio	The ratio of **current assets** divided by **current liabilities**. It indicates a company's ability to meet its short-term obligations.
Debenture	A loan secured on assets which is usually issued at a fixed rate of interest and repayable on a specific date.
Debtors	Amounts owed to a company by its customers and usually collectable within one year.
Debts	Amounts owed to loan providers.
Depreciation	An accounting estimate to take account of the diminution in value of a **fixed asset** and to spread its cost over its estimated useful life. (See also **reducing-balance depreciation; straight-line depreciation**.)
Direct costs	Costs such as **raw materials** specifically used in the creation of a product or service.
Director	A member of a company's board who is appointed by the shareholders as a steward of their investment. A director has responsibility for running a company and setting and implementing its strategy.
Direct labour	Labour costs specifically associated with the provision of a product or service.
Discounted cash flow	A technique used to value future cash flows (see **time value of money, net present value** and **internal rate of return**).
Dividend	The distribution in cash of company profits to shareholders.
Dividend cover	A ratio multiple showing the number of times the **dividend** of a company could be paid out of the profit attributable to shareholders.

Dividend yield	A measure of the cash return to investors in a company. It is calculated by taking the ordinary **dividend** as a percentage of the market price of the share.
Earnings per share	Profit attributable to shareholders divided by the average number of shares in issue during the year.
EBITDA	Earnings before interest, tax, depreciation and amortisation, an approximation for cash generation by a business.
Entrepreneur	An individual who creates a business to capitalise on a perceived market opportunity.
Equity	Also known as shareholders' funds, or net worth, it is the sum of issued share capital and **reserves**.
Factoring	The process of letting another party assume responsibility for collecting receivables.
Financial statements	The **income statement**, the **statement of financial position** and the **cash flow statement**.
Finished goods	Goods ready for sale to customers as distinct from **work in progress** (unfinished goods).
Fixed assets	The infrastructure of a business consisting of **tangible assets**, such as property, plant and equipment, fixtures and fittings, and **intangible assets**, such as **goodwill** and brands.
Fixed charge	The security provided for a debt that is tied to a specific asset or group of assets.
Fixed costs	Costs which are unaffected by the level of business activity (within a **relevant range**).
Gearing	A UK term for **leverage**.

Goodwill	The difference between the amount paid for a company and the fair value of the net assets acquired.
Horizontal analysis	Comparing actual or budgeted revenue and costs with previous years in the form of percentage growth.
Income statement	A statement showing the **revenue** minus the costs for the period under review. Formerly known as the profit and loss account.
Indirect costs	Costs or overheads incurred in running a business that are not directly attributable to a product or service.
Intangible assets	Assets which have no physical form, such as brands and patents.
Internal rate of return (IRR)	The average rate of return achieved over the life of a project, calculated by finding the discount rate where the sum of the **discounted cash flows** minus the capital outlay is equal to zero.
International Accounting Standards Board (IASB)	An organisation that produces the guidance on accounting – **International Financial Reporting Standards** – used in reports and accounts.
International Financial Reporting Standards (IFRS)	The prescriptive rules on preparing and presenting financial statements.
Inventory	The US term for stock, which includes **raw materials**, **work in progress** and **finished goods**. Inventory is valued at the lower of cost or market value.
Investment appraisal	The evaluation of proposed capital projects using a **business case**.
Letter of credit (LOC)	A payment guarantee from a customer's bank that is used in international trade.

Leverage	The proportion of investment provided to a company by its shareholders versus the proportion of investment provided by other sources which usually bears interest. High leverage (gearing) means there is a high proportion of debt.
Liability	A claim on a business as a result of a past transaction or event.
Loans	Bank borrowings.
Margin of safety	The volume of sales above the **break-even point.**
Market capitalisation	The market value of shares multiplied by the number of shares issued. This is the value of the company.
Minority interest	The shares in subsidiary companies which are not owned by the holding company.
Net present value (NPV)	The sum of the future cash flows discounted at the **cost of capital** minus the capital outlay.
Operating expenditure (opex)	The cost of day-to-day items such as payroll, rent, marketing, distribution and so on.
Ordinary shares	Shares which are entitled to the profits after all other costs. The US term is common stock.
Payables	Amounts owing to suppliers and usually payable within one year.
Payback period	The time taken for the cash receipts from a project to exceed the cash payments. It is normally expressed in years.
Prepayment	A type of **receivable** where the payment for goods has taken place in one accounting period but the goods and services will not be received until a subsequent accounting period.

Price/earnings ratio (P/E)	The share price divided by the last reported **earnings per share**. The P/E is a multiple which shows the number of years' earnings the market is willing to pay for a company's shares.
Profit	Surplus of revenue less costs.
Profit margin	The profit of a product or service expressed as a percentage of revenue.
Profit and loss account	Now known as the **income statement**.
Provision	An estimated amount to cover an expected **liability** even if the exact amount of the liability or its timing is uncertain.
Raw materials	Unprocessed **inventory**, which forms the input to the production process for conversion to finished products.
Receivables	A US term for **debtors**.
Reducing-balance depreciation	A method of **depreciation** whereby the annual amount written off is a percentage of the reduced balance. This results in higher charges for depreciation during the earlier years of the **fixed asset** and lower charges in the later years.
Reforecast	A process carried out part way through the budget year to produce an estimate of the anticipated results for the whole year.
Relevant costs	Costs that will change as a consequence of making a decision.
Relevant range	The range of production volumes over which revenue and cost relationships do not change.

Reserves: capital	Reserves which are not generated through normal trading activities. They include one-off items such as **share premium** and revaluation of properties. There are limits on their distribution.
Reserves: revenue	The accumulated undistributed income, also known as retained earnings.
Residual value	The anticipated value of a **fixed asset** at the end of its useful life.
Retained earnings	See **reserves: revenue**.
Return on investment (ROI)	Operating income expressed as a percentage of the investment used to earn that income.
Revenue	Income receivable from selling products or services, net of sales taxes. Revenue is reported in the **income statement**.
Rights issue	An issue of **ordinary shares** to existing shareholders who have a right to a number of new shares in proportion to their existing holding. The new shares are normally issued at a price below the current trading price.
Run rate	The average monthly cost for an item of expenditure.
Sales	A term for **revenue** or **turnover**.
Sarbanes-Oxley Act	US law that came into force in 2002 and established new standards for corporate governance with regard to internal financial controls.
Scrip issue	See **bonus issue**.
Securitise	The process of building a portfolio of receivables and selling them to a group of investors.

Sensitivity analysis	A technique used when appraising investments to explore the risk inherent in the assumptions.
Share premium	The difference between the price paid for a share and its nominal value.
Shareholders' funds	A term for **equity**.
Shareholder value	The generation of an investment return greater than **WACC**.
Statement of financial position	A statement at a specified date showing a business's assets, liabilities and shareholders' funds (**equity**). Formerly known as the balance sheet.
Stock	A UK term for **inventory**. In the US the term is used to describe shares.
Stock turn	A ratio calculated from **cost of sales** divided by **inventory**. It indicates the number of times inventory is sold in one year.
Straight-line depreciation	A method of **depreciation** where an equal amount is written off a **fixed asset** during its estimated useful life.
Sunk costs	Costs that have already been spent and will not change as result of making a decision.
Tangible assets	Assets with a physical form, such as property, plant and equipment.
Time value of money	A concept used in **discounted cash flow** analysis. Cash flows in the future are less valuable than those today.
Turnover	A term for **sales** or **revenue**.
Value	Creation of a consumer perception where the benefits of a product or service are greater than its cost.
Variable costs	Costs which vary in proportion to the volume of activity.

Variance	The difference between an actual result and a budgeted result.
Vendor-managed inventory (VMI)	The process of letting a supplier have responsibility to replenish inventory on your site.
Vertical analysis	Expressing costs as a proportion of revenue or of total cost.
Weighted average cost of capital (WACC)	The average return that is required by investors in the business.
Work in progress	Goods in the process of being manufactured. The value of work in progress is based on the materials and labour invested.
Working capital	The sum of **inventory** plus **receivables** minus **payables**.
Zero-based budgeting	A budgeting process which requires all resources to be justified and no reference is made to continuing with budgets from previous years.

List of companies

THESE COMPANIES ARE used as examples in the book. The names are those in existence at the time of writing; merger and acquisition activity will inevitably change this.

Company	Sector	Page
Airbus	Aerospace	113
AkzoNobel	Chemicals	73
Amazon	Retail	6, 293
Anglo American	Mining	4
Apple	Consumer electronics	5, 146, 265
Autonomy	Software	72, 323
Avon	Cosmetics	7
AXA	Insurance	75
BA (British Airways)	Airline	11, 144
BAE Systems	Defence, security and aerospace	325
Barings Bank	Banking	28
BAT (British American Tobacco)	Tobacco	73
Ben & Jerry	Ice cream	8
Best Foods	Food	92
BMW	Automotive	203
Boeing	Aerospace	63, 68, 113
Boston Consulting Group	Consultancy	147
BP (British Petroleum)	Oil	69, 329

References

Atrill, P. and McLaney, E., *Accounting and Finance for Non-specialists*, 4th edition, Financial Times/ Prentice Hall, 2003.

Ehrenberg, A.S.C., *A Primer in Data Reduction*, John Wiley, 1982.

Friend, G. and Zehle, S., *The Economist Guide to Business Planning*, 2nd edition, Profile Books, 2009.

Kaplan, R.S. and Norton, D.P., *The Balanced Scorecard – Translating Strategy into Action*, Harvard Business School Press, 1996.

Mills, R.W. and Robertson, J., *Fundamentals of Managerial Accounting and Finance*, 4th edition, Mars Business Associates, 1999.

Porter, M., *Competitive Strategy*, Free Press, 1998.

Tennent, J. and Friend, G., *The Economist Guide to Business Modelling*, 3rd edition, Profile Books, 2011.

Tennent, J., *The Economist Guide to Cash Management*, Profile Books, 2012.

Vause, Bob, *The Economist Guide to Analysing Companies*, 5th edition, Profile Books, 2009.

Additional information has been drawn from numerous websites, both corporate and encyclopaedic.

Index

PublicAffairs is a publishing house founded in 1997. It is a tribute to the standards, values, and flair of three persons who have served as mentors to countless reporters, writers, editors, and book people of all kinds, including me.

I. F. STONE, proprietor of *I. F. Stone's Weekly*, combined a commitment to the First Amendment with entrepreneurial zeal and reporting skill and became one of the great independent journalists in American history. At the age of eighty, Izzy published *The Trial of Socrates*, which was a national bestseller. He wrote the book after he taught himself ancient Greek.

BENJAMIN C. BRADLEE was for nearly thirty years the charismatic editorial leader of *The Washington Post*. It was Ben who gave the *Post* the range and courage to pursue such historic issues as Watergate. He supported his reporters with a tenacity that made them fearless and it is no accident that so many became authors of influential, best-selling books.

ROBERT L. BERNSTEIN, the chief executive of Random House for more than a quarter century, guided one of the nation's premier publishing houses. Bob was personally responsible for many books of political dissent and argument that challenged tyranny around the globe. He is also the founder and longtime chair of Human Rights Watch, one of the most respected human rights organizations in the world.

· · ·

For fifty years, the banner of Public Affairs Press was carried by its owner Morris B. Schnapper, who published Gandhi, Nasser, Toynbee, Truman, and about 1,500 other authors. In 1983, Schnapper was described by *The Washington Post* as "a redoubtable gadfly." His legacy will endure in the books to come.

Peter Osnos, *Founder and Editor-at-Large*